What a wonderful contribution t(covery to getting along with others, **Sh** vides refreshing insights and practica. ~~gg~~ communication, reducing conflicts and understanding why people behave as they do.

-John Gray, author,
Men are from Mars, Women are from Venus

Showing Our True Colors by Mary Miscisin is both informative and entertaining with immediately useful concepts that work. An incredibly practical approach to understanding yourself and getting along with others better.

-Dr. Tony Alessandra author of
The Platinum Rule and Charisma

Enlightening! This wonderfully insightful book offers practical keys for unlocking relationship challenges and enhancing your personal effectiveness.

-Jack Canfield, founder
California Self Esteem Task Force

Showing Our True Colors has been one of the most valuable books that I have read for improving relationships and communication in the workplace. In fact, I have read it several times and learned something new each time! The insights that I have now, from understanding how and why people view the same situation differently, are invaluable. Understanding WHY people act or respond the way they do enables us as managers to work with our staff in a way that works for THEM which results in ALL of us being successful.

-Sue Allen, Risk Manager,
El Dorado County Office of Education

True Colors has become a key component of our "Learning Environment" Program and is the heart of our teambuilding and diversity training...We now realize that it is a good thing we are not all just alike. This has been a major influence on our ability to work together to achieve goals and to appreciate what each individual brings to the table. We are stronger and happier as a result. And, as an added bonus, this training has enriched our personal lives. It is a gift to our associates that benefits them, their families, and the company as a whole.

-Nikki Hanna, Vice President,
Blue Cross and Blue Shield of Oklahoma

Mary's book showed us things about each other that had been right in front of us for years. It helped us to recognize the obvious and show us how to better deal with each other in our daily lives.

-John Markey,
California Association Highway Patrol

True Colors has changed my life...for the better. I now better understand my family, friends, co-workers and self. It has made me appreciate differences in people, recognize these differences as strengths and tap into them. I have been exposed to several personality type instruments in the past, none of which has had the impact of True Colors.

-Tim Schmidt, Trainer,
California State Department of Consumer Affairs

As an educator with 30 years experience in the classroom and in coaching, I wish I could have read Mary Miscisin's book **Showing Our True Colors** 30 years ago! I would have been a much better teacher and coach because I would have had a much better understanding of my students and athletes and how to more effectively communicate with them based on their colors. Every parent, teacher, and coach ought to read the book. It is a must for couples and anyone who wants to communicate more effectively. Where was this book when I needed it? Oh, yeah, I still do need it today.

-Tom Doyle, Athletic Director, Washington

The concepts Mary presents in **Showing Our True Colors** have been extremely successful in improving work relationships and resolving conflicts throughout the organization. Being recognized for their unique personalities and contributions has lowered stress levels and helped our employees gain a better understanding of everyone's part in the communication process.

-Sandy Masters, CPCU, CPIW,
CalFarm (Allied) Insurance Company

If you want to Show Your True Colors, read, absorb and use the BRILLIANCE in this book!

- Mark Victor Hansen, co-author,
Chicken Soup for the Soul

Third Edition

SHOWING OUR TRUE COLORS

A Fun, Easy Guide for Understanding and
Appreciating Yourself and Others

By Mary Miscisin

Illustrated by Jeff Haines

Author contact:
Mary Miscisin
PO Box 277453
Sacramento, CA 95827
Mary@PositivelyMary.com
www.PositivelyMary.com

Published by:
True Colors, Inc. Publishing
3605 West MacArthur Blvd., Ste.702
Santa Ana, CA 92704
www.True-Colors.com

Editor: Jennifer Adams
Illustrations: Jeff Haines
Cover Design & Typography: John Valdez, Company West
Printed in The United States of America by Offset Solutions

ISBN: 1-893320-23-5
Library of Congress Catalog Number: 2001-089728

**Dedicated with love
to my daughter
Crescentia.**

Contents

About True Colors

True Colors has been empowering individuals and organizations to succeed for over twenty years. Through workshops, skits, and a variety of training and "edutainment" formats, millions of people have gone through an exciting shift in thinking that has improved their lives and enhanced their professional and personal relationships. Just ask companies like Xerox, Boeing, and Microsoft, who have reaped the benefits of this powerful tool.

True Colors works because it's simple, enjoyable, and based on true principles. Successful people seem to know who they are, what their True Colors are, and what their values, needs, strengths, and joys are. They know and trust themselves, and behave accordingly. They appreciate the needs and strengths of others, and behave compassionately. Their integrity inspires trust and productivity in everyone around them.

When you know what your core values and needs are, and feel good about them, you can perform at your highest potential in every area of life. And when you share a working, mutual understanding of others' core values and needs, you have the basis to communicate, motivate, and achieve common goals with utmost dignity, efficacy, and mutual respect.

—Don Lowry
Creator of True Colors

Acknowledgments

There are so many people whom I would like to thank for their contributions to this book, beginning with the pioneers in the field of typology, from its roots to its many branches. They have paved the way for those who have carried on to explore, expand, and involve the original methods and theories.

A special appreciation goes to Don Lowry, whose genius developed the True Colors concept.

A heartfelt thanks to the thousands of participants in my True Colors workshops who have supplied the fuel for the material in this book by their involvement in the workshops, and especially those who asked, "Okay, I know my True Colors, now how can I learn more?"

Joe and Elaine Sullivan, along with Fred Leafgren, who brought True Colors into my life via the National Wellness Conference.

Cliff Gillies, who from the beginning provided enthusiasm, motivation, and words of encouragement.

Erica Echols for her devotion to excellence. Larry Barkdull for his tenacity. Jennifer Adams for her finesse in refinement and editing talents and Brian Carter for his typesetting contributions.

Jeff Haines, whose artistic flare is truly remarkable. Thank you for your patience and diligence in working with my demanding and detailed requirements for the illustrations that make the words of this book come alive.

Ed Redard, my best friend and soul mate, who stuck with me through the piles of papers and books in the office, late night typing, and numerous revisions. Thank you for supporting me through thick and thin, helping me reach my goals, accepting my different methods, and finding ways to help me increase my knowledge, grow in my skills, and foster my self-expression.

John Butler for being helpful, patient, and kind. Mike Berry and Michael Church for their creative talents. D.S. Fields for his artistic contributions.

John Valdez for your innovative panache and continued patronage to my success throughout the years and many phases of my career. Your artistic expertise and willingness to keep diving into projects have supplied vital fuel to keep the dreams alive.

Connie Jennings and Kim Heflin at True Colors for pulling things together on short notice, connecting me with others, taking care of so many different details, and especially for their friendship.

Mom (Jean Marie) and Dad (Ron) and my sisters and brothers: Evelyn, David, Therese, Martin, John, Michelle, Karen, Matthew, and Michael for providing a plethora of experiences that have helped to form who I am. Manuel, who is like a son to me.

Those who read sections of my several manuscript versions: Dave Manahan, Michael Peart, Joanie Stephen, Helen Scully, David Lee, Tim Schmidt, Paul McKay, Bobbie Lewis, Teresa Gibson, Jackie Mead, and Cherrise Knapp.

And others who contributed stories, ideas, or advice: Dave Roberts, Lisa Konarski, Martin Brady, Lyle Groen, Rick Jenkins, Karen Martins, Steve Steuart, Nikki Lynn Ahrens, and Jessica Dolge.

A big thank you to Dr. Katsuyo Howard and her team for translating my book into Japanese and her diligence in encouraging me to revise and elaborate on the Gold sections of my book.

I would also like to acknowledge you, the reader, for your willingness to learn and expand your appreciation of human behavior.

Foreword

I once went to a seminar where the instructor presented the components of a "hero" story. This format is used for many popular movies and books:

1. A person or group comes up against a formidable obstacle(s)

2. To get past the obstacle, they must learn a lesson they may not yet be aware they need to learn.

3. They attempt several ways of solving the challenge.

4. After much trial and tribulation, they gain skills, abilities, or insights and learn an unexpected lesson.

5. Using this newfound knowledge, they solve the challenge and emerge triumphant!

It wasn't until later that I realized how those components paralleled my own situation and the role True Colors played in it. I had attended True Colors presentations numerous times at national conferences and saw how people's lives were transformed by the experience. I, myself, had begun to speak in "color" and view the behaviors of people in my life differently. My relationships improved and my communication skills matured.

Later still, while involved in long-range planning at work, I raised the possibility of a few of our staff getting trained to present the True Colors system for our then 33,000 employees. After I was trained as a certified instructor of True Colors and began teaching it to others, my life began to change even more. The True Colors concepts were quickly learned and adopted by my co-workers. This had an immediate effect on staff communication and morale. We now had a common language to speak when we needed to solve conflicts or discuss challenges. It wasn't long before employees were requesting workshops for their family and friends so they too could learn to show their True Colors and appreciate the True Colors of others.

Members of my family, of course, began using True Colors to understand behaviors that they had before found annoying with other family members, or certain people at work.

Circumstances were explained in a color context and problems solved at a much faster rate—with feelings spared and values respected in the process.

Participants in my seminars have often shared with me—months or even years later—the dramatic impact True Colors has made on their relationships, both in their personal and work lives. A frequent comment is "I finally understand my husband (or wife) for the first time." They were really able to hear and embrace the message of True Colors. My life, as well as the lives of those around me, took a leap forward without our even planning it.

Now, you may or may not experience the life changing benefits of True Colors in as quick and permeating a way as I did. But this easy-to-learn, fun-to-use system has the possibility of changing forever the way you view and relate to the world.

As you read through the pages and chapters to come, realize that you too are on a journey. Have fun discovering how True Colors plays a part in your life, and when you're ready, travel to the next page and enjoy your True Colors journey!

Part I - Introduction

EVER WONDER . . . ABOUT HUMAN BEHAVIOR?

I know I do! For instance, have you ever noticed that some people are very punctual? They make it to places on time or even early. Yet others have a tough time being on time. It doesn't seem to matter if they give themselves half an hour or five hours to get ready—they still end up being five minutes late. What is it that makes someone very uncomfortable if they are running late, while others take it in stride and actually find it stimulating to race the clock?

Or, have you ever observed how some people speak their mind even before they know what is on it, while others are more reserved and think before they speak? Why do some people speak out spontaneously, and others hold thoughts in?

It is funny to watch the behaviors of people on the highway, too. If someone is driving slower than us, we may think to ourselves, or even out loud, "What a slowpoke!" Or if someone happens to be driving faster than us, we might think they are a "crazy driver." How do we gauge what is the "right" speed for us and others to drive?

Philosophers have been pondering human behavior for centuries and researchers have been studying it for decades. People definitely have different preferences, communication styles, and ways of behaving. For society, there are certain laws that govern what is "right" and "wrong." Whether we agree with the laws or not, it would be foolish to ignore them. However, as individuals we often judge the world by what *we* would do in a certain situation. If another person's way of doing things differs from ours, there is a natural tendency to regard it as the "wrong" way.

True, we as human beings have an innate tendency to try to understand and regulate the behaviors of others. And—if we admit it—we have all tried to get another person to behave differently. Sometimes we have been successful and other times not. Yet I've heard over and over that "one cannot change the behaviors of others, they can only change themselves." If this is true, then where did we ever get the notion that we could or would even want to change the behaviors of others? Think about it. We've been shaped, formed, and sculpted practically since the day we were born. Our parents tried their best to guide us; teachers attempted to educate and train us; relatives, friends, and even society as a whole have an influence on our behaviors and choices almost constantly. No wonder we try, too!

Specific habits or manners can be conditioned into people

to a certain extent. However, even with all the poking, prodding, and encouraging, some natural behaviors keep emerging. When individuals get around people they are fully comfortable with and let down their guard, or even during times of stress (when it can be difficult to concentrate), they have a tendency to "let their True Colors show." Their conditioned behavior gives way to what comes more naturally.

So what are our True Colors? Are they something innate? Something that exists deeper or before any training begins?

Showing Our True Colors

As the second oldest child in a family of ten children, I was often intrigued that although the same parents raised us, we all seemed to have distinct personalities early on in life. As an infant, my sister, Evelyn,

loved to be held, cuddled, and rocked. I, on the other hand (my mother reports), would buck and kick when picked up and would squiggle about unless I was held facing outward.

One of my brothers, John, was always quite fascinated with money. He found ways to earn it, count it, and save it. My sister, Therese, was quite proper and neat. She would sort her sock drawer according to colors, arrange her toys in their "correct" places, and always waited her turn.

Then and Now

Nearly forty years later, times have changed, but some things have not. Evelyn still loves to be held, I squiggle and kick if I am in one place too long, John is a successful banker, and Therese is a homemaker with everything in its place.

Our True Colors were obvious in childhood and still shine as adults. Being able to recognize our True Colors enables all of us to realize that other people are not "wrong" for having different preferences or doing what comes naturally, they are simply different.

Knowing our True Colors, and how to discover the True Colors of others, helps us recognize differences and similarities in communication styles, behaviors, and preferences and how to use this information to solve conflicts, increase respect, and bring out the best in everyone.

When I was a little girl, we used to sing this song in Girl Scouts. It eloquently sums up the concept behind True Colors:

I'm proud to be me,
but I also see
you're just as proud to be you.
We may look at things
a bit differently,
but lots of good people do.
It's just human nature,
so why should I hate you
for being as human as I?
We'll live and let live.
And, we'll get as we give.
And, we'll all get along
if we try!
I'm proud to be me,
but I also see
you're just as proud to be you.
We may look at things
a bit differently,
but lots of good people do.

Chapter 1
THE HISTORY OF
TRUE COLORS

𝕸𝖊𝖑𝖆𝖓𝖈𝖍𝖔𝖑𝖎𝖈 𝕾𝖆𝖓𝖌𝖚𝖎𝖓𝖊 𝕻𝖍𝖑𝖊𝖌𝖒𝖆𝖙𝖎𝖈 𝕮𝖍𝖔𝖑𝖊𝖗𝖎𝖈

In the Beginning...

Watching human behavior and trying to understand the basis of personality can be traced at least as far back as 460 B.C. It is interesting to note that the discernment of four groupings is a common theme that connects many of the most predominant personality theories. Although there are numerous systems for explaining our behaviors

1

and the origin of our personalities, for brevity only the ones most influential in the creation of the True Colors system will be mentioned here.

One of the most widely known philosophers in history, Hippocrates, observed that people in general seemed to have one of four humors, or approaches to life: Phlegmatic, Choleric, Melancholic, or Sanguine.

In the 1920s, noted psychologist Carl Jung offered his findings from years of observation and research. He noted that people displayed "functions" that also fell into one of four areas: Feeling, Thinking, Sensation, or Intuition. He theorized that for the most part, these functions were innate. Yet, the culture and environment in which a person is raised will also influence his or her behavior and choices. We can develop our nondominant, or least natural functions, to the extent that it can become difficult to tell which is natural and which is learned.

Myers/Briggs			
ISTJ	ISFJ	INFJ	INTJ
ISTP	ISFP	INFP	INTP
ESTP	ESFP	ENFP	ENTP
ESTJ	ESFJ	ENFJ	ENTF

Katherine Briggs and her daughter, Isabel Myers, studied the research of Jung, and in the 1950s expanded his work to include sixteen personality types. They developed the famous Myers/Briggs Type Indicator, which is used extensively in business, education, and counseling for personal as well as professional growth.

David Keirsey, based on his continued research in the field of psychology, returned to classifying personality and temperament into four types: Apollonian, Promethean, Epimethean, and Dionysian. In 1967, David Keirsey and Marilyn Bates published *Please Understand Me*, which has become another cornerstone in personality typing.

Apollonian Promethean Epimethean Dionysian

Please Understand Me.

Along Came Don!

Studying the work of Keirsey, Don Lowry was astounded by the benefits that resulted from recognizing personality types. Since his own natural temperament compelled him to derive fun from every experience, explore the endless possibilities in ideas, and contribute to others, he used the temperament model to develop the metaphor "True Colors."

He studied the various meanings associated with colors such as "good as gold" and "true blue friend." He also explored existing research on the effects of colors, such as the calming properties of green and the stimulating effects of orange. He carefully chose the colors that resembled the characteristics they would be representing.

In 1978, Don introduced the world to the True Colors concept. Initially, Don selected theater as a fun, entertaining way to acquaint people with the incredibly powerful insights of temperament typing.

He developed four playing cards illustrating the characteristics of the four different temperament types or "personality styles." The cards offered participants a gratifying, hands-on experience in discovering their personality traits. Individuals placed the cards in order from the one most like them to the one least like them. This method of self-determining type avoids the forced-choice questions of the written tests that many other personality typing systems employ.

After determining their own color type, participants then watched a humorous and entertaining theater production designed to portray extremes of the temperament types. Not only did people have fun watching the show, they laughed as they learned to understand themselves more fully. In addition, it helped them appreciate and support differences among others. The cards and theater production were, and still are, a powerful combination for learning what was once understood only by those who studied it. Now the rewarding benefits of this method are readily available and easily understood by all who experience it.

Approximate Comparison of Systems

Hippocrates:	melancholic	choleric	phlegmatic	sanguine
Carl Jung:	feeling	thinking	sensation	intuition
Myers/Briggs:	ENFJ, INFJ ENFP, INFP	ENTJ, INTJ ENTP, INTP	ESTJ, ISTJ ESFJ, ISFJ	ESFP, ISFP ESTP, ISTP
Keirsey:	Apollonian (NF)	Promethean (NT)	Epimethean (SJ)	Dionysian (SP)
Lowry:	Blue	Green	Gold	Orange

True Colors Today

Millions of people throughout the world have been taught the True Colors concept. True Colors knows no ethnic or gender boundaries. There are thousands of True Colors certified trainers in the United States, Canada, Brazil, Japan, Costa Rica, Australia, Europe, and the U.K. Materials have been translated into Spanish, Portuguese, Japanese, French, and Russian.

Over 500,000 people annually are being educated in the benefits of True Colors in the contexts of business, education, healthcare, criminal justice, mental health, personal and career counseling, and communities.

True Colors is presented in a variety of ways, including theater, written materials, video, audio, electronic media, card sorts, presentations, and workshops. Once you've learned True Colors, you can use it in virtually every aspect of your life, from personal and workplace relationships to your community and beyond.

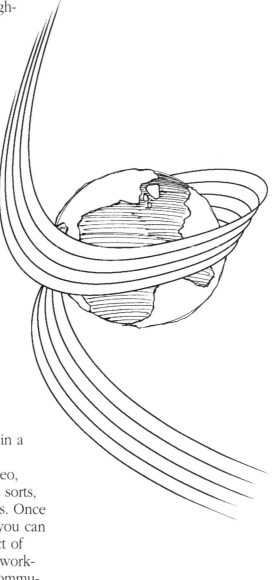

Chapter 2

DON'T
PUT ME IN A
BOX

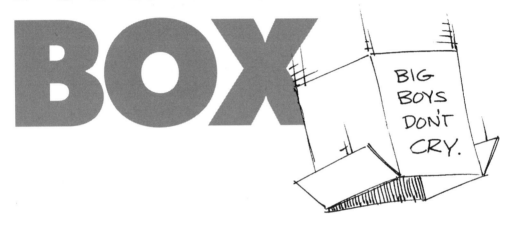

BIG
BOYS
DON'T
CRY.

As children, we may or may not have grown up in environments that encouraged us to let our True Colors shine. Some parents may have admired and fostered creativity, imagination, and self-expression. Some supported conventionality, while others promoted risk-taking. Still others taught the cultivation of competence in intellectual pursuits. It is common for parents, teachers, and even communities to attempt to instill their own values in others. If they are not aware of the importance of supporting an individual's own gifts and preferences, these individuals or groups may end up rewarding the behaviors they label as "good" or "appropriate" and punishing behaviors they do not understand or approve of. When children think they have not lived up to their parents', teachers', or community's expectations they may feel inadequate or even defective.

As adults we can have more control over the behaviors we choose. However, some of us still believe the old labels and behave accordingly.

Many of us have held jobs we hated—just to make a living. Some of us were criticized by our spouses, family members, bosses, or friends for behaving or *not* behaving in manners they deemed appropriate. We may have even felt we must pursue activities or causes that others considered suitable, enjoyable, or worthwhile. Many of us have lived up to—or

> I WANT TO BE AN ARTIST!

> DREAMER! GET A REAL JOB!

down to—our labels. Fortunately, many people have at least some family or friends that they can "be themselves" with and let their True Colors show. Others are not that lucky. They may never have been validated for their own unique values, abilities, and preferences.

Now it is your opportunity to shine—to be esteemed for being who you are and to foster self-expression in others so they may shine too.

What? More Boxes?

It is important to discern the difference between stereotyping people, which is restrictive, and identifying commonalities and differences, which expands possibilities for more understanding and appreciation.

Sometimes people misuse personality typing as a way of labeling others or putting people into boxes. Because the benefits of knowing and using True Colors are so tremendous, it is tempting to try and use True Colors to explain or "fix" challenges by constantly putting people or situations into neat little labeled boxes.

This is both the beauty and the shortcoming of type watching. It is easy, fun, and revealing to identify people's personality types, yet, if taken to the extreme, it can become restrictive. Attractive as it may be, take care not to oversimplify your entire world by boxing it all up into four rigid stereotypes. Contrary to stereotyping, which is a "fixed conventional representation," True Colors recognizes that all people are a unique blend of characteristics. There are four categories in True Colors— Blue, Gold, Orange, and Green—but

7

these four colors blend in a variety of ways to form endless combinations.

We do generally refer to people as being dominant in one of the four colors for ease of identification. However, this is not stereotyping. It is just identification. What category people are identified with is determined by the characteristics they have in common. Think in terms of automobiles. A Chevrolet Corvette and a Toyota Corolla are not the same, yet both are put into the category of "cars." Similarly, dogs and elephants are both "animals," but nobody would mistake one for the other. Every noun in the English language is essentially a label—a way of identifying what we are talking about.

Knowing a Little Can Tell You a Lot

Just as with being able to identify certain characteristics of animals or cars, the benefits of identifying certain characteristics of people are endless. For example, if you know someone is a vegetarian, how is this information of benefit to you? What do you know about this "category" of people? The number one thing you could be sure of is that they do not eat meat!

Simply knowing this one thing—someone does not eat meat—provides you with a variety of information. However, take heed to make sure you are not simply stereotyping. Would it be safe to assume that vegetarians would choose whole wheat bread over white bread or that they enjoy eating sprouts? Could you conclude that they own a comfortable pair of blue jeans? Would you expect to find that they recycle? Although the probability is higher that these things are also true, one could not assume so with 100% accuracy.

All vegetarians are not "sprout-eatin', blue jeans wearin' recyclers." This is stereotyping. However, just knowing that a person is vegetarian does give you specific information about that person. For instance, if you are inviting vegetarians over for dinner and really want to impress them and make them feel welcome, would you cook a roast for dinner? During conversation, how interested would they be about the butcher sale at the local grocery store? How much rapport will be built if you talk about the "delicious" taste of a good steak or the "scrumptious" recipe you have for

8

meatballs or lamb chops? How much would they be able to contribute to the conversation? How much do you think they would want to contribute?

Now, if you are one of those people who really enjoy making your guests as uncomfortable as possible, you could still choose to serve meat and make it your topic of conversation throughout the evening. Although your guests will have to forego the roast at dinner, and may be polite enough to listen to the conversation about meat, they will probably not have much of a chance to be themselves.

Just knowing your dinner guests are vegetarian gives you plenty of information to assist you in knowing how to make them feel as comfortable and welcome as possible. You can either ignore this information because you feel calling someone a vegetarian is labeling them, or choose to use it because you know it can assist you in building rapport, opening lines of

communication, and increasing self-expression.

So, when people are not comfortable with the use of systems like True Colors because they don't want to be labeled, it is for a good reason. They just want to be sure that people are not getting unfairly stereotyped. We do too. Just like any tool, it can be used to destroy or build.

True Colors is a way for you to break out of boxes, self-imposed or otherwise. It's a way of recognizing your gifts as just that—gifts! It's also a way of acknowledging that others are distinctive individuals with different gifts to contribute; and different does not mean wrong.

True Colors is one of the easiest, most convenient methods for understanding and appreciating human behavior. Don't miss out on the benefits because you might not understand it yet. You will. Use it to build self-esteem, enhance relationships, and bring out the best in everyone.

9

Chapter 3

DISCOVERING YOUR TRUE COLORS

On with the Show...

In the following chapters, I will use the terms Blue, Gold, Orange, and Green. These are the colors that make up the True Colors concept. As you will learn, people usually have various characteristics from all four of the color styles in their personality. However, one color is typically more dominant. So when we speak of a "Gold," we are referring to a person who has many of the character traits associated with the Gold temperament. They wouldn't necessarily have all of the Gold traits to be considered a "Gold," just more Gold traits than Blue, Orange, or Green.

As you learn more about and embrace the True Colors concept, you will begin to experience people, places, and events in relationship to their "color." You may notice the "colors" becoming integrated into your vocabulary. You'll find this awareness empowers you to avoid conflicts you would have otherwise run into head-on. You will be able to perceive behaviors as Blue, Gold, Orange, or Green automatically. And, instead of trying to change others' behaviors, you easily can find ways to value their methods as right for them.

Are you excited to find out more about yourself and others? At the back of the book you'll find cards with characteristics of the four different color types that make up the True Colors concept.

Notice that the cards are made to be removed so you can do your own "hands-on" sort for yourself or others. Carefully remove the cards and place them in front of you, picture side up.

Color Card Sort...

Once you have your cards in front of you, look at the pictures. Which ones do you relate to the most? Notice which one(s) remind you most of yourself and your own interests or motivations. Next, turn the cards over

and read through the information on each one. Rank them in order from most like you to least like you. For instance, you might decide that Green is most like you, Orange is second, Blue is third, and Gold is last or least like you. So, your color order or *spectrum* would be:

Green–Orange–Blue–Gold.

What Is Your Spectrum?

As mentioned, most of us are a combination of color style characteristics. If you read the cards and feel that you are equally strong in two or more styles, this is natural. We each have the capacity to excel in various areas exhibited by the different color characteristics. If after reading this section you still want further clarification of your color order, turn to Part II, "Color Watching," and read through the characteristics of each color style. If you follow your gut, you'll be able to recognize your colors more easily than if you try to scrutinize each one too closely.

First: Your Primary, Most Dominant...

The characteristics listed for this number one spot on your color spectrum indicate the ones you feel most comfortable operating with. They are the attributes most like you; the ones you use when you are being your most natural self, the ones that happen automatically.

Sometimes people may order their cards incorrectly because they choose the skills they *must* use on a daily basis, instead of the ones they *prefer* to use. For example, one woman I remember quite vividly was a principal for an elementary school. During a True Colors training at her school, she chose Gold as her primary, most dominant color. When she announced this to her staff, they roared with laughter and insisted she belonged in the Orange group instead. She argued that all she did all day was enforce rules, maintain schedules, and keep the school organized. Although this was true for the most part, her staff had a different point of view. They suggested that although it was her job to do so, she went about it in a strained, haphazard way. A bit taken aback by this information, she begrudgingly (at first) joined the Orange group. Throughout the rest of the session it was obvious to all that she was enjoying herself. By the end of the session she testified to her staff that she had never felt such a rapport

and freedom to be herself as she did with that Orange group. She realized that just because she had to enforce rules all day did not mean it was natural for her.

Second: As Meaningful as Your First...

Your second color will have a major influence on your first. Many times, it shines just as brightly as your most dominant color. In fact, for those whose colors shine inward (introvert) it may be hard to tell which is their first color and which is their second. (See Chapter 4 for more on introverts.) This is because they may use their most dominant color to process internally. The rest of the world may experience their second color as their most dominant, because that is the one they may use to operate in the external world. Take this into consideration if you are confused about your own or another person's behaviors. Some consider their second color as being almost interchangeable with their first.

Third...

You may or may not recognize some of the characteristics of your third color as being part of your temperament. Many times these traits will not be as obvious as the more dominant ones but will come in handy when needed. Sometimes when an individual's first color is extremely dominant, the second and third colors can be closely related to each other.

Fourth...

The last color in your spectrum is significant too. Because these characteristics are the least natural to you, you may admire them in others. Or, on the contrary, because they are the least natural, chances are that they are also the least understood, and therefore they are the characteristics that cause the most conflict with others.

This lack of understanding can cause us to criticize instead of appreciate others that have characteristics that are the least natural for us and vice versa. For example, a person who is very organized may have a tendency to criticize those who are not. And, those individuals for whom organization is not a priority may criticize those for whom it is.

People often condemn what they have not had much experience with or lack most in themselves.

Are You a Rainbow?

All of us, at one time or another, can recognize characteristics we have that are from any one of the four color styles. *Everyone* has all four of the color styles in their spectrum in differing amounts. On occasion some people feel their traits are evenly spread—one color not be any more dominant than another. This very well could be true. Some people who have had a lot of life experiences have had the opportunity to develop many aspects of their varying temperaments and therefore may appear to be quite balanced in characteristics. Others have conscientiously gone about developing their non-dominant traits so they feel comfortable with virtually all of them.

Many times however, if individuals are having a difficult time deciding their True Colors, it's because they are in a transition period in their life and are trying to figure out what's happening to them. Or, they may have seldom been able to truly be themselves and therefore only vaguely have a sense of what comes naturally for them. They may have lost touch with their True Colors. In addition, Greens are prone to thinking they do not have a dominant color because of their tendency to extensively analyze things.

Nonetheless, years of research have shown that people are born with one temperament that is stronger than the others. It's just a matter of recognizing which one it truly is.

For now, rank the colors from most like you to least like you below:

My Color Spectrum:

1. _____ 2. _____ 3. _____ 4. _____

Chapter 4

DO YOUR COLORS SHINE

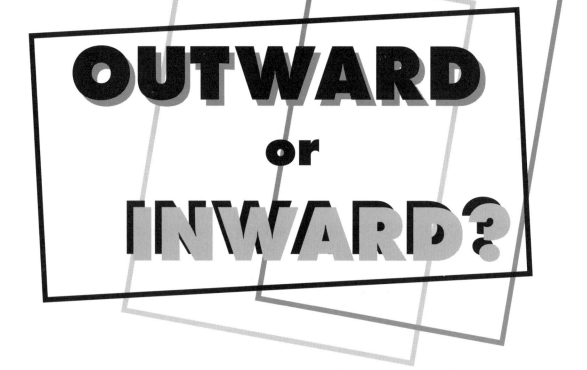

OUTWARD or INWARD?

A Note about Extroversion and Introversion...

Some people's most dominant color shines brightly for everyone to see. Others may not show their domi-nant color readily. For this reason, we might not recognize our True Colors immediately or may sometimes misin-terpret the True Colors of others. For instance, many Oranges are very loud and straightforward. You definitely know when they are in the room.

But some Oranges are quiet, passive, and don't call attention to themselves. That is what is usually expected for Greens. Typically a Green doesn't like to be in the limelight. However, some Greens are energetic, enthusiastic, and take the initiative to motivate others to action. So why the difference? The difference is whether their Colors are shining outward or inward.

Shining Outward— Extroverted...

Extroverts are generally fairly easy to spot. They are usually very approachable—if they haven't approached you first. They typically are comfortable meeting new people and will readily talk to strangers. They enjoy interaction with others and gain energy from it. The more they talk and share, the more energetic they become. Extroverts will ask others for their opinions and take pleasure in sharing their own. They have a tendency to get bored if they are not contributing to the conversation. In fact, if some extroverts don't self-regulate they may end up dominating the entire conversation. Given the opportunity, extroverts will speak before or as they think. They can blurt things out without much thought.

Some extroverts can have an entire conversation with themselves while you are in the room and thank you for your input, when in reality you said nothing!

Another way to look at extroverts is to say that their colors shine outward for the world to experience. Their attention is focused on the external environment of people, activities, and things.

HI BOB! WHAT DO YOU THINK OF MY PEARLS, AREN'T THEY WONDERFUL, DON'T YOU JUST LOVE THEM! ME TOO! BYE!!

Shining Inward—Introverted...

Introverts choose solitude to gain their energy. They prefer to think and reflect before sharing their opinions with others. They cherish their privacy and therefore honor the privacy of others. They are often thought of as good listeners because they wait to communicate until they have given the topic at hand some consideration.

This is not to say that introverts are not very talkative. With individuals that they have known for a while, they can be very verbal. In addition, they may muster up the resolution to be more verbal because they know it

can help bolster rapport with extroverts. However talkative or social they are, a great amount of interaction can be draining to an introvert who eventually needs their private time to recoup their energy. Even a long commute from work can be enough "alone time" to reenergize introverts by the time they arrive home.

Overall, introverts shine their colors inward to gather their energy. They focus much of their attention on the inside world of thoughts, ideas, and reflections.

Outside, Inside, In Between...

An introvert can seem to be an extrovert to someone who does not know them and vice versa. We all have times when we behave more introverted or extroverted, depending on our mood, experiences, and phase of life.

Sometimes people may question themselves and think that it is better to be one way or the other. For instance, many people find extroverts refreshing and entertaining and may wish they had the same glibness. On the other hand, there are extroverted individuals who berate themselves for not pausing before speaking and admire the independence of introverts, wishing they had the ability to be content and comfortable when alone. Neither way is the better way to be. Introversion and extroversion are simply characteristics pertaining to the way a person gathers their energy.

One interesting phenomenon that does occur relating to introversion and extroversion is that extroverts have a tendency to show their True Colors more outwardly while introverts may use their dominant color traits to process things more internally and thus may show their second color more readily. Extra attention may be needed in determining the colors of introverts. For instance, introverted Blue/Greens may show their Green traits more predominantly and thus appear to others as being Green dominant. This is because they use many of their Blue characteristics to process in their internal world. What is visible to others may not be what is going on inside. This is also another reason that we sometimes refer to a person's first two colors instead of just their first. You really need to pay attention to tell which is which!

What to Watch For

Keep in mind there are degrees of extroversion and introversion. Individuals that are extremely extroverted will speak more loudly with animated facial expressions, large hand movements and ample body movement. Those extremely introverted will appear the opposite—reserved in movement and facial

expressions using minimal gesturing as to not call attention to themselves. Of course many people are somewhere in between. They may have some introverted tendencies mixed in with their dominant extroversion or visa versa. In general, some hints for determining whether someone you know is more extroverted or introverted are:

Extroverts:

Think and process out loud

Prefer to bounce ideas off others

Enjoy attention from others

Speak readily in many situations

Outwardly focus on surroundings

Seek activities involving many people

Pursue breadth of experiences

Introverts:

Process internally before sharing

Explore options independently

Avoid attention from strangers

Pause and think before speaking

Inwardly focus and ponder

Seek solo, intimate experiences with select individuals

Pursue depth of experiences

17

COLOR WATCHING

An In-Depth Look At Color Characteristics

We all know that every single snowflake is unique and different, each one remarkably individual. However, they all have some features in common. The most obvious, they are all made from snow! And snow, of course, is made from water, and water from hydrogen and oxygen.

18

We also know that when exposed to temperatures over 32 degrees Fahrenheit, a snowflake will melt. Even with these similarities snowflakes can become discolored by dirt, pets, pollution, and people. Depending on the environment and the air it fell through, it will pick up different particles along its journey to the earth and may end up looking different on the outside than when it started. Yet on the inside the same basic ingredients still exist.

It is the same for human beings. We are also unique and different, each one remarkably individual, yet possessing commonalities, if you are willing to look for them. Since there are billions of people, it stands to reason that there are probably billions of variations in personalities, especially since no two people (even twins) were raised exactly alike. Even if they were, we all know that two people can go through the same situation yet have totally different experiences and responses. Nonetheless, as you may have noticed by now, there are some similarities in the natural tendencies of yourself and others. I often ask my workshop participants, "Who here is unpredictable?" I rarely, if ever, have someone raise their hand. Barring any mental illness, most of us have aspects of our personalities that are predictable to a certain extent. Just like vegetarians are similar to each other in that they avoid meat, you can recognize traits the color types have in common. Knowing these characteristics can help guide your own actions when relating to others.

We may change the color we operate in depending on the circumstances.

Determining the colors of ourselves and others may not always be simple because when we shift roles, we may shift what colors we show accordingly. For instance, some people find it is pretty natural for them to behave quite Gold at work, yet as parents they seem to shift to Blue. With friends, the Orange in them is brought forth. Yes, the people in our environment definitely have an influ-

19

ence on our behaviors. Our basic character ingredients may remain the same, but who we are with or what role we are in may influence what color is in operation at any given time. Sometimes we even find ourselves pressured to act in certain ways to be accepted or fit in.

Keep this in mind when determining your True Colors or the colors of others. Look for the underlying motivation for the behavior. If a person is following the rules because it is the appropriate and responsible thing to do, it is different than someone following the rules to keep harmony or to be liked or accepted by others. Notice the action is the same but the motivation behind it is different.

This section gives you a more in-depth look at the different color characteristics. Be aware that as you read each color chapter and review these characteristics you won't necessarily agree with every word of your own color profile. You may be reading along, saying to yourself, "Oh yes, this is me!" or "Yes, I do that," then look at the next trait and pause. You may discover that a particular characteristic is not one that pertains to you. That's okay! You are looking for a general trend. We are all a blend of a variety of traits. Amazingly enough, though, many people find several, if not all, of the attributes in a color style apply to them in one way or another.

The stories in this section show only a few ways that the True Colors characteristics might be demonstrated. You may have a very different way of showing the very same characteristic. The stories are provided to assist you in recognizing and understanding the different motivations for people's behaviors. Notice as you read who you know that fits the various descriptions. Pay attention to the ways they are similar to or diverse from each other. And most importantly, realize how you can use this information in your life and relationships.

If you are curious and want even more clarification, ask a friend or co-worker to read the profile you think applies to you. Frequently, you'll get a resounding "Oh yes!" or "Oh no!" Either way you will receive valuable feedback on your journey to discovering your True Colors.

Chapter 5

SHADES OF BLUE BLUE

BLUE

If you've ever seen the movie *Dead Poets Society,* starring Robin Williams, then you have experienced the motivating enthusiasm of a passionate Blue. In the movie, the character acts as a mentor to lead his students down the path of their own calling. He stimulates their imagination through his assignments and encouragement. He acts as a catalyst to thrust them in the direction of being the best they can be at being true to themselves.

The character that Robin Williams portrays in this movie is only one hue of the many shades of Blues. Frequently, extroverted Blues seem to make their way to the front lines of motivation, while many introverted Blues may choose to support others more behind the scenes. Whatever Blues decide to do with their lives, it must involve people. They have an inner drive to connect with others as well as to connect with themselves. Blues feel a never-ending tug to explore their own identity and find a sense of who they are from what they do.

The following pages will capture the essence of a Blue's style, values, and motivations. They are simply observations of some common traits shared by many Blues. You or the people you know may have any combination of the several characteristics. The important thing to keep in mind, however, is that the reason for determining which characteristics apply to you or others is to gain understanding and appreciation for the differences in all of us. And, instead of trying to change each other, we will choose to welcome and nurture the differences.

Blue Characteristics

The following qualities are associated with the Blue color style. Since all of us are unique individuals, the characteristics will manifest themselves a bit differently for each person. However, the general theme will remain. Keep in mind that a person can still be considered to be Blue dominant without having all of the characteristics listed.

Caretaker—Nurturing, sensitive to the needs of others. Usually, the first one to notice that someone isn't feeling well or needs help and will want to offer assistance. Frequently puts the needs of others before self.

Optimistic—Looks on the bright side of things. Likely to be the one who sees "the light at the end of the tunnel" during a crisis. Motivates and encourages others.

Passionate—Devoted to and intoxicated by their interests. Whether it's collecting antiques, motivating a team, or building a relationship, they throw their heart and soul into it. Can be very dramatic.

Enthusiastic—Speaks kindly and compliments freely. Expressive, persuasive, stimulating, and inspirational. Lives to have everyone around them happy and comfortable. Often feels it is their duty to cheer up others or provide motivation.

Imaginative—Creative, expressive, and inspired. May be drawn towards art, music, or drama. Possibly will write and speak with poetic flair or use metaphors. Sees possibility, hope, future potential.

Cause Oriented—May volunteer time and get involved in causes such as recycling, helping victims of violent crimes, feeding the hungry, raising consciousness, self-improvement, spiritual growth, and so on.

True Romantic—Enjoys gestures of romance. Needs to know that they are loved. Likes to feel special. Derives immense pleasure by providing romance for their lover. May enjoy reading romance novels or poetry.

Needs to Be Unique—Strives for genuine self-expression and their own identity. Although they may be good at modifying their behavior like a chameleon to fit the needs of the person they are relating to at the moment, they aspire to be unique in

their own way. Are able to spot, and like to bring out, the best in others. Will take any opportunity to bolster someone else's self-esteem or acknowledge others' uniqueness or talents.

Cooperative Rather than Competitive—Encourages team-building rather than "may the best man win" attitude. Good group or team participant. Enjoys the friendship and camaraderie of working together on a project or goal.

Strong Sense of Spirituality—Whether or not this is a belief in God or a higher power, Blues feel they have a larger purpose in life, a connection somehow to the rest of the universe. Growth oriented and self-searching. Life must have meaning, significance, and contribution. Wants to make a difference.

People Oriented—Accepting of differences, friendly, and affirming. Relates well with people. Makes an effort to connect with and acknowledge others. Most every decision made is determined by how it will affect the people involved. Promotes growth and development of others.

Peacemaker—Most comfortable when everyone is getting along with each other. When conflicts arise, can become distracted from work or even affected physically. Will go to great lengths to restore harmony, even if it means holding quiet their own point of view for the moment. The relationship is more important than being right.

Understanding and Appreciating Blues

Blue's core values are relationships and self-expression. One of the best ways to understand and appreciate them is to recognize some of their strengths.

Blue Strengths:

Accepting
Acting as a catalyst
Communicating
Cooperating
Counseling
Creating
Guiding
Imagination
Intuition
Leading
Listening
Mentoring
Motivating
Optimism
Recruiting
Speaking
Supportiveness
Teaching
Tolerance
Training

There are endless possibilities for how the strengths and preferences of Blues might be drawn upon. The following stories are provided to illustrate how just a few of these traits might be demonstrated by the Blues in our lives. You may see yourself or people you know in these individuals and circumstances.

Of course, it is impossible to capture every nuance of what makes up any human being, but hopefully, in reading these stories, you will better understand the motivations behind the person's actions and increase your appreciation for their way of doing things.

Why Am I Doing This?

"This is a scary move," Steve thought to himself, " but I just have to do it. I know it is right; I can feel it."

For the past three years Steve has worked as a sales representative for a nationwide technology development company. He took the job because he could work part-time and get paid quite well. It was a means to an end. He always kept the future in front of him. He was so associated with his future that he felt as though he were already there, living it. That's how he was able to work for the company as long as he did. Working minimal hours and receiving a good salary made it possible for him to spend time learning more about himself by reading, traveling, and connecting with others. He was able to take many classes in areas that he was drawn toward: mastering emotions, mind/body/spirit, meditation, yoga, tai chi, breath work, and hypnosis.

But his present was catching up to his future. Although he was actually an outstanding sales person—top in his field—he just couldn't do it

anymore. His heart wasn't in it. He felt like a hypocrite. For this reason, he decided to leave his position to explore other avenues. "I have to be passionate," he confided in his co-worker Mindy, "and truly believe in something to sell a product or work for a company. I need to work in an area where I know I am contributing to others on a daily basis, where I can connect and bring out the best in people."

"But you do contribute, Steve," she assured him. "Everyone around here benefits from your compassion and energy. Even those that others find hard to work with, you are able to appreciate. You're everyone's friend."

It was true. Steve was definitely there for the people he worked with. Just this morning he was scheduled to meet with a big client and was heading out of his office when his co-worker Shelby appeared. Shelby was involved in a very intense situation and needed a listening ear. Steve thought of his pending appointment, then noticed the look on Shelby's face. He pushed the thought of the appointment to the back of his mind and sat down to give Shelby his full attention. Although Steve heard the words that were coming out of Shelby's mouth, what he was really experiencing was Shelby's emotions, the feelings behind the words. He felt good about being there for Shelby and giving him the opportunity to vent. Helping others was virtually irresistible to Steve. He was aware that he was supposed to be at his appointment, which was important to his own financial well-being, but at the same time he knew *this* was where he really needed to be. This was more important.

Steve paid attention to Shelby's physiology, tone of voice, and facial expressions. He felt as though he was a conduit for Shelby's emotions. Shelby must have felt it too. After twenty minutes of venting, he was freshly liberated. He stood and shook Steve's hand, obviously relieved to have gotten things off his chest to someone who was so empathetic.

Steve felt exhilarated, taking pleasure that he could be of some help. Yet at the same time he had a sinking feeling inside, knowing he had let down his appointment. At this point he was only fifteen minutes late, but that was late enough. Steve had already made up his mind to be more cooperative in his negotiations with the customer. He felt as though he had to make it up to him somehow. He quickly ran over options of what he could do. Perhaps he could come down on his

price, throw in free shipping, or offer an upgrade. He picked up the phone to apologize.

The other person was very understanding and reassured Steve that it was perfectly okay, that he had appreciated the extra time. But this did not allay Steve's guilt. He had made up his mind. The other person would be rewarded for his patience.

Who Am I?

Many Blues are fascinated by human behavior and relationships. They seek understanding of themselves and how they fit into the world around them. They may be drawn to the self-help and psychology sections of bookstores and are on a constant quest of self-exploration. As they are seeking to find themselves, they are also engaged in understanding how they can connect effectively with those around them. They seek a connection on a much deeper level than the other color styles typically do. When listening to

27

others, their attention goes beyond the words. They respond to the emotional needs of others. They will try to read for deeper meaning than the question or issue at hand, sometimes uncovering a land mine of untapped feelings. When this happens, Blues are there to listen compassionately.

Since they have a genuine acceptance for most everyone they come in contact with, they look for the positive attributes in others and usually find them. This is why they are able to get along with and appreciate the approach of individuals that others may find intolerable. Blues truly feel uplifted when they are able to contribute to others, be it a simple compliment, acknowledgment, or praise for a job well done.

Blues also enjoy being needed and liked. They aim to please. They have a habit of trying to be everything to everybody. If they are not careful, they can get overwhelmed by spreading themselves too thinly.

The Object of the Game Is to Feel Good

Two second-graders, Justin and Trey, were playing *The Phonics Game®* called "Silent Partners" with their reading teacher. There were two decks of cards, deck A and deck B. The teacher had started the game with deck A, and each student

had won one round. Trey won the first time and was so excited that he jumped up and down. Justin looked almost as excited as Trey as he reached over and patted him on the back, saying, "Good job!" The next round, Justin won and Trey congratulated him.

Deck B was a little harder. Justin won the first round. Trey looked disappointed this time and did not congratulate Justin as he had previously. During the second round of deck B, Justin had the opportunity to take more than half of Trey's cards, which would assure him a winning game. That would be three games in a row! Justin looked at Trey and his cards. Then he looked at the teacher, who knew from his body language and eyes that he knew exactly what he was doing. Instead of drawing from Trey's pile he drew from the center pile, ending his turn.

On the next hand, Trey won. As a smile burst across Trey's face, a smile shone on Justin's.

Because it is the player's option whether or not to take cards, it is not considered cheating to refrain. The primary objective is to learn phonics, not just to win points.

Trey had already gone back to his seat and Justin was helping the teacher put the cards away when she told Justin, "I noticed you didn't choose to take Trey's cards and that's okay. That's your choice."

Justin bubbled, "It's fun, even when Trey wins."

Cooperation and Seeing Others Happy

As depicted in the story about the card game, from the Blue perspective, harmony, happiness, and friendship are valued more highly than personal victory. Blues derive joy from seeing others happy. When it comes to competition, they seek the pleasure that comes from participating with others. Playing together becomes their objective over winning. If winning will bring joy to other team members, then Blues will be more motivated to win.

Spreading Smiles

"Wow! That's beautiful," commented a co-worker.

Lisa looked up from her work. "Thank you," she beamed as she hastened to finish up the bulletin board she was designing so she could make it to her next meeting on time.

Lisa coordinates the Loss Control Department for her company. She is in charge of employee safety. Each month she tries to pick a safety theme

appropriate for the month. Since it was now mid-summer, her theme was fire safety. She had cut flames from red, orange, and yellow paper and had creatively positioned them around some information about preventing fires. One corner of the board was always reserved for announcing birthdays. There she had placed a cut-out picture of a small birthday cake and had arranged around it the names of staff members whose birthdays landed in August.

"Oh no!" she gasped. "It's August 3rd today and Lynn's birthday was yesterday. I didn't get the names up in time for everyone else to know." Lisa felt awful. She tried so hard each month to come up with good themes, make them eye-catching, and get the board up on time. She rushed to her meeting, thinking about what she could do for Lynn.

Lisa had volunteered to be a member of the Events Committee. Because she spent most of her days working on rules, regulations, and other paperwork, the bulletin board and this particular committee were a welcome break from her heavier responsibilities. The committee had been formed to bring some "fun" to the work environment. Members were involved in activities such as decorating the office for holidays, implementing events for employee recognition, and planning the company picnic. She enjoyed being a part of making the work environment more festive and welcoming. It really brought the employees together and gave them a sense of family and belonging.

Because her laughter can be heard ringing out at any given moment throughout the day, Lisa is often referred to by her co-workers as "Laughing Lisa." She is friendly and positive; a smile seems to be a permanent fixture on her face. People like her the moment that they meet her.

But today Lisa's smile slowly faded from her face. The committee members had strayed from the agenda and were chatting about various situations and people. Lisa was uncomfortable with gossip and never participated in it. She felt sorry for the people they were discussing—after all, they were not there to defend themselves. Her thoughts flitted for a moment to whether these same people also talked about her behind her back. She sat there quietly, not wanting to interrupt their camaraderie but at the same time wishing they would stop.

She was relieved when the committee chair finally called everyone's attention back to the agenda. By the end of the meeting Lisa had volunteered to create a flyer announcing their next event as well as shop for some particular items they would

need. A tiny smile returned to her face.

The next day Lisa quietly placed a special birthday card on Lynn's desk.

Creativity, Acknowledgment, and Empathy

Naturally creative, Blues often have an eye for color and aesthetics. They like to have their environment look nice and fashion things so they are pleasant. Since creativity can come in endless forms, Blues may sometimes be too humble to recognize their own variation of creativity. It doesn't always come in the shape of creating art and beautiful surroundings, but it is there nonetheless.

Blues are warm and friendly. They will go to great lengths to make sure others feel comfortable around them.

Because they are conscientious about the feelings of others, they make sure to give acknowledgment. Blues enjoy making a person feel recognized and special and can feel horribly guilty if they miss an opportunity. They make it a point to remember others' special occasions such as birthdays and

30

anniversaries, and other personal details.

Although some Blues enjoy the social connecting they derive from gossip or "sharing," other Blues will not participate unless it is of a positive nature. Being empathetic, they can put themselves in the shoes of others and may think, "How would I feel if this were happening to me?" They may keep quiet about their opinion on certain matters if they feel it would hurt the feelings of others, spoil their mood, or create disharmony.

Self-Expression

Nikki remembers when she was eight years old. It was Christmas and she could feel the excitement well up inside of her. She had written a special poem as a gift for her family. It came from a pure place in her heart; it was something she had created. She remembered kneeling on the bedroom floor, writing. "It just came flowing out of me. I felt so mature as I read the words. They sounded so grown up, so unique, so spiritual. I was almost impressed with myself. I couldn't wait to share my gift, to share myself."

But when Nikki read her special Christmas poem to her family she did not get the reaction she had anticipated.

"They didn't believe me. 'You didn't write that, you got that out of a book,'" she recalled them saying. "Then they all dispersed! They got up and left, and I was just standing there all alone. I was crushed. They didn't acknowledge my gift; a gift from my heart. It was so painful. I swore right then I would never share again."

Now, years later, Nikki confides, "I didn't see it for all these years. I could have looked at the underlying message—that they thought it was so good they didn't believe an eight-year-old could write it. Instead I chose the pain of the illusion that they didn't care about my gift."

Nikki continued to write, but she never shared it with anyone. She kept a journal at night and poured her heart and soul onto the pages. This way she could write freely, without judgment.

One time one of her girlfriends had to write a story for an assignment at school and shared with Nikki that she was at a loss for ideas. Without even thinking, the words popped out of Nikki's mouth, "I'll write it!"

Nikki wrote a story that earned her friend an "A." (Keeping the story tucked away since childhood, she now plans to publish it as a children's book.)

Another joy of Nikki's was singing. "By the time I was twelve, I was belting out Streisand in our family room. I used to hop up on the step in front of the fireplace and give a show, but always in private, where no one could hear me. I was very shy with my voice."

In her mid-twenties she hooked up with musicians and formed a rock band. "It was easy to get out there and sing my lungs out. There was all this loud music, and I was part of a whole so it was more comfortable."

Over time Nikki played with several bands, and she was asked to write songs for them to play. She was up for the challenge. As a group they would brainstorm ideas for her to write about. She said about her writing, "It was always fun but some of it felt contrived. I was writing about something that *others* wanted me to write about, things that didn't matter to me personally. It didn't feel completely natural. Still, it was rewarding yet scary. It was definitely a stretch for me."

In her thirties she decided to help a friend promote his music and songs. She could no longer hide behind the band and the loud music. It was only her singing and Joe on the acoustic guitar. "It felt good to help a friend, but I still needed to fulfill what was inside of me."

Now Nikki has decided to write and play her own music. "I feel like I am going backwards. I haven't played a guitar in twenty years. I'm taking what I learned in the eighth grade and trying to put it together with my songs. The hardest part is being patient with the process. It's personally challenging. The whole journey

has been to get me here to express what is inside of me. It feels more rewarding, more personally fulfilling, and a lot more intimate. Playing my own music is when I feel the most at home, in myself and in the world. I feel connected up with the spirit, the most complete and whole; expressing my deepest sense of purpose."

True Blues

Blues shine the brightest and feel the most alive and fulfilled when they are expressing their true selves, showing their True Colors. Creative and passionate about their interests, they may not share their talents with the rest of the world for fear of rejection.

Nonetheless, they feel a drive or calling to fulfill their purpose to be "at home" with themselves and the rest of the world.

Another Hue of Blue

Blues have generous natures and a love of people that makes them pleasant company for most anyone. However, sometimes the motivations and actions of Blues are misunderstood. The same traits that are viewed as positive by some, especially other Blues, may actually be irritating to others. It is human nature to evaluate the actions of others. Our values, judgments, and beliefs influence our perception of those actions. It is a matter of perspective. For example, you may observe a person to be "incredibly sensitive" because they cry at movies. Another person observing the same behavior would call it "over-emotional." Which is true? Neither! A behavior is a behavior—period.

There are multiple ways to label any given behavior, so why would it be beneficial for us to know how other people may view ours? When we are aware of how our own behavior is affecting others, we can make choices. We may think, "Yes, I do that and it is a part of myself that I cherish." Or, "Gee, I didn't know I did that. Thank you for pointing that out to me so that I can become aware and change it if I wish." For example, have you ever had the opportunity to hear yourself on a tape machine? If so, did you sound the way you thought you did? Most likely not. Many times when people hear their voices played back, they are surprised at the speed, style, or even accent of their words. Frequently, after individuals hear something in their speech they were not aware of before, they end up making some kind of modifications based on the feedback they received.

Keeping this in mind as you read, think of situations in which the following may apply. Notice whether you are coming across to others in ways other than you intended. Instead of hoping others will change and clearly understand your intentions, pay attention to the contributions you are bringing to the situation. Remember, it is your choice whether to modify your behaviors or not. Feedback is a gift. You may choose to use this gift in any way you desire. Validate yourself for *who you are* and know *when, where,* and *how* you wish to best express yourself.

Others May See Blues as:

Over-Emotional—Sensitive. Takes things too personally. Hard to give feedback to because they can become easily hurt by criticism. Often reads between the lines of communication and misinterprets things to mean something else. Creates chaos out of an average circumstance by being overly dramatic.

Mushy—Gets carried away in the romance department. Makes "puppy dog eyes," writes poetry, sends love notes, sings songs, caresses, hugs, and wants to hold hands any chance they get. Yearns to hear "I love you," to see it written, to feel it in their soul. When it comes to love, dives in headfirst without checking to see if there is even water in the pool. Over-romanticizes the simplest gesture to mean a sign of true love.

Other-Worldly—Can be found taking or teaching yoga classes, meditation sessions, and retreats. From traditional religion to psychic readers to hypnotherapy, enjoys looking for and helping others find the meaning of life. Promotes "touchy-feely" subjects. May spend money for a personal growth seminar instead of paying bills.

Unrealistic—Says "yes" to too much and then cannot follow through on promises. Believes they can be everything to everyone, all of the time. Naïve. When all evidence suggests otherwise, still believes in a person. Wants their relationships to be the number one priority of their significant other. When priorities of others line up differently, doesn't understand. Dreamers.

Too Tenderhearted—Sees everything as subjective. Is easily swayed by emotions and opinions of others. Makes exceptions to rules and may ignore policies depending on the situation at hand. Can be easily duped. Soft; too nice; someone who will let others "walk all over them."

Wishy-Washy—Can't make a decision for themselves. Changes mind according to what will make people happiest.

Smothering—Attaches to people and fosters dependency by not allowing them to do for themselves. May be labeled as "co-dependent."

Manipulative—Instead of coming straight out and making their desires known, drops hints. Pouts if others do something they don't agree with. Passive-aggressive. Makes it known indirectly what a martyr they are to get acknowledgment.

Groveling—Overly apologizes or supplicates. Says "I'm sorry" too much. Overuses softeners such as, "If it is not too much trouble, could you please?" or "I mean only if it is not an inconvenience, would you mind . . . ?"

Bleeding Heart—Motivated by pity. Gives up life for a cause that has nothing to do with their own plight. Wants to rescue others.

Talking Too Much—Makes conversation about anything and everything with anyone. Carries on after cues are given that the conversation has ended. Gossips.

Nosy—Asks too many personal questions about other people's business. Busybody.

Blues May See Self as:

Caring—Of course Blues take things personally. It's because they care. Warm, compassionate, and considerate. They try their best, so when they are criticized they feel it deeply. Pays attention to the nuances of conversation and has the sensory acuity to notice what people really mean. In touch with feelings; alive and expressive. Thinks going through life without intense feelings and drama would be boring!

Romantic—Loves the excitement of being in love. It awakens the senses. Enjoys all the trappings that come with being in love. Why wouldn't a person want to hug, hold, and hang out with the one they love? It's fun to notice when someone sends out a signal that they are interested. It's all part of the intrigue and excitement of romance.

Spiritual—Blues know they have a greater purpose. They would not have been put on this earth to merely exist. They may meditate, pray, or participate in other spiritual practices to get closer in touch with their higher power, themselves and others. They search for the meaning of life and know that powers exist beyond what some people might believe.

Having Faith—When they take on projects, Blues truly desire to complete them all and have the faith that they will find a way. They have faith in people and give them numerous chances to demonstrate their worth. Put relationships as top priority and can't imagine why other people would be any different. After all, isn't that what life is about . . . people?

Nice—Pleasant, cheerful, and wants people to be happy. Trusting, gives the benefit of the doubt and believes in others. Affirming. Sees the need for exceptions. Will go the extra mile for others. A good friend.

Flexible—Goes with the flow. Empathetic, they can put themselves in the shoes of others. Really can see many sides of an issue. Taking a firm stand is not worth jeopardizing a relationship. Harmonizer.

Caretaker—Sensitive to the needs of others. Will help in any way possible. Enjoys being depended upon and bringing joy to others.

Pleasant, Not Pushy—Has needs but puts others' first. Does not believe in being aggressive. Would rather make needs known in a non-confrontive manner.

Polite—Wants to make other people feel comfortable; lets them know they are important and that their feelings count. Interprets bluntness as uncaring or purposefully hurtful.

Willing to Work Tirelessly for a Cause—Sympathetic to the needs of others. Knows when others need help. If they won't lead the crusade, who will?

Great Communicator—Friendly. Has a great ability to put anyone at ease and help them feel welcome, important, and recognized. Wants to be interesting and acknowledge others.

Genuinely Interested in the Welfare of Others—Wants to know how people are feeling and what they need and want. If they don't know what's going on, how will they know whether to bake a cake, bring a gift, or offer help?

As you can see, depending on which lens you are looking through, what can seem like less than desirable qualities to one can be held as redeeming qualities to another. If you find yourself beginning to make a negative judgment about another person's behavior, stop, and see how you can reframe the behavior to view it in a more positive light. Also, when you are more aware of how your own actions are being perceived by others, it can help you more effectively choose the situations in which you can be most comfortable sharing those aspects of yourself.

Relating to Blues

First and foremost, Blues are some of the best friends a person can have. They will be there for you through thick and thin. When others have given up on you, they will keep giving you encouragement. Even though they have their own priorities, they will set them aside to help.

Individuals with Blue as their first or second color tend to be communicative. They want to interact with others in a warm, caring way. They respond well to kindness and place a high priority on relationships. If you can consider some of their needs important to you, then you will be able to relate to them in such a way that they will naturally be motivated to want to cooperate with you. Typically, Blues relate well with other Blues. They like Gold's predictable style and structure. They enjoy Green's imagination and intellectual discussions, and they take pleasure in Orange's active, entertaining approach.

Maintain a Pleasant Environment

Pay attention to ways in which you can help put a Blue at ease. Blues look for opportunities to be a source of help in creating a cooperative and harmonious atmosphere. Not only do they want to cooperate and please, they will try to encourage others to do the same. They will usually conform to whatever group, organization, or structure is set up for them, although fitting into that structure is not as important as their desire to feel valued and unique. Acknowledge them for their support and distinctiveness.

38

Point out How Others Will Benefit

Blues are naturally drawn to individuals who seem to be having difficulty—social, personal, or otherwise. They often side with the underdog and support various human rights movements. In their element—when they are helping people—Blues have a knack for cultivating the potential of others. They are self-sacrificing and will forgo the luxuries in life to contribute to others more in need.

Blues may be reluctant to get involved in something in which they do not see value. When they realize that their participation really would help others, something transforms inside of them. Simply re-framing the situation compels Blues to want to do the things they may have been trying to avoid just minutes before. Suddenly, they're on a mission.

Understand Their Zest for Vitality Includes Emotions

Blues like to act out and participate fully in the human dramas of life. They tend to get immersed in the experiences of living such as love, strife, success, sorrow, joy, and so on. A lot of their energy is spent paying attention to how they and those around them feel and what they are going through personally and emotionally. Step into their world to appreciate their enthusiasm. Show care when they are sharing to promote a receptive atmosphere for them to express their feelings. Make sure your body language and facial expressions are congruent with theirs. Support them through strong participation and interaction.

Grant Opportunities for Personal Growth

Interested in self-awareness and self-improvement, Blues look for meaning in life. Understand their yearning for their life to have purpose. Supply avenues for self-expression. They strive to be authentic, unique, truly themselves. They are on a constant and never-ending journey to self-discovery. Encourage them to find avenues to present their ideas and be creative, for them to be at home with themselves.

Give Individual Attention

Blues seek to connect with others. They enjoy forming lasting relationships, having close friends, and feeling loved. Remember their birthday and other personal matters they have shared. Offer a story about yourself. Often the smallest gesture of friendship towards them can go a very long way. They like to enlist and excite others. Provide opportunities for them to train, guide, recruit, and mentor

Blues Need:

- acceptance
- empathy
- harmony
- self-expression
- inspiration
- affection
- to contribute
- understanding
- meaning
- validation

Blues Need to Be:

- authentic
- dramatic
- free to find meaning
- nurturing
- personal

Blues Value:

- compassion
- friendship
- teamwork
- sensitivity
- sharing
- tolerance
- trust
- kindness
- relationships
- possibility

Blues Find Joy in:

- acceptance
- affection
- conversations
- family
- friendships
- groups
- love
- music

With Blues Be:

- caring
- communicative
- humanistic
- nice
- open
- people-oriented
- personal
- respectful of their feelings
- sincere
- approachable

Bringing Out the Blue

To allow Blues to show their True Colors, turn to them for actions that bring out the best in themselves and others.

Miranda sat at a table outside her favorite café enjoying lunch in the sunshine. As she dined she took in her surroundings. There was a park nearby with several benches that seemed to be occupied quite frequently with homeless individuals. A glimpse of an elderly gentleman in ragged, dirty clothes approaching her table startled her. She turned towards him, feeling a bit unsettled.

"Got any spare change for a hungry man?" he implored.

"How about some food?" Miranda asked. "Would you like to join me for lunch?"

"I wouldn't want to impose, ma'am", he said apologetically. "But if you have some change that would truly help me out."

"Really," she said with the sweetest, soothing tone, "I would really enjoy your company."

After a bit more encouragement the man took a seat with her. They shared a wonderful lunch together. He talked about aspects of his history as well as his present living conditions. Miranda gave him some money and vowed to him that she would somehow help to make things better. Truly moved by the encounter at lunch, Miranda started thinking about what she could possibly do. "I know," she thought, "I'll call Sharmila. She'll have some ideas."

Sharmila was Miranda's best friend. She was a sociology student and part-time instructor for toddlers at a Montessori school. She, too, had thought about helping out somehow, and the call from Miranda was the impetus she needed to charge ahead. The first thing Sharmila did was to contact organizations that already existed to help feed and shelter the homeless to find out what was being done in their area. Finding out that they were short-staffed and short-funded, the answer was not a surprise; not much could be done with the resources they had available to them at the time.

Miranda and Sharmila decided to dig up some of their own resources. They held fund-raisers in front of grocery stores and at the university. They put together a concert of local bands and accepted donations to benefit the hungry. They finally got permission from the city to hold a Saturday afternoon weekly picnic. They gathered volunteers to help them make posters and flyers, contact markets for food donations, and help set up the area at the park. Sharmila and Miranda personally made soup and sandwiches and served them to anyone who showed up with an appetite.

Turn to a Blue for:

Validation—When you need a little praise, acceptance, and understanding a Blue usually has plenty to offer.

Cheering Up—Blues are optimistic and have a way of making you feel that everything will be okay. They look for the silver lining in a cloud and will help you see how practically any situation can be used to learn and grow.

A Confidant—If you need someone to listen empathetically, Blues will lend an ear. They try hard to not judge others for their actions and have an immense amount of understanding and tolerance.

A Mentor—Blues like to foster growth in others. It feels wonderful for them to be a role model, inspiration, or other positive influence on the lives of others.

Understanding Affects on People—If you need to know how your project will affect the people involved, ask a Blue. They are connected with people and know their needs and how they might react to changes.

Help!—If you need a volunteer to pitch in, if you are overwhelmed and need assistance or a favor—turn to a Blue. If they are not already stretched to the limit, they find pleasure in contributing to others. It makes them feel wanted, included, and needed. Many Blues seek out service professions such as nursing, social work, and teaching.

Creative Ideas—Blues are full of possibility. Find a Blue to help you brainstorm ideas. Original, unique, and inspiring, they can also help unlock the creativity in those around them.

42

Training—Blues make great trainers, especially in "people" skills such as customer service, morale, team-building, and communication.

Leading a Human-Needs Cause—When it comes to the charitable organizations—if humanly possible, Blues will lend a hand. This is especially true if they can see their help will benefit others.

Sharing—Most Blues enjoy hearing a personal anecdote. Some even use what others refer to as "gossip" as a form of staying connected with friends.

Affection—Whether you are looking for a mate or a friend, you'll find that Blues are usually very generous with their affection. Many will give hugs freely, smile, and touch or even give massages to those that they feel a kinship with.

A Friend—Relationships are the number one value to Blues. They seek out friendships and alliances with others. They can provide encouragement, motivation, and support.

Chapter 6

SHADES OF
GOLD
GOLD GOLD

Lyle has been married for thirty-four years. He and his wife, Gloria, have two children, a son and a daughter. Growing up, each child had his or her own chores to complete, including keeping their own rooms clean. They were required to make their beds in the morning before going to school. Lyle had a "policy" that his children should finish what they start. When they were making decisions to join little league or take swimming lessons, for instance, they knew they had to stick with it until the end. No dropping out allowed. Since Lyle and Gloria both worked for schools, and had summers off, they frequently went on camping trips together as a family. Gloria's parents lived close by so they were able to visit them on a regular basis. Every three years they would travel to Minnesota to visit Lyle's family, always the last week in July or the first week in August.

When their son became a cub scout, Lyle became the cub master. When their daughter joined softball, Lyle became the coach. Joining organizations and teams soon turned into an integral part of Lyle's life. Since he worked as the director of transportation for a local school district, Lyle also joined the California Association for School Transportation Officials. The first year as a member he took the position of vice president, the second year he was an active member, and the third year he became presi-dent of the chapter. He remained president for five consecutive years, then spent another year as a member before becoming the president again for four more years. Currently he holds the position of past president and is still a very active member. Lyle has also been a member of the American Legion for twenty-eight years, the first year as a member and the next seventeen as commander. He is a good coordinator and finds it easiest to be the head of organizations so that he can designate policies and projects, delegate assignments, and ensure ventures are responsibly brought to completion.

Lyle has many Gold qualities. As traditional, rule-abiding citizens, Golds are hard-working and dedicated to their families. Their children are raised to adhere to set rules and are taught a strong sense of what is right and wrong. They are encouraged to be responsible, respectful, conservative, and stable.

Golds have a strong sense of loyalty, not only to their families but also to the organizations they work for. They are drawn to service organizations, community action groups, churches, and volunteer associations. Golds derive a sense of great satisfaction from being useful and responsible. Their superb eye for detail and finesse for planning make them excellent coordinators of events and supervisors of projects. Well organized and punctual, Golds thrive on regularity, efficient use of time, and predictability. They derive great pleasure knowing that they can be counted on to follow through. Their work and nature are "as good as Gold."

Gold Characteristics

Prepared—Thinks ahead to be ready in advance. Uncomfortable putting things off until the last minute. Carries backups just in case. Usually has a contingency plan.

Loves to Plan—Can see every step that needs to be taken to reach the goal. Is able to realistically determine timelines. Good at linear thinking, one thing leads to another. Often has checklists to follow on projects.

Detail Oriented—Notices particulars that others may never think of. Sees the trees in the forest as well as the bark, bugs, and leaves!

Punctual—Makes every effort to be on time and appreciates it when others are also.

Strong Sense of Duty—Enjoys being useful and responsible. Service oriented, very helpful, and dependable. Reliable, supports family, organization, and community. Can be counted on to implement, execute, and follow through.

Belief in Policies—Supports procedures and rules. Most likely of all the color styles to drive the speed limit or even under it. Implements, administers, and supports requirements.

Values Family Traditions—Usually likes to celebrate holidays the way they have been done for generations. If they own a family business they tend to want to pass it down to offspring. Enjoys family-related gatherings; may even plan them.

Conscientious—Does not litter and is bothered when others do. Tries to conserve resources and keep things tidy. Is trustworthy and honest, loyal to spouse. Has a strong work ethic. Hard on themselves if they don't follow through.

Conservative and Stable—Predictable and consistent. Likes having a sense of security or safety net. Values order and the status quo. Chooses to save for a rainy day instead of spending in the moment.

Well-Organized—Comfortable within an orderly, consistent environment. "A place for everything and everything in its place" is a motto that many Golds try to live by at home as well as at work. Has a knack for knowing the most efficient place and method for storing or arranging things.

Strong "Shoulds" and "Should Nots"—Knows the difference between right and wrong. Is aware of what would be appropriate in various circumstances. Gets upset or concerned when other people violate customary norms.

Most Comfortable with a Structured Environment—Likes to know what to expect and what is expected from them. It puts them at ease to know who is in authority and what the rules are so they can follow them.

Understanding and Appreciating Golds

Gold's core value is responsibility. One of the best ways to understand them is to appreciate their strengths.

Gold Strengths:

Accounting
Belonging
Caretaking
Collecting data
Contributing
Coordinating
Dispatching
Family
Following directions
Guarding
Handling detail
Organizing
Planning ahead
Securing
Supervising

Planning Is Golden

Sarah was heading to a conference for work. She registered for the conference three months in advance to take advantage of the reduced rate for early registration. From the moment she registered, she felt an urgency to plan and confirm other arrangements she would also need for the trip. She began a list:

✔ Reserve hotel room—make sure it is non-smoking

✔ Reserve rental car—call around for best prices

✔ Get complete driving directions—check whether there is any road construction or detours en route

✔ Where to park—how close to conference site, best prices, safest

✔ Good restaurants in the area

✔ Will there be food available at the conference site—need a meal ticket?

✔ How much cash to carry? Credit?

✔ Is it casual dress? What is the weather in the area?

47

So much to do, so little time. Sarah was disappointed that she would not be getting an official agenda of events until she picked up her registration packet at the conference, so she could plan in advance what workshops she would attend. She started another list for the clothes and other items she would need to pack.

✔ Alarm clock—in case the hotel one isn't working
✔ Special stain remover wipes

Clothes for the following:
   ✔ Warm weather
   ✔ Cool weather
   ✔ In between weather
   ✔ Rainy weather
      ✔ Casual events
      ✔ Dress-up events

Sarah plans when to leave, what stops she will be making along the way, approximate length of each stop, and when she expects to arrive at her hotel. She will depart a day early just so

she can check out the conference site and know where she will be going. Before she leaves she makes sure the house is clean and all the plants are watered. As a special treat to herself, she likes to put clean sheets on the bed so when she returns she has a fresh bed. Sarah calls to cancel her newspaper for the week and makes sure to give a checklist to the neighbor who will be watching the house.

Golds are most comfortable when they know what to expect.

Golds often anticipate what possibly could go wrong and try to prepare ahead for it. Their joy is feeling "in control." They may worry about events and others, getting stressed if things don't go as planned.

Respect

When Charlie originally took a position as school principal in 1974, he was troubled by the deteriorating respect he noticed in the students. He further observed that although the teachers and administrators of the district were addressed by their proper names such as Mr. Gonzales or Mrs. Kowalski, the bus drivers, as well as custodians and maintenance personnel, were called by their first names by the children and their co-workers alike. It made it harder for these staff members to enforce the rules and elicit the appropriate respect if they were perceived as buddies instead of authority figures commensurate with their positions. Charlie decided to enact a new policy starting immediately. Because he surmised it was a deeply ingrained habit with the older children, he chose to start with the kindergarten through fourth graders to have them address every employee of the school district with a proper greeting.

It took about five years to establish the new norms, but it eventually brought back the respect they had been losing. Long after the students graduated, even though many are now married with families of their own and it is perfectly appropriate to use first names, some of them still call their former bus drivers and other school staff by their last name and proper title.

Work-time, *then* Play-time

Charlie is a dedicated and committed worker and believes in work before play. And, when the work is done . . . he plays! Charlie's number one favorite joy is spending time with his family. He has a camper and loves to travel to the mountains, the coast, and just about anywhere in between. He also enjoys cruises. Charlie even takes the grandkids to Las Vegas a couple of times of year. He can be found karaoke singing at conferences, sharing a good story, and making new friends. His cordial attitude, playful manner, and smile are warm and contagious.

Golds place a high importance on preservation of respect for authority and consideration for the hierarchical procedures of organizations.

Individuals with a these Gold characteristics often look to the past for information about how to deal with present challenges. If they feel that a value they regard is deteriorating, they will establish new protocol or help to revive previous standards to restore consistency. They value fairness and strive to treat everyone around them appropriately, paying close attention to the chain of command and specific roles of each individual. Recreation with their family is often one of their favorite pleasures. They also enjoy participating in organizational and community events.

Following the Rules

Clyde dropped into the grocery store on the way home from work to pick up a few things that his wife Emily needed to complete dinner. He navigated through the store, picking up the items she had listed in order of the isles in their favorite grocery store. They always shopped at the same market because they knew they would get the quality and service they had come to rely on.

As Clyde approached the checkout stand he counted his items once again to make sure he could use the "Quick Check—Cash Only" line. He counted nine items altogether. "That fit the ten items or less limit most definitely," Clyde confirmed to himself. Just as Clyde maneuvered his basket into the appropriate line, another customer whisked in ahead of him. Since there were already two customers in line before them, Clyde had a while to wait. He could not help but notice that the man who pushed ahead of him in line seemed to have well over the ten item limit. Clyde started to get a bit irritated. First the man cut ahead of him, then to add insult to injury, the man was violating the ten item limit. "I could be wrong," Clyde thought to himself. "I'd better count to make sure." Clyde peered into the man's cart and quickly counted its contents. "Twenty-one items!" Clyde almost yelled out loud. "The man is in the wrong line," Clyde thought to himself. "Perhaps he is not aware of the rules. I would want to know if I were him." Clyde then leaned over and gently tapped the man on the shoulder. "Excuse me, sir, but this is the ten items or less line," he said very politely.

He no sooner got the words out of his mouth when the lady at the checkstand motioned to the man that he was next. Without responding to Clyde, the man turned his back and started piling his groceries on the belt.

A Matter of Principle

Clyde stood dumbfounded. He didn't know whether he was more embarrassed or mad. The checker was not enforcing the store policy. She acted as if it didn't even matter that he had twenty-one items. Why did the store even have a policy if they weren't going to enforce it? Thoughts ran through his head of not shopping there anymore. If they could not be consistent with their service, what else would they slack on next? He got his answer. The checker let the man write a check!

CASH ONLY
10 items or
less.

Clyde seethed. He did not want to be inappropriate and make a scene, but he also did not want to just stand there and say nothing. He decided to wait until his turn. He asked the woman why she let the man continue in line when he had too many items and then write a check. She had no "good" explanation for him, so Clyde asked to speak to the manager. He gathered his groceries (as to not hold up the line) and stepped aside with the store manager. Clyde voiced his concerns to the manager, who apologetically assured him that it would not happen again. For some reason Clyde found that a little hard to believe. When he got home, Clyde discussed the matter with his wife. They decided they would give the store one more chance—after all, they did apologize. But if it happened again, they would take their business elsewhere.

Not many things will annoy a Gold as much as when people, especially "reputable" organizations, violate their own rules.

This is one reason they may get upset when rules are not enforced. They like to be able to rely upon the stability of knowing the "right" way of behaving in a situation. If everyone followed the rules then everyone would be treated fairly.

"Shoulds" and "Should Nots"

When Jasmine was planning her wedding, she shared some creative ideas with her friend, Delores. "I think it would be fun to have a potluck and camp overnight," proposed Jasmine. "I know this great campground up in the woods. It's only about a three-hour drive from here."

"What?" gasped Delores. "That's not a wedding, it's a camping trip! You shouldn't make people bring their own food to your wedding. At my wedding we had family members cook for a week to prepare for the guests. People expect to be able to dress up, not wear jeans and sit in the dirt. It would be outright disrespectful to dress so casually. Your friends and relatives will want to choose gifts from a registry so they know it is something you will like and can use. That way they won't waste their time and money. My husband and I had a traditional wedding and people raved about it for years."

Delores is a strong Gold. She believes there is a right and a wrong way to do things, especially traditional things such as weddings. Since Golds themselves make an effort to always be appropriate, they imagine that others would want to know when they are not—so that they can adjust their behavior accordingly. Golds may offer considerate advice about what people should or should not do in certain situations.

51

A Place for Everything

Debbie is a fun-loving Gold who expresses her emotions and enthusiasm freely. While shopping with her husband, Debbie spotted an item on sale that she had been looking for for months. She shrieked with excitement as she grabbed it off the shelf. Pulling it close to her chest as if hugging the item, she jumped up and down giggling. "I found one! At last! It's perfect! It's just what I wanted!"

"What is it?" her husband inquired with curiosity.

"A label-maker! A label-maker! And such a great price too! What a find!"

Her husband smiled in anticipation of what projects would be accomplished with this new tool.

It wasn't long before he found out. Debbie left no room unlabeled. In the kitchen she labeled the soap dispensers by the sink "hand soap" and "dishwashing liquid." She labeled shelves in her cupboard for dishes, pots and pans, food items, and spices. The bathroom medicine cabinet got its share, as well as the drawers and shelves. The children's rooms got stickers with labels on toy boxes, shelves, and in closets. Her boxes of "hand-me-downs" were appropriately labeled with descriptions of size, color, style and designer, as well as date outgrown. Even her suitcase-sized diaper bag got labels for diapers, pacifier, bottles, ointments, etc.

She was in sheer heaven with everything clearly labeled.

Now, not only could she spot where everything should be when in its place, but her family and friends could too!

Golds value orderliness.

Golds like to have a place for everything, and everything in its place. This may not always happen, but it is something they strive for.

Another Hue of Gold

Some of the greatest contributions that Golds make to the world are to organize it and make sure things are "right." This yearning for "rightness" includes but is not limited to; the right etiquette, choosing the right words when speaking, the right moral values being upheld, things put back in the right place, things done in the right order, and following the right protocol.

In their attempt to get things "right" the first time, they may focus a great deal of time and energy on the details and preparation for an endeavor. They are able to seriously concentrate their efforts and stay on task until completion. When the demands of others threaten to interrupt the well-thought-out plans of a Gold, the Gold may increase efforts even further to meet designated timelines and begin to strongly encourage others to stay on task as well. This intense steadfastness is a gift of our reliable Golds and cherished by employers, families and the communities that depend upon them.

However, while for the most part Golds have very admirable traits that are appreciated and revered, there are times when others may view these same characteristics in a different light. To those who do not possess this drive for responsibility and "rightness," a Gold's actions may appear rigid or controlling. Golds themselves may get concerned that their efforts to uphold the rules and values of society are going unappreciated and that people misunderstand their intentions. Just because they like to finish their work before playing, does not mean they do not like to play, and some Golds even have a mischievous side that others are surprised to see when revealed. Because their powerful sense of commitment and duty usually directs their decisions toward what would be the most appropriate and responsible, they typically do not totally throw all caution to the wind, and if they happen to, they may feel tremendous guilt afterwards.

Many Golds are aware that they may seem inflexible, boring or even unfriendly to individuals that do not understand their conscientiousness and the drive for responsibility that motivates them. Comparing the descriptions of how others may at times see Golds to the descriptions of how Golds view themselves will help enhance your understanding of the way Golds operate in the world.

Others May See Golds as:

Rigid—Inflexible to other options. Refuses to deviate from a designated plan. Won't relax or allow others to relax or enjoy leisure. Adamant about everything being orderly.

Restricted— Unable to go with the flow, bend with circumstances, or keep up with the times.

Stubborn—Uncompromising, has to have things a particular way. Once a decision is made, will stick to it even if there is a better choice. Strict, stringent, unbending.

Boring—Does not like to play or have fun. Dull, lacks enthusiasm and spontaneity. Constantly monitor their behavior and the behavior of others to make sure it does not deviate from norms.

Self Righteous—Believes their way is the "right" way. Takes on the role of martyr, wanting everyone to repeatedly recognize their efforts and sacrifices. Shames and criticizes others for not adhering to the same standards or values.

54

System-bound—Unalterable adherence to policies, systems and customs. Follows rules without questioning. Gets personally insulted if others refuse to uphold the roles and rules they deem appropriate. Will not consider extenuating circumstances.

Unimaginative—Likes things status quo. Rejects innovative ideas. Resistant to change and afraid to take the risks necessary to be successful or keep up with the times. Refuses to consider new possibilities.

Judgmental—Judges others' actions as "good or bad," "right or wrong," "appropriate or inappropriate." Extremely opinionated, makes up mind and then tries to convice others. Negative attitude.

Bossy—Controlling, governs actions of others. Dominates, tries to take over and manage circumstances, people, and decisions.

Uptight—Worries too much. Limited to what would be the "responsible" thing to do. Won't let go or loosen up.

Rigid Idea of Time—Puts everyone and everything on an agenda. Tries to force others to adhere to scheduling demands. Does not approve of others who have a more casual style of time management.

Married to Task—"Work-a-holic." Will not lighten up and smell the roses along the way to meeting a goal. End justifies means. Pushes self (and sometimes others) to extremes to accomplish duties.

YOU'RE THE ONLY PERSON I KNOW WHO BRINGS A RULEBOOK TO PLAY CHECKERS!

Golds May See Self as:

Firm—Solid, sturdy, not wishy-washy. Persistent in adhering to consistency. Can hold their ground when necessary.

Knows What's Best—Has realistic views of what can be accomplished and how. Establishes procedures, then articulates to others to help them stay on track.

Efficient—Thinks rules were made to be followed. If everyone did so, then things would run smoothly. It would save a lot of time, money, and energy if everyone would just obey the rules.

Realistic—Has no illusions and faces reality squarely. Sensible, practical, sane. Keeps their feet on the ground.

Stable—Organized. Likes to know where things belong in order to be efficient. Considers options but prefers to stick with what can be depended upon.

Appropriate—Knows the difference between right and wrong and can make sound decisions and determinations. Traditional and upright in values.

Providing Security—Very reliable. Wants others to be able to count on them to always follow through with no surprises. Likes sticking with the proven, confirmed, "tried and true."

Executive Type—Able to take charge and see that things get done. If someone does not take on the responsibility, who will?

Dependable—Good planner. Can be counted on. Trustworthy and credible. Takes pride in being steadfast, faithful, and steady.

Responsible—Accountable. Makes sure that duties and responsibilities are addressed before play.

56

Punctual—Very respectful of the time lines of others. Likes to be efficient; gets the job done. Does not want to waste time.

Goal-Oriented—Likes to finish what they start. Will go to great lengths to follow through on promises. Keep their word and deliver quality work.

Relating to Golds

Golds want to interact with others in a respectful, responsible way. They identify strongly with other Golds who share their need for structure. They also relate well to Blues, who are supportive; Greens, who are knowledgeable and inventive; and Oranges, who are optimistic and resourceful.

Count on Them

Golds are some of the most dependable friends a person can have. They are reliable and consistent. They want you to place full confidence in them because they are very serious about doing a good job. Golds enjoy opportunities for leadership; give them the responsibility of coordinating events. When they say they will do something they will follow through, making sure they have addressed every detail.

When interacting with Golds, remember that they enjoy hero stories and anecdotes of honesty, patriotism, and courageous people. They take pleasure in keeping up with current events and receive satisfaction in knowing they are providing support and structure to relationships, organizations, communities, and society as a whole.

Appeal to their Strong Sense of Right and Wrong

When discussing or introducing ideas, use examples relating to traditional approaches, sense of community, responsibility, and moral values. Golds place a high priority on academic achievement and relate very well to authority, rules, and procedures. Make sure to mention how your goal supports the family, organization, or existing norms.

Be Mindful in Your Use of Resources

Golds enjoy goals to save time, effort, and money. They like to organize their thoughts and ideas and prepare for their future. There is no excuse for waste in their book. They admire others who are careful to use their resources wisely. Be thoughtful in what you choose to discard and where. Make sure to honor their time and resources. They thrive on being prepared. They put a lot of effort into making sure everything will turn out "right." When their preparations conflict with your spontaneity and desire for options, stop and think before charging ahead with a different agenda. A little notice time before changes goes a long way with a Gold.

Offer Opportunities for Expression of Traditional Values

Golds are interested in family and moral values. If they will not bend a rule or make an exception to something you find dated or silly, understand their well-meaning intentions in enforcing such rules or traditions. Let them know you would like to pitch in and do your part, especially if you realize that carrying out the custom or task is beginning to cause them stress, drain their energy, or even make them physically sick. They will continue their efforts at great cost to themselves unless they feel it is appropriate to ask for or accept help from others.

Show How Much You Value Their Efforts

As with most people, Golds especially enjoy knowing their contributions are appreciated. Be specific when giving compliments or praise, and mention their actual accomplishments of fulfilling their responsibilities well. They also welcome recognition in the form of plaques, certificates, and ceremonies.

Golds Need:
consistency
reliability
timelines
structure
clear expectations
responsibility
respect
rules & standards
organization
closure

Golds Need to Be:
appropriate
appreciated
aware of who is in control
clear on requirements
responsible

Golds Value:
commitment
security
professionalism
etiquette
duty
loyalty
honesty
membership
time & resources
tradition

Golds Find Joy in:
belonging
home

a sense of order

a task well done

time for family

tradition

doing the "right thing"

acknowledgement

With Golds Be:

accurate

consistent

rule-abiding

fair

organized

thorough

reverent of traditions

respectful

reliable

conscientious

Bringing Out the Gold

To bring out the best in Golds, rely on them for their responsible nature.

Laura had a knack for arranging events. Her family often counted on her to be the one to plan and organize family get-togethers and vacations. In the early '90s she had the foresight to realize that New Year's 2000 would be a very special occasion, so she set about making plans. She considered places from past events that held special significance.

After careful contemplation she chose the perfect place, a huge inn located right in the heart of a festive island. It had plenty of restaurants and night clubs as well as sightseeing spots within a short distance. People could bring their own cars with them over on the ferry.

With no time to waste, she promptly placed a down payment—ten years in advance! She commenced inviting her friends and family and collecting deposits for their "reservation" in the event. Each year, twice a year, Laura would reconfirm the reservation with the inn, just in case the staffing or policies had changed. She wanted to make sure the reservation would stay firm.

Six months prior to the event she held a "planning party" with the guests that would be attending. They brainstormed what activities they would like to have and how to best make it a memorable experience. Laura asked each couple or group attending to come up with some form of "entertainment" for the night, such as a skit, magic act, or karaoke singing. To make sure that the events were coordinated smoothly and everyone was included, Laura kept a notebook of information for each person attending such as home phone; e-mail; cell phone; make, model, color, and license plate number of the car they would be driving; reservation confirmation; room number; and any medical conditions like allergies, asthma, or diabetes. She also included any other emergency information she might need, such as family and physician phone numbers. Just in case anything happened to this notebook, she kept a back-up copy.

The event went beautifully. It was a grand occasion that was special in the hearts of all those who attended. After the event, Laura thoughtfully created a scrapbook of pictures and stories for each group in attendance for a keepsake.

Turn to a Gold for:

Planning—When arranging an event or project, look for a Gold. They are amazingly gifted at knowing what needs to be done to accomplish a goal. They can think of items and arrangements that need to be addressed and be realistic in setting time lines for completion.

Responsibility—If you have something very important that you need

accomplished on time in a quality manner, turn to a Gold. They derive pleasure from taking on duties and doing an excellent job. Because they are very dependable, you can count on them to follow through. They will be respectful, appropriate, and timely. They will keep you apprised of their progress and find a way to complete the task at hand.

Supervision—Golds enjoy taking care of business and others. They easily take on a leadership role when necessary and will direct and motivate others to appropriate action.

Trust—Golds will rarely, if ever, tell a lie, or pass on slander or gossip. They go to great lengths to save face for others they respect and who share the same values. They are conscientious in their endeavors. You can entrust your confidences to them.

Details—If you want directions for doing something or need particulars, refer to a Gold. They have the ability to speculate as to what particulars, articles, or elements are necessary for completion of a task.

The Correct Way to Do Something—If you are wondering what the rules of etiquette might dictate under certain circumstances, of all the colors, a Gold will be your best bet for finding out. They usually know what is the appropriate tradition or norm for behavior in many different circumstances.

The Rules or Policy—If you are unsure of a procedure, policy, or rule, ask a Gold. If they do not know the answer, they certainly know where to find it. They most likely know how to access the information needed to find out what the procedure is for most anything in their organization. If a policy does not exist, they can be instrumental in the implementation of one.

Accuracy—Golds do not slack when it comes to accuracy. They check and double check their work to make sure everything is correct. It is uncommon for them to guess or make up something when they do not know the answer to a question. They will find out and get back to you. They like to do a good job.

Tradition—Golds keep track of the customs relating to families, institutions, and places. They enjoy upholding legacy and heritage. If you want to make sure a tradition stays alive and gets carried out, enlist the help of a Gold.

Fairness—Golds' characters are distinguished by their honesty, justice, and freedom from improper influence. They pay careful attention to what would

be most equitable in situations. As long as it follows the rules, they try to be reasonable.

If You Need Someone to Be on Time or Enforce an Agenda—With their great organizational skills and dependability it is natural for a Gold to be punctual. If they say they will be somewhere at a certain time, they will. They also make fantastic timekeepers for meetings and presentations to make sure things are running according to schedule.

Organization—If you are having a hard time locating files you have tucked away, are constantly digging through your clutter to find things, or can't quite figure out how to establish a system for organizing thoughts, words, or things, find a Gold. They have a knack for systemizing and categorizing items for easy access.

Chapter 7

SHADES OF
ORANGE
ORANGE
ORANGE

Individuals with large amounts of Orange characteristics in their temperament boldly seize opportunities when they arise. They need a great amount of freedom and flexibility in relationships, work, and life in general. They are usually very straightforward in their communication. As very physical individuals, they fade fast if they must endure routine or inertia for extended periods. The words to a popular '70s disco song portray a certain attitude of Orange quite succinctly: "I want to go where the action is, I want some action, I want to live!"

The difference between extroverted Oranges and introverted Oranges can be quite drastic. The storybook character Winnie the Pooh is most likely an introverted Orange—he just sort of goes with the flow. His major concern in life is satisfying his voracious hunger for honey. His attitude is "I'm here, life happens."

Now the character Tigger, in contrast, is a great example of an extroverted Orange. Everyone knows when he is around. He comes bouncing in, full of energy, announcing his presence to all. He prides himself on being the only Tigger in the world and is always ready for the next adventure. Very little stresses him out, except being stuck somewhere.

Orange Characteristics

The following are characteristics that generally describe the style of Oranges. They can show up in a variety of ways. Remember, just because certain individuals consider themselves to be Orange dominant, it does not mean that they have every characteristic described. All it means is that they have more of these traits than traits of any of the other color styles.

Energetic—High need for mobility. Likes to get movement somehow throughout the day. Usually enjoys recreational activities, for example: skiing, boating, dirt biking, skateboarding, dancing, and so on. May be drawn to competitive sports.

Desires Change—Enjoys variety, flexibility, and resourcefulness. This could include many aspects of life such as jobs, projects, relationships, and environment. Questions the status quo, expects others to adapt to situational requirements. Enjoys surprises; takes chances.

Playful—Quick-witted and humorous, likes to bring fun to a situation. Can be flirtatious. Is interested in the process of reaching a goal as much as achieving it.

Master Negotiator—Charming, enjoys making a deal. "No" is often interpreted as "maybe." Tries to find a way to accomplish desires.

Natural Entertainer—Can be a bit flamboyant. May call attention to themselves by the way they dress, act, or speak. Likes to have the interest of others. May give extravagant gifts and takes pleasure in seeing the reaction of the receiver.

Pushes Boundaries—
Tests limits, natural non-conformist and risk taker. May live on the edge. Seeks excitement. Can get bogged down by red tape and rules. Many times can find loopholes in the system and may bend the rules if necessary to accomplish goals.

Accepts Challenges—
Derives pleasure in solving problems. Thrives on competition and likes adapting to last-minute changes. Able to trouble-shoot and act in a crisis. May get involved in situations just to see if they can be successful where others have failed.

Impulsive and Spontaneous—
Likes to leave options open so that they have the freedom to choose. May easily get distracted from task at hand if interruptions aren't kept to a minimum. Likes to live in the moment; may arrange life to include making on-the-spot decisions.

"Just Do It"—
Finds planning tedious. Makes decisions and takes action quickly. Hates to wait. Wants to "get the show on the road." May also change their mind as instantly as they made it up.

Appreciates Immediate Feedback—
Delayed feedback is almost meaningless. Prefers giving as well as getting straight responses at once, instead of waiting.

Most Productive in Non-Structured Environments—
Likes to be able to kick off shoes and be comfortable. Enjoys an environment that is changing and unpredictable.

Self-Confident—Takes initiative. May jump in and take over leadership role if others are perceived as ineffective or hesitant.

Understanding and Appreciating Oranges

Oranges' core value is freedom. One of the best ways to understand them is to recognize some of their strengths.

Orange Strengths:

Able to take charge
Being the master of tools
Carefree
Dealing with chaos
Determination
Direct communicator
Doing many things at once
Eclectic, diverse, changing
Going with the situation
Hands-on
Keeping options open
Negotiating
Proficient, capable
Receptive to opportunities
Risk-taking
Trouble-shooting
Welcomes new ideas

These strengths may show up in a variety of ways. The following stories illustrate many of the characteristics, strengths, and preferred ways of operating of Oranges. You may ask yourself, "How would I act in the same situation?" Your answer to this question will help you determine the level of Orange characteristics you possess or already appreciate in others. By paying close attention to the underlying force behind the actions of the characters in the stories, you will gain further insights into the motivations and values of Oranges.

Living Moment to Moment

Rachel, in her mid-fifties, is quite a head-turner. She has blonde hair cut in a classy, yet playful, style. She usually wears her trademark red lipstick with matching nail polish and dresses quite fashionably. She also drives a white Corvette.

This car will come in handy today. She will be leaving in a few hours for a business trip she booked last month. She will be gone for an entire week, and she really needs the break.

Rachel scrambled to tie up some last-minute projects at the office before stopping at home to pack on her way to the airport. She quickly stuffed everything she would need into one roller suitcase so she would not have to wait in line at the baggage claim later. The contents of the case were mostly shoes and a minimal amount of mix-and-match clothes made of low-maintenance, wrinkle-free fabrics. She had to push the speed limit just a bit to make it to the airport, but she had the right car to do it. On the way to the airport she started thinking of a few other arrangements she needed to make such as rent a car, get a hotel, and figure out where the conference site was. She hoped she had packed the information about where the conference was being held. If not, she could always call the office when her plane landed.

Arriving at the gate moments before the plane was to take off, she sprinted to the check-in counter. They had just made the final announcement for boarding. Good thing she didn't have any luggage to check. As she climbed aboard the plane, the flight attendant closed the door behind her and the engines were started. Noticing an empty seat in first class, she asked the flight attendant if she could have it. The attendant agreed, and Rachel settled back in her seat. "Ahhh," she sighed, "I made it just in time."

Style, Convenience, and Time Management

Many Oranges have a certain eye for style and may dress with flair, flamboyance, or flirt. The way in which they dress can send a message (blatant or subtle) that says "look at me," "notice me," "I am fun." Even

the cars they drive and "toys" they own imply a more playful over practical priority.

Especially when traveling, convenience counts. They don't want to be bogged down with too much stuff or too many "inconveniences." If it does not add to their fun, they don't want it along. Their aim is mobility and freedom. Some Oranges may pack ahead and even use a list, but for many Oranges, planning or packing ahead of time is simply not a priority. More often than not, Oranges get in the habit of putting things off until the last minute. Sometimes they want to leave their options open or their schedule is jam-packed with other "priorities," but many times it's just for the fun of it. Many Oranges enjoy the challenge of trying to beat the clock and push the "limits."

"I have the most fun being on the edge of out-of-control."

Manuel loves to play a variety of sports and get involved in recreational activities. "Whether I'm playing football, soccer or baseball," he declares, "it's the same for everything. You've got to go full out. It's a competition with myself and others."

His latest love is motorcycle dirt biking. "It's pretty intense," he describes. "The whole thing is to try *not* to get hurt, but to go fast enough to know that you *could*. I like being in control of the direction of the machine. It's such freedom. It's like being on top of a car going 60 miles-per-hour—you're not in it, you're on it, and you could fall off at any time. It's exciting. I'm not really thinking— I'm totally present in the moment. I'm looking for lines and pointing the bike where it is supposed to go. I'm trying to avoid rocks. You run on pure instinct, reactions, and reflex. If they don't work, you're in trouble.

"When you're in the air," he continues, "fighting for your life to stay on that bike, that's 100% what it's all about. Getting dirty, feeling the rush of the wind on my face and body, the smell of the gasoline, the sound of the motor and the vibration, it's exhilarating. It lets you know you are alive."

The Rush of Feeling Alive

What Manuel describes is how many Oranges feel about life. Oranges enjoy their senses. Whether it is dirt and mud on their skin or the rush of the wind, they like to experience the sensations of smell, touch, taste, hearing, and sight. Often, they aim to feel a certain "edge" or "rush." There are many ways to get this "rush"; it doesn't have to be partaking in high-risk activities or contact sports. It can be things like negotiating their way into or out of a situation, performing on stage, or having ten contracts to close on the same day. One thing for sure is this "rush" or "edge"

is what makes them feel alive. If they don't have it in certain areas of their life, they will seek to find or create it in other aspects: work, relationships, or added activities. It is perhaps the main reason they seem driven to push their physical limits, relationship margins, or societal boundaries.

Recognizing and Seizing Opportunities

Brad and Shirley wanted to cement in a portion of their side yard as a patio. Shirley kept asking her husband, Brad, when he was going to put the patio in. He kept getting distracted with other jobs that cropped up at the moment and spent the money Shirley had budgeted for the patio on those jobs instead.

One cloudy night at about 3 a.m., Brad drove up to the corner gas station to buy some cigarettes.

"Looks like rain," the clerk behind the counter was commenting when a loud screeching of tires interrupted their conversation. He and Brad both looked out of the windows of the store front in time to see a truck skidding around a corner to catch the entrance ramp of the highway. As the truck barely made the curve, several bags of something came flying off the back of the truck. They watched as the truck sped off into the distance.

The clerk and Brad looked at each other. "Well, whatever it is will be worthless when it gets rained on," the clerk offered. "Why don't you check it out?"

Brad was game. He ran across the street to investigate. As he approached the corner he could not believe his eyes. There were about 100 sacks of cement strewn off the side of the road!

The clerk made his way to the door of the store. He lit up a cigarette and, taking a big drag, shouted, "Hey, what is it?"

"Cement," yelled Brad.

"What a waste," the clerk said, shaking his head. "The rain's gonna soak it."

Brad lit his cigarette. There was a moment of silence. The night air was crisp. The wind was blowing as the cloud-filled sky loomed overhead. It appeared by now that the driver was not returning. The clerk could tell Brad was thinking.

"Wish I could help you," he said to Brad as he tossed his cigarette to the ground and stepped on it, grinding it into the dirt. "Good luck!" he hollered as he turned and went back in the store.

Brad quickly snuffed out his cigarette and went to work. He drove his van over to the piles of cement and started loading them up. Brad labored diligently, working up a sweat. As the van filled, it became lowered with the extra weight. A misty moisture started to driz-

zle ever so slightly from the sky. Brad's adrenaline surged as he drove his first cargo home to unload. His back and arms ached as he lifted bag after bag. His heart beat faster and he worked harder. "All that cement will go to waste if I don't hurry back," he thought to himself. Picking up his pace even more, he hurled the sacks of cement into his garage, then sped back to retrieve the rest.

Brad's body was beginning to hit the edges of fatigue. He fought to push past his pains to salvage what he could of the remaining cement. Trembling and exhausted, Brad finally decided enough would have to be enough. He had salvaged about 80 bags of the cement before the sky started to pour rain. His body ached all over from fatigue. "Wow!" he thought, "What a night! Won't Honey Bunny be pleased. We've got our patio!"

Urges, Opportunities, and Action

Oranges may not keep customary hours or predictable schedules. In fact, some Oranges are predictably unpredictable. They may think nothing of heading to the store at 3 a.m. if an urge hits them. They may even say they will be "right back" and get distracted by another priority that just "came up." When circumstances present themselves to an Orange, they are quick to grab hold of the moment if they are motivated to do so. For example, have you ever noticed that while some people are still mulling over options, others have already dived into action? This is typical for Oranges. They are quick decision makers (and can be equally quick at changing their minds too) and will seize an opportunity when it arises. They may ignore physical discomfort to accomplish their goal. Triumph over this discomfort may even add to the fun and the challenge.

Show and Tell

Crystal was a very excited volunteer. She had joined the Overdose Aid Program through the YMCA. This was a program in which volunteers were trained in what to do for victims of drug overdose. When rock concerts came to town, the volunteers would don a green arm band with a white cross on it and were allowed in the concert for free in exchange for patrolling the crowds for drug overdosing concert-goers and taking care of them as needed. They would meet in the Overdose Aid (ODA) room, designated for taking care of the more serious victims.

At the concerts, Crystal always had a flamboyant story to tell her director, Jeanette. Crystal would explode into the ODA room, shouting to anyone within earshot, "You should have seen this guy, he was barfing bright pink! He had fallen down the stairs and . . ."

Jeanette, interpreting Crystal's tone of voice as panic and her explicit accounts as a cry for help, would practically come unglued. She would think to herself, "Crystal is trained in this. Why can't she handle it?" Usually overwhelmed with her own emergencies, Jeanette would offer some quick advice: "What are you doing in here? Go help him up! Find someone to help you if you need it. Get the vomit off the floor so no one else slips in it!"

Crystal would usually pause for just a second, looking confused, and then say, "Oh, I already got Maurice to clean it up. The guy was fine. I walked him back out to the concert. He was nice; his name was Billy. I gave him my phone number."

Several times throughout the evening Crystal would have to be reminded of her purpose for being at the concert. She could be found bouncing to the music, sitting on

69

some guy's shoulders up in the first rows of seats, stage front. Often, when Crystal brought "victims" to the ODA room, she was assisted by other male concert-goers she had recruited to help her.

One night, Jeanette had a revelation. After about five outrageously descriptive "crisis stories" from Crystal describing various rescues involving convulsions, vomiting, and hallucinations, Jeanette exclaimed, "I've got it, Crystal! I've finally figured it out! You are not complaining . . . you're bragging!"

Getting Excited

Oranges like circumstances that are larger than life. They enjoy trouble-shooting and creatively emerging triumphant from a situation. They also have a knack for eliciting the help of others and having fun along the way. If they can squeeze just an ounce of juice from a situation to liven things up a bit and add some fun, they will.

Another Hue of Orange

As you know by now, Oranges (especially the extroverts) are usually fairly easy to spot. They are most likely fast-paced and where the action is. If they are interested, they are involved. They may act in a dramatic or flamboyant manner. Whether they are the center of attention or other-

wise helping to stir up a little excitement, you know it when they are around. You'll see plenty of active body movement and vivid facial expressions. They appear excited and may even fidget. Many will speak in a loud, fast-paced, or direct manner. They have an air of confidence about them and yet are playful.

Often, people who don't have large amounts of Orange characteristics themselves have a tendency to view those who *do* as acting in unacceptable ways. As is true with all the colors to a certain extent, Oranges in particular have a different style that can be greatly misunderstood by others.

Do you notice how you are perceived through the eyes of others? Many of us may strive to make sure our actions are acceptable to others and society. But try as we might, people may label any of our admirable characteristics as being less than appealing if they would never act that way.

Recently, I was at a conference that had nearly 6,000 attendees. I had given a True Colors workshop in the morning for about 150 people. The evening entertainment happened to be dancing. I, myself, look for any opportunity to dance, so of course I went. When I arrived, I headed straight to the dance floor and was pleased to find a group of individuals gathered already dancing in a group. I recognized them as participants from the earlier workshop who had determined that they had a predominance of Orange and Blue characteristics in their color spectrums. An intriguing phenomena seems to happen after individuals find out what their True Colors are: they start to shine much brighter, especially around others who also know their color spectrum. The Oranges in particular were no exception tonight. They were dancing wildly and playfully, skipping around the floor—some with arms outstretched as if in flight. They started rumba lines and dance trains, diving between other dancers on the floor, laughing and giggling and having a great time.

By the time the band took their first break, the Oranges were just getting revved up. As a group they decided to stay on the floor during the intermission DJ music. They continued to smile, laugh, and act goofy—providing plenty of entertainment for those people who chose to take a recess from dancing.

I had to rip myself away from the dance floor to get a drink of water and use the restroom. While in the closed confines of a restroom stall, I could hear a couple of women chatting while they washed their hands.

"Did you check out that crazy group on the dance floor? They remind me of the acid-droppers of the '60s, skipping around and pretending to fly."

"I know, they're probably all high or drunk or both!"

At that moment, I thought about how misunderstood Oranges are sometimes. Their playful, carefree style can be mistaken for a drug-induced high to those who do not allow themselves to experience the exhilaration of being fully in the moment. Yes, of course, some individuals may use drugs or alcohol, but a great many others are accused wrongly because others just do not understand their motivation.

When the motivation behind someone's actions is not understood, it can be interpreted in very unfavorable ways. What one might perceive as a negative quality is oftentimes an exaggeration of a good quality. Oranges can be very intimidating to those who don't appreciate their flamboyant tendencies. Sometimes Oranges are confused as to why someone would view them that way; other Oranges are not surprised at all.

One or more of the following characteristics of Oranges may be true for you or the people in your life. As you read them, keep in mind that although you may not fully understand certain actions and may find these traits unfavorable or perhaps even inexcusable, Oranges pride themselves on their abilities and gifts. These "gifts," of course, vary from person to person. However, taking a more objective point of view will enable you to discover that even the traits that may seem unfavorable at first glance have merit in the right context.

71

Others May See Oranges as:

Rude—Blunt. Doesn't take into consideration the feelings of others. Uses foul language. Pushy, loud, and boisterous. Interrupts.

Irresponsible—Slackers. Doesn't do fair share. Pushes responsibilities off on others. Does not feel obligated or conscientious enough to finish work before play. Neglects to consider past or future. Does not think of consequences to actions.

Not Serious—Makes a joke out of everything. Puts more effort into fun than into work.

Selfish or Self-Centered—Spends time doing only what pleases them. If it's not fun or a turn-on at the moment, it gets postponed or neglected. Doesn't take into account what others want and need.

72

Ignoring the Rules—Feels rules were made to be broken. The rules don't apply to them; if they can get around rules they are proud of themselves. Likes to "beat the system." Takes shortcuts. Uncontrollable—lives by their own rules. Minimal respect for authority.

Manipulative—Wants to have things their way. Will go to great lengths to control others or the situation. Lies, cheats, exaggerates, minimizes.

Impatient—Won't wait. Demanding, hasty, edgy. Continuously rushed or in a hurry.

Easily Distracted—Unable to stay on task, scatterbrained. Works on other things when people are trying to talk to them. Cluttered. Has too many irons in the fire.

Unprepared—Flies by the seat of their pants. Pushes things to the last minute. Disregards time lines. Constantly late.

Flirtatious—Pushes personal boundaries. Uses innuendo. Attempts to attract admiration for amusement.

Taking Advantage of Others—Dishonest, disrespectful, untrustworthy. Uses others for personal gain without reciprocation.

Flaky—Doesn't remember promises made and doesn't follow through. Changes mind at the last minute and neglects to let others know in a timely manner. Unreliable.

Oranges May See Self as:

I'LL GIVE YOU $2000 TAKE IT OR LEAVE IT.

Now-Oriented—Believes in living life to the fullest, squeezing the juice out of every moment. Self-fulfilling and independent, looks out for "number one." Why compromise immediate needs when tomorrow may never come?

Productive Freedom—Gets things done in any way they can. If they need to push a few limits, so be it. Proficient. Does not like to be bogged down by too many restrictions. Wants choices.

Straightforward—Tells it like it is. Honest. Comfortable with self and others, so uses casual language. Does not put on pretenses.

Easy-Going—Thinks a goal isn't worth achieving if it's not fun along the way. Efficiency experts, proficient at delegation. Adept at drawing upon other people's resources. Master motivator for enrolling others in helping with projects.

Enjoying the Process—Very serious about producing desired results, yet believes in having fun along the way.

Good Negotiator—Sees possibilities when others may think the doors are closed. Helps others open their minds and think outside the box. Inspires others to agree. Convincing. Innovative, people-pleaser. Able to establish rapport with others. Knows that people embrace a leader, someone who is self-assured and confident.

Mover and Shaker—Eager, enthusiastic, efficient. Doesn't believe in wasting time. Wants to make things happen, not merely *watch* things happen—or worse, sit around discussing it. Doesn't like to be slowed down. Takes the bull by the horns.

74

Multitasker—Enjoys working on several things at once. Highly mobile; switches gears quickly. Is stimulated by variety and change.

Spontaneous—Energized by crisis or chaos. Able to troubleshoot and is prepared for anything. Creative.

Friendly—Bolsters self-esteem of others and builds rapport. Makes others feel at ease and acknowledged.

Succeeding—Believes the ends justify the means. Seeks to accomplish outcomes and will do whatever it takes to reach goals.

Flexible—Adaptable, spontaneous. Likes to leave options open. Reprioritizes instantly, according to the situation at hand. Goes with flow and seizes the opportunity at hand.

Relating to Oranges

Oranges want to engage others in a mutual, fun-loving way. You can relate to them most effectively when you are active and in the moment. They are naturally drawn to the energy and flexibility of other Oranges. They get along well with Blues who are friendly and patient, enjoy the knowledge and great ideas of Greens, and appreciate Golds who are productive and goal-oriented.

If you want Oranges to go along with your ideas then make sure they are in on the decision-making process.

Oranges hate feeling stuck. Let them know your preferences and then encourage them to come up with some other options for accomplishing the goal. Determine which ones you would be willing to accept if it came down to it. Just knowing they have choices puts an Orange at ease. They won't necessarily take advantage of the other options, but somehow just knowing they could if they wanted to allows them to feel content going along with yours.

Expect some spice

Remember that Oranges are instinctive trouble-shooters. There is something about rising to the moment that entices them to take action. They welcome change and new ideas and are rarely set back by defeats because they take them as being only temporary, a new challenge to face and conquer.

Oranges can deal with chaos and are apt to create some if there isn't enough in their lives. Don't panic! They like to test the limits. They might just be stirring up some chaos so that they can figure a way out of it. It is a fun contest to them.

Don't take it personally if Oranges don't always make their relationship with you their number one priority. You may be highly important to them, whether it seems that way or not. Frequently, Oranges enjoy the comfort of knowing you are in their lives and may turn their attention to other avenues for the moment. It does not mean that you are not valued by them. It simply means that their concentration is temporarily directed elsewhere.

Understand their impulse to take each moment as it comes

When left to their natural expression, Oranges are carefree, playful, and spontaneous. Their craving for action, variety, and excitement may pull their attention elsewhere in an instant. Because they are most comfortable in environments that are unstructured, it can be a challenge to get them to adhere to a fixed schedule or plan. If you know the Oranges in your life have a tendency to forget or "blow off" appointments and plans for something that has come up at the moment, a gentle reminder or double check on your part may help save you from disappointment.

Allow them to show off their skills without condemning them for their process

As natural performers, Oranges need the freedom to express themselves. Their lighthearted charm, wit, and fun can be irresistible. You may find yourself being motivated by the charisma and style of an Orange. They are good negotiators and persuaders. As natural fun-seekers, they like to recruit others to play along with them. For the most part, whether they admit it or not, they enjoy being the center of attention. They often feel there isn't anything that they cannot do. They love any opportunity to show their skillfulness, cleverness, agility, and precision.

They are proficient, capable, hands-on people. They have a love of tools and are masterful with them. Give them immediate feedback and praise for the clever way they handled a situation.

76

Avoid slowing them down when they are on a quest

Oranges like immediate results and therefore complete tasks quickly. Because they consider waiting and routine as emotional death, they may take shortcuts to accomplish their goals. If things take too long or remain static, they are apt to get frustrated and are prone to taking off for somewhere else to follow the "action." As excellent multitaskers, they are capable of, as well as rather enjoy, doing a variety of things at once. For best results, don't insist that they drop what they are doing and give you their full attention. Instead, figure out what you can do to help them finish their projects or otherwise fit into their world.

Oranges Need:

action and activity
freedom
flexibility
make an impact
attention
adrenaline rush
variety
physical contact
fun & play
competition

Oranges Need to Be:

appreciated
doing
resourceful

given options
recognized for their skillfulness

Oranges Value:

adventure
forthrightness
options
experience
flair
spontaneity
productivity
opportunity
winning
expediency

Oranges Find Joy in:

being the best
excitement
moving their body
performing
putting plans into action
taking risks
troubleshooting
saving the day

With Oranges Be:

dynamic
clear and direct
confident
entertaining
flexible
open-minded
skillful
spontaneous
ready for change
energetic

Oranges are "doers" and not content to sit on the sidelines for very long. Offer hands-on assignments that can be completed quickly and proficiently using their skills and flair. Encourage them to promote their ideas and products. Establish methods of immediate payoff. Create games or challenges out of otherwise mundane tasks or obligations.

Bringing Out the Orange

To draw out the greatest from Oranges, call upon their innate preferences for action.

At 12:30 in the afternoon, Trudy (an Orange/Blue) got a call from her sister Rose (a Gold/Blue). Their brother George (a Green/Blue) was in a tight spot and needed some help. The health club he managed was supposed to have a CPR training that afternoon and the instructor had just called in sick. They had set this date aside for months and meticulously coordinated schedules with their other three clubs to make sure that all forty employees could attend.

It just happened that both Rose and Trudy were certified instructors of CPR. George had called Rose at noon to see if there was any possibility that she or her sister or both could teach the class at 2:00 that afternoon.

Before Rose called her sister Trudy, she spent a half-hour going over the requirements for teaching a class that size. There are many regulations that must be met in order to teach a CPR class. First of all, there is an instructor-to-student ratio of one-to-ten that must be met. That means they would need to find four instructors. Then they would have to get equipment and books. The instructor that called in sick was not willing to lend his equipment. It was Saturday and the local Red Cross's switchboard was closed to the public except for disaster emergencies, which obviously this was not. Rose could not call to reserve equipment, which should be reserved two weeks prior anyway. The stock room was closed on Saturdays, and equipment must be picked up on weekdays. To top it off, she did not have the videotapes that were used to instruct the class. All the brainstorming and decision-making had already taken up a half-hour of the two hours they originally had, leaving her only an hour and a half to find two to three other instructors, acquire the equipment, find a video, get to the gym (which was a forty-five minute drive in itself) and get set up for the class, which usually takes a minimum of thirty minutes. The way she figured it—No Way! But with a bit of urging from George, she called Trudy to see if she had any ideas or resources.

Open to Options

Trudy had a different response to George's request. Although she had a full day of obligations and projects she had promised to address, Trudy could not pass up an urgent challenge. When she heard the situation, her mind started spinning. "If we could find two other people at the gym that already know CPR we could use them as assistants. Add that to Rose and me, and it will pass for the one-to-ten instructor ratio. I have a friend who owns equipment; maybe I can talk her into lending it to me. If I can't get hold of her, maybe we could use stuffed toys or dolls, or some other props they have at the gym as mannequins. We really don't need the video: I can ad lib," she thought, running over the possibilities in her mind.

Going for It, Finding a Way

Trudy tried to call her friend who owned the equipment but was only able to leave a message on her machine. Trudy wouldn't give up that easily. Her mind raced, searching for solutions. Although Rose thought it would be better to give a firm "no" than to leave someone hanging until the last minute, Trudy called her brother and said, "If we can pull something together in the next hour we'll be there. Otherwise, we can't do it."

The class did happen. They were able to get equipment, videos, and even certified assistants. Forty students were trained that day. Trudy and Rose spent nine hours of their Saturday, on a moment's notice, contributing to others. Although Rose would have preferred to plan further ahead and follow the customary protocol, she gave her full support to help. Trudy admitted she would not have wanted to do it at all if it hadn't been a "full-out, fun emergency."

You may have noticed the tendencies of the Oranges in your life and already know where some of their skills are best utilized. Sometimes we don't recognize the potential or usefulness of an Orange's energy, panache, and drive. For example, some teachers and parents may suspect their child has Attention Deficit Hyperactivity Disorder (ADHD), when in reality it *could* be that the child has strong Orange tendencies. You may find it useful to look into the possibility of channeling their energy using True Colors.

I CAN DO THIS.

To obtain methods for keeping attention at school, you may want to read *The Art of Teaching to Their True Colors* by Jean Miscisin, or *Effective Learning: Making the Personality Connection in Your Classroom* by Fairhurst and Fairhurst.

Turn to an Orange for:

Leadership—If you need someone to take charge of a situation with confidence, ask an Orange. Oranges are able to take over and manage a situation with flare, even when they have little experience with the circumstances at hand.

Trouble-Shooting—Oranges are quick decision makers. When faced with a challenge, they find it almost irresistible. Their minds go straight to work figuring out a way to make things happen. They are flexible, innovative, and not afraid of trying something new.

Tasks Requiring Risk and Chance—Many "daredevils" are Orange. Race car drivers, bungee jumpers, and firefighters tend to be Oranges. If you need someone to go first in an activity or try something uncertain, chances are an Orange will volunteer before you even get the opportunity to ask. They enjoy a good adrenaline rush.

Fun Ideas—When brainstorming for events—from family reunions to conferences—Oranges can contribute a plethora of suggestions for outrageously fun activities.

Action—If you want something done *now*, ask an Orange. They have the ability to easily stop what they are doing mid-stream and change tasks. They are ready for action and aren't hesitant to do what it takes to accomplish their immediate goal. They realize that quickness is important and usually are aware of all the shortcuts.

Proficiency with Tools—
Skillfulness, agility, and precision can be quite natural to Oranges. Frequently, they are able to build or make something with ease and accuracy. Talents they take for granted may be difficult for others.

Variety—When you want a change of pace, find an Orange. They arrange their world to ensure diversity and are even known to create a crisis or two just to stir things up. If you want a new or different way of doing something, you need only observe an Orange in action.

Negotiation—If you run up against a "no" from someone and need a "yes," enlist the help of an Orange. They have a charming way of gaining cooperation from others. They are full of options and choices and won't usually let up until they get their way, or a close compromise.

Entertainment—Oranges relish telling a great story, adventure, or even some juicy gossip. They can describe situations in larger-than-life representations. They are expressive and energetic. They are involved in a virtual kaleidoscope of pursuits.

A Good Laugh—Practical jokes, cartoons, and other forms of humor are part of the nature of Oranges. They can reframe the most mundane or even unfortunate circumstance into something to jest about. They love to laugh and to make others laugh, as well.

Attention—Many Oranges exude a tremendous amount of playful energy. And, since they crave variety and love to have fun, they are often comfortable flirting and bantering in a care-free manner.

Straight Answers—Oranges will "tell it like it is." While others are being careful to be politically correct, Oranges like to give it unadulterated. Often, they will speak their mind on a subject even if no one else agrees or is even listening. If you want to cut to the chase and get some frank, forthright responses, ask an Orange.

81

Chapter 8

SHADES OF
GREEN
GREEN
GREEN

Joyce went to see her doctor about her son. She thought he might be depressed and was gravely concerned. "He's a loner," she explained. "He really doesn't like to play with other children. He spends hours alone, reading, playing on the computer, or taking things apart like the telephone or vacuum cleaner, then putting them back together again. If I make him go out and play with other kids, I notice that instead of playing he's looking at an ant hill or exploring something by himself. When I ask him why he isn't playing with the other kids, he just shrugs his shoulders and says, 'don't want to.' What am I doing wrong? I don't want him growing up a misfit!"

After asking the usual questions about eating, sleeping, and other patterns, the doctor, an avid user of True Colors, smiled and told Joyce he would be right back. He returned to the room with a card describing a "Green." Joyce got wide-eyed as she read the description. "This is my son," she said, looking up. "This is him all the way!" she emphasized, pointing at the card. She didn't know whether to be relieved or worried.

The doctor explained that far from being abnormal, her son was quite "normal," yet had a temperament type that happened to be different from hers. "In fact," he continued, "most Greens are quite intelligent and many grow up to be doctors!"

The following are characteristics that many Greens have in common. As with all of the colors, some Greens have more of the traits than others, and some traits may also be stronger and more obvious. In addition, there can be quite noticeable differences between introverted and extroverted Greens. Introverted Greens are much more common than extroverted Greens. Bill Gates, the founder of Microsoft, is a great example of someone with many of the qualities of an introverted Green. He is a visionary, full of ideas, very complex, and willing to experiment. He holds himself and others to high standards of competency. On the other extreme, Steve Jobs, the founder of Apple Computer, is a prime example of an extroverted Green. He has many of the same qualities just mentioned; however, as an extrovert he shows his colors in a much more flamboyant and outspoken manner.

Green Characteristics

Keep in mind that just like the other color styles, Greens come in many shades. There are many aspects to a Green's temperament, and how you decide that you or someone else is Green depends on the combination of the characteristics below. Use your imagination to explore the possible ways these traits might describe the Greens in your life.

Problem Solver—Diligently works at finding a way to accomplish the task at hand. Has a tremendous amount of tenacity for figuring out solutions and enjoys the challenge.

"Why" Mentality—Wants to know the reasons why things must be done a certain way. "Because we've always done it that way" is not a good reason. Desires to know the logic or theory behind things. Very philosophical, interested in the "why" of human behavior. Inquisitive.

Very Complex—Abstract, theoretical, conceptual. Global thinker, looks at the big picture. Uses systematic approaches to situations or activities, including personal relationships.

Standard-Setter—Visionary, futurist, idea person, insightful. Often an inventor, technician, scientist, or engineer. Establishes new protocols and systems, especially for technological advances, that may influence society as a whole. The Einsteins and Edisons.

Cool, Calm, Collected—Maintains composure in situations where others may become outwardly emotional. Considers expression of feelings, such as crying, as getting in the way of

relationships instead of enhancing them. Looks at the principles involved in the situation; can work without harmony. Decides objectively. Firm-minded and can give criticism when appropriate.

Intellectual—Can never know enough. Constantly seeking information. Enjoys investigating matters further. Many Greens have a rather expansive vocabulary—know a tremendous number of "big words" and how to pronounce and use them.

Work Is Play and Play Is Work—Enjoys work so much it may be considered play. Can find "socializing" taxing unless interacting with someone sharing similar interests. Greens are often misunderstood as children because of their inclination towards solo activities.

Need for Independence and Private Time—Seeks autonomy. Doesn't necessarily enjoy or see the value in teamwork. Usually prefers to work alone. Works best without constant direction or coaching. Likes to be able to try new ways outside the norm.

Driven by Competence—Proficient and capable, feels rewarded when job is done well. Strives for expertise in field or areas of interest. Measurable success is motivating.

Perfectionist—
Explores all aspects before making a decision. Takes pride in getting it right the first time and every time.

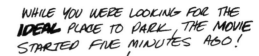

WHILE YOU WERE LOOKING FOR THE **IDEAL** PLACE TO PARK, THE MOVIE STARTED FIVE MINUTES AGO!

Analytical—
Naturally investigative; able to find flaws and imperfections. Critical thinker—does not take things at face value. Diagnostic, systematic.

Approaches Interpersonal Relationships in a Logical Manner—Can find it cumbersome to keep up with social expectations. Usually doesn't chitchat about personal matters. Speaks for a purpose, not simply to keep up social ties. May seek "formulas" for personal relationships.

Understanding and Appreciating Greens

Green's core value is competency. They are good at what they do and take pride in doing it perfectly. Following are some of their strengths.

Green Strengths:

Analyzing
Conceptualizing
Confidence
Designing
Determination
Developing
Diagnosing
Intellectualizing
Inventing
Mapping out
Problem solving
Reasoning
Researching
Technical know-how
Thinking

Greens have vision and creativity; they take their pursuits seriously. Their interests and quests may be drastically different from the general population. What is fun to them may seem like work to others. They may spend hours on what others may dub as "hair-brained" ideas or invent systems for things they think are important. While others never think about it, Greens will ponder the "why" of the world. For the most part, they like to keep their feelings on the inside so they can get on with other things. When it's time to analyze their feelings they will do so, but they don't make it a habit to share them with everyone they encounter.

Mr. Fix It

Lydia started to watch a television program on her older model TV. The picture color was yellowish and had some faint wavy lines running through it. She tried to adjust all the knobs and dials she could find to improve the picture but nothing seemed to help. Eventually she gave up and decided she'd just have to watch it the way it was. She had just settled down in her spot on the couch when her husband, Larry, walked into the room to get something out of a desk drawer. Glancing at the TV, he said to Lydia, "We should be able to get a better picture than that."

"I know, I know," she responded. "I tried everything already—this is as good as it gets."

"Everything?" he questioned, walking towards the set.

"Leave it alone, Larry," Lydia insisted, anticipating what would come next. "You can fix it later, after my program is finished."

"This will only take a minute," Larry said, as he started exploring all angles of the TV to gather data for his plan of action. Within moments he

had the set turned around and had taken the back of it off to take a look at the circuitry inside. There was no tearing him away from the set now. Lydia trudged upstairs to finish watching her program on the small black and white set in their bedroom.

Meanwhile, Larry worked diligently. He took a trip to the hardware store to try to locate a tiny electronic component. He hadn't even noticed that a couple of hours had passed. Lydia was finished with her program and already had dinner on the table.

"Honey, come and eat," she called to him from the kitchen.

"Almost there," was his response.

After about fifteen minutes or so Lydia came into the living room. There stood Larry triumphantly. "Well, what do you think?" he asked, motioning towards the set.

"Amazing!" commented Lydia, duly impressed. The picture was crystal clear and the color was perfect.

Finding a Way

Solving a problem is nearly irresistible to a Green. Their strong drive to have things work "right" can compel them to spend a tremendous amount of time trying to fix things or find solutions to conditions that others might not concern themselves with or may have given up on. Green's innate talent for figuring out how things work can be uncanny. Unraveling mysteries and working out puzzles fascinate them. They see it as a game, an intrigue, a challenge.

The Perfect Gift

Troy was deliberating about what to get his girlfriend, Helen, for her birthday. He knew a gift would mean a lot to her. He had picked up on her hint that she wanted flowers—the *first* time she alluded to it. "I just don't see the logic in buying something so useless," he thought to himself. "Thirty-five dollars on something that is just going to die in a week and have to be thrown out seems so ridiculous." Troy remembered that Helen had also mentioned several times how much she loved chocolate. "But she's always complaining about her weight. I don't want to make matters worse by buying her some chocolate so that every time she eats it she feels guilty," he pondered helpfully. "I know what I would want—a gift certificate. That way I would have options to buy whatever I wanted." He smiled, content with his choice, as he set off to pick up a gift certificate.

After purchasing the certificate Troy stopped by a store to get Helen a birthday card. Taking nearly a half-hour to sift through the selection, he found one that made him laugh out loud. "Perfect," Troy grinned. Reading it once again for pleasure, he recited the words on the front of the card, "On your birthday remember, you're not getting older, you're getting . . ." He opened it to reveal the punch line, "Well, I guess you are getting older! Happy Birthday anyway!" He chuckled all the way up to the cashier.

The look on Helen's face when she read the card and examined the gift certificate was not one of joy and amusement as he had expected. Instead she barked, "You call this a gift? How much thought went into this? Where is the 'I love you?' You don't love me, you just like making fun of me!"

Bewildered, Troy defended himself. "Of course I love you." It seemed obvious to him by all the thought and time he put into buying the gift certificate and picking out the card that it was an indication of his love for her. Why wasn't it obvious to Helen? He wouldn't do that for just *anyone*.

"You don't *tell* me that you love me," came Helen's counter response.

"I told you I loved you just last month," he replied. "If things had changed I would have let you know."

"But you don't say it often enough," Helen complained.

"Specifically how many times is enough?" Troy asked. "Twice a day and three times on Sunday?"

Exasperated, Helen sighed heavily. "I want you to *want* to say it, not give you a number. You just don't understand."

"Honey, just tell me precisely what you need and I'm sure I can figure out a system for providing it!"

Practical Love

Greens like to establish a personal relationship and then leave it to maintain itself while they pursue more intellectual accomplishments. For this reason, some Greens may not want to direct a lot of attention to making sure their relationship stays alive. They assume it will. Why wouldn't it?

Other Greens may try to devise a strategy for keeping their partner satisfied. For instance, if they know their partner wants to hear "I love you," they will try to make a conscious effort to say it, but it usually is an effort. They prefer not to be so redundant. Many Greens think that once they have stated something it should stand until they say otherwise.

When it comes to gift giving and receiving, Greens enjoy options. Therefore, many Greens assume that others do also. A gift certificate is a great gift for a Green to receive because it does just that—gives them options. Often, they put many hours and a lot of thought into picking out the "perfect" gift for their mate. The only trouble is that it might just be perfect for them. It may be hard for Greens to override their deeply embedded value system and sense of logic to purchase something they view as frivolous.

A Quest for Information

Kirk and Sophie had been going out for four years now. Kirk was

88

always amazed by the tremendous amount of trivia Sophie had at her fingertips. It came in very handy at social gatherings, where she always seemed to know something about every topic discussed. Be it politics, science, wine, or gardening—it seemed that Sophie had a never-ending fund of knowledge. Yet at other times, it was frustrating—not because of the information she possessed, but because of the lengths that she went to to acquire it. Kirk related one of those times.

"We were at a dance and they were playing a song that was just *awesome.* I leaned over to Sophie and let her know how much I liked it, and not a second later she was walking up to the DJ and asking the name of the song. Later that night when we got home I found her in our study sitting in front of the computer, searching for the song on an Internet record store. 'Sophie, what are you doing? It's two o'clock in the morning!' I exclaimed. She told me that she had found the song on a search engine that led to a site about the band. The site told the story of how the band got started, what other albums they had put out, what additional artists the band had recruited for backup drums, as well as the symbolism behind the artwork on the cover. She was even able to play samples of the record right off the Internet. Agghh! It was too much for

me at two in the morning. I felt kind of bad when I couldn't match her enthusiasm for her "project." I just went to bed and, to tell you the truth, forgot about the whole thing. About a week later a package came for me in the mail. She had bought me the CD off the Internet! I can still remember the first time I played the CD. Knowing all that information about the band that Sophie had told me really did make listening to the music more enjoyable. One day I took the CD to work and left it on my desk. Someone from Sales came over and picked it up, and soon I was going on about where the band had come from, who the band members were, what the artwork on the cover symbolized . . ."

Hmmm . . . That's Interesting!

Greens enjoy gathering interesting details about various subjects. Before watching a sporting event they may look up the history and statistics on the players, as well as particulars about the event itself. Before making a decision, like a purchase, Greens want to gather *all* of the facts, and then some! They want to make sure they have all of the information possible so they can make a sound decision. Sometimes even after a decision has been made, they will continue to gather data to back up the fact that they made the best decision.

The Excitement of Learning

"San Francisco Amateur Astronomers Club—Mount Tamalpais Astronomy Program," Ceni read out loud from a flyer posted on a bulletin board in the hallway of the Student Services building at her college. "A popular series of lectures, slide presentations, and night sky viewing," she continued. "Presenters are from the NASA/AMES research center, the SETI Institute, the Morrison Planetarium, and nearby universities. Dr. John Miles from Lockheed will be discussing Extraterrestrial Planet Finders. Telescopes will be available after the lecture for night viewing."

Grabbing a mechanical pencil from her backpack, she copied down the contact information. "Wow! That sounds like fun," she thought. "If I

went this weekend, I could get a head start on my Astronomy class. It would be great to be familiar with some of the information before I get into the classroom. I would love to get a membership so I could get the newsletter and stay informed on the latest discoveries on a continual basis." Her thoughts reeled, thinking of possibilities. Then, suddenly realizing that she had stood there thinking longer than she meant to, Ceni snapped her attention back to the present moment. She hurried down the hall to the tutoring center where she worked as a calculus tutor.

Just last week she had brainstormed ideas with the instructor trainer about how to take the program to a new level. They wanted to improve the old instructors' manual (that the tutors used) to incorporate methods for teaching to the various learning styles of the students. With this new tool, the tutors could ascertain various techniques to help the students learn faster, increase their comprehension, and retain the information longer. Once the manual was written, they could test its effectiveness and determine if it were a valid instrument. After they proved its validity they could publish it, so that other universities across the state and possibly the nation could incorporate it into their own programs. Ceni had already purchased a few carefully selected manuals and checked out several books from the library to study the various theories. She wanted to do a good job of integrating the learning styles material into the existing tutoring curriculum. She was confident she could assist the trainer in putting together a usable manual for the program.

Besides having a knack for incorporating information, she also seemed to have an intuitive eye for being able to display the information in a usable format. Just last year, she was a teacher's assistant for her chemistry lab. The students were confused as to how to arrange their lab notebooks and the instructor turned to her for help. He asked her if she could put something together as an example for them to review. Ceni knew she could not just show them her notebook because it would have all the answers to the lab problems, so she made up one with mock data points and calculations. It was fantastic. The students were delighted to have an example of how to organize their manuals, and the chemistry instructor enjoyed receiving well-organized notebooks from the students all year.

Ceni decided this year, instead of assisting in the chemistry lab itself, she would take a position as a teacher's assistant for correcting homework and test papers. She figured that correcting papers would help her know the concepts inside and out. This would prepare her more thoroughly for her next chemistry class. This position was not a paid

one like the classroom tutoring. She thought of a quotation she had heard earlier that day and felt it summed up her philosophy quite well: "Symbolic Analysts are people who manipulate symbols. Their jobs are something they would do even if they were not getting paid for it."

"Yep, that's me!" she reconfirmed, as she scurried off to her next class.

New and Improved! Better than Before!

Greens are on a never-ending quest for improvement of the status quo. They enjoy developing concepts and are intrigued by advances in progress, especially of an intellectual or scientific nature. Very complex individuals, not only do they think about how an issue affects them, they think of how it affects the world . . . and even beyond! For them, "work" is play, as long as they have an interest in what they are doing. They will sometimes spend a great amount of time on projects that others may perceive as "work," such as reading, attending lectures, and studying. Embarking on ventures that require them to investigate data, figure things out, or test theories is exciting and can be spellbinding. Many Greens take pride in the display of information they have gathered. They derive gratification from a well-designed spreadsheet, charts, graphs, or reports. Mastering their subjects is a great source of pleasure to Greens, and they will seek avenues for enhancement of their competence.

Books, Books, Books

Dwayne, a self-professed "Pure Green," shared his philosophy on owning books. Because he believes in recycling and sharing the knowledge contained in the pages of books, he limits himself to owning only approximately 200 books at any given time.

Although he never went on to college after high school because he did not like "conforming to the rigid structure of our educational institutions and being stifled in my thinking," he continues to read and study on his own. Some of his interests include math, from algebra through calculus, non-linear dynamics, fractal and chaos theory, magic, biology, psychology, and philosophy. He enjoys religion and has read the Bahagavad Gita, Koran, Bible, Book of Mormon, and Cabala, just to name a few.

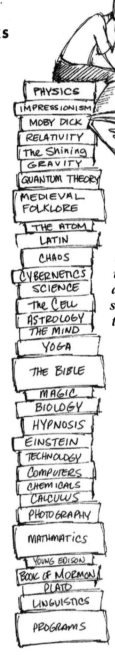

PHYSICS
IMPRESSIONISM
MOBY DICK
RELATIVITY
The Shining
GRAVITY
QUANTUM THEORY
MEDIEVAL FOLKLORE
THE ATOM
LATIN
CHAOS
CYBERNETICS
SCIENCE
The Cell
ASTROLOGY
THE MIND
YOGA
THE BIBLE
MAGIC
BIOLOGY
HYPNOSIS
EINSTEIN
TECHNOLOGY
Computers
CHEMICALS
CALCULUS
PHOTOGRAPHY
MATHMATICS
YOUNG EDISON
BOOK OF MORMON
PLATO
LINGUISTICS
PROGRAMS

He has also read *The Lord of the Rings* trilogy and a variety of books about astrology, yoga, and human anatomy. He likes to keep a 50 percent "roll over." In other words, he reads at least 50 percent of his books before purchasing a new one. Dwayne keeps a book in his car, at work, and at home to read during increments of time when there is nothing else he can do. He always has three or four going at a time.

Since Greens have a variety of interests, love exploring ideas and theories, and are adept at storing wisdom and knowledge, they often read.

Greens that read a tremendous amount have an extensive vocabulary. Other people can read the same book as a Green and have no idea what the author is talking about because the words and concepts are not familiar to them. Greens' abstract thinking makes it easier to understand highly theoretical material.

Another Hue of Green

Greens are perhaps the most misunderstood of the Color profiles. Their ability to make objective decisions with a high degree of independence leads others to misread them as cold and uncaring. Because Greens are big thinkers, their minds are sometimes not in the same room—or even plane of existence—as the people they are with. Oftentimes they are internally focused on creating an idea or working on a problem instead of outside connecting. Their gift for critique compels them to seek perfection and may alienate those that don't understand or share a similar drive.

The following are ways that people sometimes interpret Greens. If you are Green, you have probably been accused of having one or more of these attributes.

These characteristics may or may not be true; the amusing thing is that it's the perspective of the person observing that shades the qualities as negative or positive. What comes naturally for Greens can get misinterpreted by others as something Greens purposely "do" to put themselves above or to control others. The fact is they have some natural abilities that may be misunderstood by the general public.

If you are Green, pay attention to the way you may be perceived by others. It could answer some questions you may have about why people respond and relate to you as they do.

Others May See Greens as:

Intellectual Snobs—Know-it-all. Uses big words. Refers to books that aren't read by the general public. Speaks of structures, systems, and techniques.

Arrogant—Condescending. Gets irritated if perceives others don't have the same competence or knowledge. Thinks they are always right.

Heartless—Uncaring. Devalues emotional pleas. Ignores people's values.

Unrealistic—Uses technology extensively and assumes others should want to also. Always wants to change or improve things. Expects others to adhere to unbearably high standards of performance.

Eccentric, Weird—Has strange ideas and opinions. Behaves out of the ordinary.

Unfeeling—Without emotions. Doesn't allow others to express their emotions.

Anti-Social—Doesn't like people or entertaining activities. Not a team-player. Afraid to open up. Won't allow others to get to know them. Does not share feelings. Not interested in others as people.

Cool, Aloof—Does not bother to acknowledge others. Unfriendly, serious, doesn't smile very much, controlled demeanor.

Sarcastic—Mean. Has a biting, demeaning, put-others-down sense of humor. Makes fun of others.

Critical—Fault-finding, not on your side. Looks for errors and mistakes. Points out exceptions. Instead of focusing on what has been accomplished, hones in on what is lacking.

Lacking Mercy—Hatchet man. Does not consider extenuating circumstances.

Unappreciative—Stingy with praise. Doesn't compliment or encourage.

Greens May See Self as:

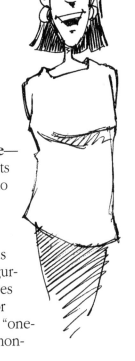

WHAT SOME SEE AS **PEDANTIC,**
I SEE AS **FELICITOUS,** TO
QUOTE **SOCRATES**...

Knowledgeable— Has varied interests and spends time to research curiosities. Adept at designing and using systems. Has keen sense for figuring things out. Uses accurate words for precision—not to "one-up" others or demonstrate superiority.

98% Right—Unless extremely extroverted and thinking out loud, or playing "devil's advocate," Greens rarely speak on a subject they are not acquainted with. They pride themselves on their expert competence and seldom risk jeopardizing their reputation for being right. In fact, if a Green makes a bet with someone, chances are it's a well-calculated conjecture. They usually don't bet unless they are fairly certain they will win.

Expedient—When on a mission to accomplish a goal, may not notice (or chooses to disregard) that others are seeking acknowledgment or personal connection. Generally more task-focused than people-focused at work or when engaged in a project.

96

Visionary—Sees the need and value for technology and change. Able to anticipate the future consequences of actions and inventions. Open-minded; recognizes possibility, relevance, and usefulness in areas incomprehensible to others.

Innovative—Creative, original, unique. Work is play. Would rather spend time on worthwhile endeavors than to fritter it away on mere common entertainment. Has the ingenuity and resourcefulness to take ideas to fruition when others would have given up.

Rational—Eminently reasonable. Once relationships are established, prefers to let them maintain themselves. Does not feel the need to constantly reestablish them. Cares deeply and prefers to share intense emotions only in close relationships.

Independent—Able to work alone proficiently. Gathers energy from internal world of thoughts and ideas.

Deep Thinkers—Under control, serious, and logical. Concentrates on other things and has different priorities than the general public. Focused.

Able to Find Flaws—Views it as a favor to point out discrepancies and imperfections. Often driven to find the exception to the rule.

Witty—Entertaining, funny, amusing. Enjoys word puns, dichotomies, and dark or sarcastic humor.

Fair—Seeks justice, able to reprimand. Gathers information before making judgments. Takes into consideration the whole picture. Knows the nature of human behavior and that things may not always be as they seem. Able to look beyond the obvious. In this quest to know all sides of an issue, Greens may reach information overload and find it difficult to choose one side or another.

Assume Things Will Be Done Well—Doesn't like to point out the obvious. Likes to think everyone is working to the very best of their ability and *that* is reward enough. Thinks commending trivial tasks would be equivalent to an insult.

Relating to Greens

Greens seek to express themselves through their ability to be competent in everything they do.

The secret to relating to Greens lies in stimulating them to use their minds in an atmosphere of rationality and freedom. They have the ability to acquire the skills and knowledge required to perfect any product or system they choose to focus on, from computers to world peace. Their ability to conceptualize is a gift that they contribute, given the opportunity to do so. They relate well to creative Blues, helpful Golds, and resourceful Oranges.

Honor their need for privacy

Greens are most comfortable in an environment that is unstructured, creative, and allows for privacy and independent discovery. Their loved ones, friends, and co-workers must understand their need for independence and private time. They like to sit by themselves and think without noise or intrusion. Don't insist they share without first allowing them time to gather their thoughts. Once they have collected their thoughts, they are more ready to interact with others. Insisting that they sit and listen to you tell about your day before allowing them this solo period could prove to be rather futile, as well as frustrating.

Understand their necessity to question your knowledge and facts

Greens are extremely curious; they have a need to learn and comprehend. You can gain their cooperation by being objective and avoiding power struggles when their strong sense of logic challenges your ideas and data. Admire their intelligence; let them know you value their wisdom. When you make it a point to

WHY?
BECAUSE I SAID.
WHY?
JUST BECAUSE.
WHY?
PLEASE JUST DO IT.
WHY? . . .

ask for their opinion and supporting arguments on a topic, you will enlist their cooperation and maintain a positive atmosphere.

Realize they too have feelings

Because many Greens don't show their emotions readily, they can appear rather serious or businesslike. Especially introverted Greens may be more reserved in demeanor or seem difficult to approach. Although they feel their emotions deeply, they usually do not show many of their feelings about situations, people, or stress.

When discussing problems with Greens, remember they enjoy playing on words and demonstrating their large vocabulary, but have little tolerance for redundancy or stating the obvious. Their sense of humor can throw non-Greens off guard. Keep in mind that their sarcasm and wit is for amusement, not to hurt.

Greens generally pay little attention to verbal cues and have often become accustomed to others failing to grasp what they are saying or thinking. Therefore, to focus their attention on problems concerning them, be logical and objective. In privacy, explain the reason for a rule, stick to the issue, avoid sarcasm, and let them share in determining corrective action.

Encourage and reward achievements by commenting on their creativity, competence, and ability to gather data.

Greens pride themselves on their intellectual ability to investigate, analyze, and understand new ideas and concepts. Realize they need validation for their own ideas. They take mistakes very seriously, so don't take it personally when they focus their attention on problem solving instead of relationship building.

Appreciate their varied interests

Greens often notice and are intrigued by things that some people simply don't even think about. They may be concerned with developing models, admiring intelligence, being a perfectionist, utilizing precise language, exploring ideas, striving for competency, storing wisdom and knowledge, handling complexity, and understanding human systems and the environment. They are interested in analytical processes and abstract thinking. They know how to work, or even invent, equipment to meet their needs. They are also good at figuring out a way to get things to work. Often, they take initiative on things that are important to them, even if others are not in agreement. They act with confidence and a sense of urgency to solve such problems.

Don't be mad at them because they don't embrace your interests. It can be equally frustrating for them when you lack interest in their ideas and conversations. Instead, encourage them in their endeavors and provide avenues for exploration and contribution.

Greens Need:

intellectual stimulation
autonomy
challenge
to question
time to ponder
information
competence
privacy
innovation
objectivity

Greens Need to Be:

competent
well-informed
emotionally composed
recognized for their ideas
innovative

Greens Value:

expertise
intellectual achievement
knowledge
logic
technology
accuracy
ingenuity

strategy
self-sufficiency
improvement

Greens Find Joy in:

exploring new ideas
high achievement
meeting challenges
seeking new knowledge
solving problems
doing what "can't be done"
creative freedom
humor and irony

With Greens Be:

rational
precise
ready for questions
prepared to give facts
analytical
encouraging
focused
logical
objective
open-minded

Greens will be most cooperative when you provide positive feedback on the quality of their work; provide opportunities for them to display their competency; request their contributions for findings and conclusions; and encourage them to create, build, analyze, and evaluate. They appreciate it when you allow them to work on projects independently; provide opportunities to gather additional knowledge; offer experiences which will enhance written work; and ask them for additional insights and observations.

Bringing Out the Green

To elicit the finest from Greens, involve them in situations and activities where they have a chance to show their competency.

"Somebody has got to do something about the smell around here. This is getting ridiculous!" Amy was talking to her co-worker Matthew, both coaches for a gymnastics studio. You can imagine that after hundreds of children have tumbled around on the mats hour after hour working up a sweat, it would leave some effect on the air.

"I know," said Matthew. "By the end of an eight-hour day my sinuses are clogged. The problem is we're trying to cover up the odors instead of eliminating them. I've always been a bit concerned about the perfume air fresheners we have. They emit chemicals that can't be the best for us to be breathing. The other day I put a new garbage bag in a trash can and sprayed it with the citrus extract we have. The next day I noticed the can was moldy. There are so many harmful effects this could have on our health."

Amy was pleased that Matthew had taken a vested interest in her complaint. He promised her he would personally take it upon himself to get rid of the odor and mold problem once and for all.

Matthew was aware that negative ions help freshen the air and can even enhance the moods of people. So he went to his employers and told them he wanted to invest in a system. He anticipated some resistance and was prepared to talk them into it. To his surprise, they had already tried an air purification system in another location without success. They said the units "didn't work" the way they wanted them to so they weren't using them anymore. Matthew suggested they give the units a try at his location.

"When I picked up the units, I was disappointed to discover that they only had analog controls. And they had settings for both ion production and ozone production. Although ions help eliminate airborne particles, they are not completely effective against eliminating odors. I knew that ozone was an antigerm and antiviral agent. However, I also knew that breathing ozone in high amounts over long periods of time can lead to respiratory problems. I wanted to have the healthy beneficial ions in the air during the daytime while people were in the gym. I needed the ozone to be produced only at night when no one was there to be subjected to them.

In spite of the assurances on the label on the machines that they didn't produce ozone in high enough amounts to be harmful, I did not want to take the risk of exposing anyone to the potentially harmful effects. With only analog controls, I was faced with the dilemma of inconveniencing myself or someone else to climb up a ladder morning and night in order to readjust the settings.

At last I came up with another solution. Although the machines themselves did not have digital timers or the ability to change settings, I realized that I had two machines and could use them alternately. All I had to do was add my own timers. So I purchased two timers and set one machine on only ions, to be turned on during the daytime, and the other machine on only ozone, to be turned on after closing and turned off in time for the ozone to dissipate before anyone arrived in the morning."

The representative who sold the units to Matthew's employer was so impressed that he referred his other clients to Matthew. In addition, another vendor called and asked Matthew if his company could refer their clients to him to learn how he was using the units. They had never seen such sophisticated and effective use of their product.

Turn to a Green for:

Ideas—They are problem solvers, innovators. If you want to get the big picture on an idea, or concepts for improvement, Greens have a knack for creating masterpieces from mud.

Information—When you need a logical explanation or data, a Green either already has it or knows where it can be found. They pride themselves on being a storehouse of information on a variety of subjects.

Competence—Greens strive for brilliance. They want to be proficient and expert in their endeavors. If you need someone who knows what they are doing, ask a Green.

Tenacity—Although Greens have a tendency to brainstorm plenty of ideas for projects and can be content to let others finish them, if they are interested in the challenge at hand, they will not stop until they have the problem solved. Once the challenge is gone, they will move on.

Firmness—Since Greens are very objective, they are able to hold their ground without feeling threatened. If you need someone who will not be easily manipulated or duped to deliver a message, send a Green.

Objective Decision Making—Greens use their logic to examine the pros and cons of a decision. They explore issues from many angles and have the ability to see black and white or countless shades of gray.

The Right Word—If you are looking for accuracy in language—correct usage, meaning, or even spelling, a Green is one good source to turn to.

Technology—The most likely color type to have an intense interest in or passion for technology is a Green. They know how to use a variety of equipment and systems that are foreign to the average person.

Critique—Greens easily spot what can be improved in situations, people, and theories. They welcome an opportunity to share their insights on what they think is good and what could be modified to be more effective. Ask for their feedback.

To Learn—Greens are usually quite eager to enlighten others on various topics. Their main concern is whether the person they are educating has enough of a background in the subject to comprehend the information they are receiving. If you have a genuine interest in a subject that deals with ideas, systems, theories, religion, etc., ask a Green.

To Get Something Fixed—Greens have the uncanny ability to know how to fix things or create more efficient ways of using things to progress forward.

To Invent or Create Something—Got a problem and don't know where to go from here? A Green's innovative mind is always creating new possibilities for solving challenges.

103

Chapter 9
COLOR
COMBINATIONS

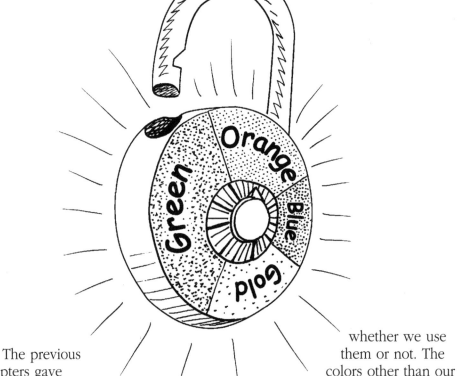

The previous chapters gave examples of the traits that are the strongest for each color style. Some individuals have a majority of their characteristics in one color and may seldom operate using traits from the other colors.

However, we all have a blend of different variations of the four colors, whether we use them or not. The colors other than our dominant color can and *do* influence our behaviors. So, even though a person may be Gold dominant, their Blue, Orange, or Green characteristics will often affect their choices and actions.

Many people find that their first and second colors are equally strong

104

and interchangeable. They are so closely intertwined that they almost merge together. It may be hard to discern whether one is really more dominant or preferred than the other. Since our most dominant colors are considerably easy to access and naturally called upon, we often refer to the top two colors in a person's line-up instead of just the top color. For instance, we might say someone is a "Green-Blue" or a "Gold-Blue." Although they still have traits from their third and fourth colors, for simplicity, we refer to only their first two colors.

For some individuals, their second color influences their first in a strong way. For others, their second color may have only a slight impact. Other people are somewhere in between. It's simple to understand how certain color combinations easily go together and how they naturally influence each other. You may recognize some of the following color combinations in yourself or people you know. The following are examples of how combinations of colors might show up.

Familiar Combinations

Orange–Blue

It's quite obvious that the wit, charm, and spontaneity of the Orange characteristics would positively enhance the enthusiasm, empathy, and genuine love for people of the Blue. When Orange is more dominant than Blue, the need for freedom and flexibility can often take precedence over the need to connect with others. When Blue is predominant, relationships will be placed ahead of the powerful tug to switch attention to whatever captures it at the moment. Those whose Blue comes first will have a stronger tendency to check with the other people involved before diving into another endeavor. Those whose Orange is first might not.

Blue–Gold

The strong desire to influence others, the need to contribute, and the caring of the Blues go well with the loyalty, dependability, and preparedness of the Golds. When Blue is first and Gold second, organization, tradition, and procedures may give way to extenuating circumstances of family members, friends, or co-workers. When Gold is first, obligation, responsibility, and duty will be prioritized along with the people involved. In either case, this is a friendly, dedicated combination.

Gold–Green

A Gold's thoroughness, sensibility, and punctuality blend nicely with the objectivity, proficiency, and tenacity of the Greens. When Gold is foremost, attention and efforts will be focused first on the completion of tasks, maintaining an organized and structured environment, and following procedures. The Green traits become a logical backup for objective decision making and analysis of data. Both Greens and Golds, of course, prefer to think before making a decision. When Green traits are more abundant than Gold, innovation and independence can lead to the creation of new rules and standards. This combination is great with data, details, and being forthright and firm-minded in their decisions. High expectations are usually placed upon themselves and those around them. They are competent, capable, and dependable.

Green–Orange

The visionary, non-conformist, problem solving of the Greens combines readily with the natural troubleshooter, resourcefulness, and boldness of an Orange. Those with Green dominance will strive for competence and to create a better, more advanced world than before. Their Orange provides a "charge-ahead" attitude that can propel these individuals toward high goals and expansive endeavors. Orange-Green unifications may try new challenges before they've gathered all the data or gained the high level of skill generally required by most Greens before they feel comfortable taking action. They are naturally eager to boldly dive in and "Go for it!" Their competitive, trouble-shoot-ing, risk-taking nature compels them to continuously take on new challenges. And if things don't work out, they can easily switch gears to a new undertaking. These endeavors may have a tendency to take precedence over attention to personal relationships. Their Green provides them with the big picture insights, along with the vision and ingenuity to keep trying. The non-conformist nature of this combination allows them to live by their own standards. Variety and change are familiar friends to them.

Seeing Opposites?

The previous combinations might seem to unite with each other rather naturally. However, there are some combinations that might seem to be contrary to each other. For instance, Blues make decisions based on how they will affect the relationships and people involved, yet Greens decide according to facts and logic. So, how can they both be dominant in a person? Further, Oranges seem to thrive on pushing boundaries, while Golds like to enforce the rules. Aren't these direct opposites? One might think so, at first.

Blue–Green

Individuals with a Blue-Green combination, with Blue being the most dominant, will put the feelings and needs of others ahead of theirs, in most situations. They may try to guess what the other person wants and act accordingly to accommodate them. They are caring, considerate, and kind. However, having Green as a second color may cause an internal conflict because although they love people, they will have a strong need for independence and private time. Their pursuit of information, perfectionism, and mastery for using systems may override their attention to relationships. Since intellectual competence is important to them, they will excel in their chosen field and use their broad base of knowledge to help others.

Green–Blue

Although one may think a Blue-Green and a Green-Blue would be quite similar, there are some definite differences. Individuals with Green as their primary color and Blue as their second are probably the most misunderstood of the combinations. Their ambition for perfectionism, the high standards they set for themselves and others, as well as their drive for accuracy may alienate people. They put proficiency and competency first. They may not want to be bogged down with having to say "good morning" to people or remember their birthdays. They may choose to avoid certain social functions, instead preferring to read a good book or invent a new system for doing something. But because their second color is Blue,

they may not understand why some people perceive them as cool, aloof, and unsocial. The Blue in them will take things personally and may feel hurt for long periods. Others may never know they have hurt this person because they are most likely not going to open up and share. Although others may find them unapproachable, Green-Blues may feel they are open-minded and communicative. They want people to like and understand them without having to spell it out for them.

What Blues and Greens have most in common is their ability to see endless possibilities. They usually look at the big picture before the small details. Both are very creative, imaginative, and idealistic.

Orange–Gold

These are the fun-loving, spontaneous individuals that fancy a challenge. They derive great joy from experiencing the here and now. They have an attitude that "tomorrow may never come" so they seize the moment, often without thinking of consequences for the future. This is where their second color, Gold, can haunt them with guilt. Because it is in a Gold's nature to plan ahead, the Orange-Gold has a tendency to act now, regret later. They may browbeat themselves for being irresponsible and make sure that everyone else around them is abiding by the rules. They may have the world around them super-organized so that they can take advantage of opportunities when they arise without upsetting the balance of their lives. Planning ahead and keeping organized makes it possible for them to act with more freedom and speed than if they had to wade through things to find opportunities. This way they are unencumbered and free to act on a moment's notice. They are prepared to take on any challenge that comes their way.

Gold–Orange

The Gold-Orange actually has quite the opposite challenges of the Orange-Gold. These individuals have a drive to be responsible at all costs. In order for them to play, their duties *must* be met first. They may *want* to be spontaneous and stay overnight when the time gets late, but their sense of responsibility won't allow them. They may have internal arguments with themselves about what is right and wrong. Both the Gold-Orange and Orange-Gold combinations can be powerful unifications. The self-confident, practical, take-charge traits of the Orange combine well with the plan-ahead, dependable, consistent follow-through of the Gold.

Opposites Work Together

So, what may seem like such opposite characteristics may actually combine into a synergistic alliance.

Acknowledging that every trait is one worth having and developing will help us better understand how to channel our natural tendencies to bring out the best in everyone.

Same Color Combinations— Different Personalities

Just because you have the exact same *color order* as someone else, does not mean you have the exact same *personality*.

Rick, Terry, and Aaron are good friends. It's not unusual for friends to have some commonalities in characteristics or circumstances. Often that's what ignites a friendship in the first place—having something in common, such as working at the same company, taking a class together in college, or owning the same kind of pet.

These three friends have quite a bit in common. First, they all happen to have the same color spectrum: Orange-Blue-Green-Gold. They are all very physical and like to work out with weights. Their conversations with each other are loud and open. A topic that seems to permeate their dialogues is sex. They talk and joke about it freely and often. All three love to dance-dance-dance! They are very playful, easy-going, and friendly. They like the adrenaline rush of an unpredictable situation and are constantly negotiating. It is amusing to watch any one of them at a restaurant trying to coax the server into adding some free food onto the order, or at a store, trying to get an extra discount. None of them seems to be able to drive the speed limit. In fact that's where they all met—in traffic school!

Even with so much in common, people often have distinct differences

When people with similar color combinations get together it can brighten up their colors even more. Golds are very comfortable around other Golds, Blues seem to feel freer to express themselves around other Blues, Greens articulate more with other Greens who have similar interests, and Oranges can relax and let it all hang out with other Oranges. However, when you take a look at the individual characteristics that make up a person's color spectrum, you will notice that the same trait can be expressed in very different ways.

Rick

Rick is a mechanical engineer. His job is to troubleshoot what needs to be done in situations to make machinery work. He is good at jumping in and saving the day with

his ingenuity, knowledge, and skill with tools. But the adrenaline rush does not end at work. If someone happens to cut him off in traffic on the way home or takes his parking spot when he stops at the bank, he'll jump out of his truck and pound his fists on the hood of the other car, loudly daring the driver to get out and fight. Rick seems to be the center of attention in most places he goes, usually because he is stirring up some kind of trouble. He has been in and out of several relationships. He loves the excitement of meeting a new woman. The flirt, the chase, the catch. But that is usually when things start heading downhill—after the catch. He begins to get a bit bored and finds himself more and more restless. It is not long before he is distracted by new prospects. Strangely enough, Rick is always on time or even early for appointments and events.

Terry

Terry is a motivational speaker. He thrives on standing before a large crowd and sharing passionately about how to live life to the fullest.

He enjoys the challenge of hearing an audience member share an issue and being able to think "on-the-spot" of a solution or options for resolving it. He practices what he preaches and spends his time ardently achieving his goals. Although he has moved thirty-two times in the past ten years, he maintains a long-distance relationship with a woman he has been seeing for the past five years. Though they have a child together, they have not seriously discussed any marriage plans. When Terry is not on the road, their relationship is like a whirlwind romance. They squeeze every bit of juice out of the time they spend together. Terry is occasionally late, putting things off until the last minute and rushing to meet deadlines.

Aaron

Aaron is a Ph.D. student. He is married to a designer who is busy building her own career. He loves the freedom that a committed relationship affords him. He appreciates being able to come home and share his day with his wife, equally enjoying hearing about her tribulations and triumphs. Aaron and his wife participate in many activities together such as marathons, exercising, and even taking classes. He has a part-time job as counselor at a middle school. He enjoys the one-on-one with the students and the feeling he gets when he knows he has affected their lives in a positive way. Figuring out what to do for each unique situation that arises is a fun challenge for him. He is virtually never on time for anything. You can almost count on him being late. Of course when he arrives, he is so charming and friendly, one cannot stay mad at him for long.

We may have the same characteristic in common with someone else, yet manifest it in different ways.

Isn't it interesting to note the general commonalities in the three friends while noticing how different they are

in their *specific* behaviors and lifestyle choices? For instance, all three of the friends enjoy problem solving and troubleshooting on-the-spot. Because their circumstances are different, they get this need met in different ways. Rick troubleshoots to make machinery work, Terry finds solutions to his workshop participants' questions, and Aaron figures out how to help young students with their problems. Our upbringing, culture, age, location in which we reside, and numerous other circumstances all contribute to our behaviors. Therefore, we may act specifically differently than someone else with the same color combination yet—in general—very similarly. It is important to keep this in mind when you are trying to discern your color spectrum or the colors of others.

Some people have a tendency to think that if they do not have the same interests or lifestyle they cannot possibly have the same color traits. Think again! It is the motivations behind the behaviors, not the behaviors themselves, that are the signposts that point us in the direction of our True Colors.

Part III

COMMUNICATING ACROSS THE SPECTRUM

Ways to Open Up Lines of Communication for Everyone

No matter what color style is dominant in a person or the order of one's spectrum, there are some basic communication skills that apply to all the colors. Learning these principles will enhance your interactions and allow you to communicate more easily, effectively, and eloquently with nearly everyone you encounter.

112

Do you understand what I am asking?

Susan was interested in joining a health club and asked her mother, Roberta, to come with her to look at a few places. Roberta belonged to a fitness club that allowed her to go to any of their clubs in California. One of these clubs happened to be close to Susan's apartment, so they decided to explore this one first. On the way to the club, Susan explained that she wanted to check out the atmosphere. She was looking for nice, helpful workers—people who would acknowledge her and greet her with a smile when she came in.

She wanted a place that was not too crowded, other members that were friendly and patient if it did get crowded, and clean locker rooms, as well as clean, functioning equipment.

When they walked in the door they asked the receptionist behind the front desk if they could look around the club. The receptionist handed them both clipboards, told them to have a seat and fill out the forms, and someone would be right with them. Roberta asked her if it was really necessary to fill out the forms. All they wanted to do was look around and get a feel for the place. The receptionist told them that if they were not members, then "for liability reasons" they were required to fill out the forms. Roberta told the receptionist she was indeed a member and showed her her membership card.

The receptionist barely glanced at the card and said "make sure to note that on the form," then abruptly went back to what she was doing. Susan and Roberta were already getting "bad vibes" and thinking about leaving without even seeing the place when a trainer came walking out, grinning heartily.

He motioned for them to give him their clipboards, which they did. Grabbing the clipboards, he continued to walk right past them without a word. The smile dropped from his face as he scanned the forms and talked to the receptionist behind the desk. As he turned to approach Susan and her mother, the smile suddenly reappeared.

"How are we doing today?" he asked, reaching out to shake Roberta's hand. She explained again that they just wanted to look around and see what the club had to offer. Seeming uninterested in their requests, he asked if they received their mail at the same address.

Susan and Roberta looked at each other puzzled. "Yes, we do," they said in unison.

"What does that have to do with a tour?" Roberta asked.

"Well, I see you are already a member, and in order for your daughter to be eligible to join you must receive your mail at the same address," he replied.

Suspecting he might be referring to some sort of family member- ship, Roberta was just about to clarify that her daughter would be join- ing on her own when Susan answered his question with "we do!"

The conversation went even further awry as he fired off more questions.

"Do you live in a house or apart- ment?" he asked.

"A house—"

"An apartment—"

Roberta and Susan spoke at almost the same time.

"Which is it?" he said, frowning as if they were trying to pull a fast one on him.

"I live in a house; she lives in an apartment," Roberta responded.

"I thought you said you get your mail at the same address!"

"We do! We use a PO box," they both said.

"Well that won't work unless you have some kind of utility bill with

HOUSE OR APARTMENT?

why?

114

your names on it," he said with a scowl on his face.

"We both get our utility bills there, and of course they have our names on them!" Roberta said.

Feeling interrogated and utterly flabbergasted at this point, Susan and Roberta looked at each other and said, "Let's go!" They nearly ran out of the place.

The next health club they explored was a bit further from Susan's apartment. When they walked in, the receptionist behind the counter greeted them with a big smile and said, "Hello!"

Susan said, "We are interested in looking at your facilities."

"Terrific!" responded the receptionist. "Would you like me to give you a tour or would you like to look around on your own?"

After the experience at the last gym it was no surprise when Susan said, "We'll look on our own, thanks!" Susan walked around the place. It felt cozy and friendly. Even the people exercising smiled as she walked by. It took her an entire five minutes to decide to join.

It's easy to notice that there was better communication in the few sentences spoken at the second club than in all the words spoken and forms filled out at the first club. Why?

What was the difference? If you said something like "they listened" or "they paid attention" at the second club, you're right!

When people continue with their own agenda without listening to the needs of others, a lot of words can be exchanged without any intended communication actually taking place.

Ways to Open Up Lines of Communication

#1: Share True Colors with *Everyone*

If the trainer at the first club were lucky enough to have been familiar with True Colors, he would have recognized the Blue needs of Susan right away and could have addressed them accordingly. The girl at the second gym most likely met Susan's Blue needs by happenstance. Don't leave it up to luck! Knowing True Colors helps you understand the values, needs, and actions of others. It gives you a nonjudgmental language base to enable you to communicate more freely and appreciate the uniqueness in everyone. Things that might irritate another will instead fascinate someone who knows True Colors.

#2: Pause and pay attention

The biggest mistake the trainer at the first club made was to be blind to Susan's and Roberta's needs. He didn't pay attention to what they were telling him. Instead, he went straight to figuring out how much it would cost for a family membership, which they didn't even care about! Even if the club were free, Susan wouldn't go

there if she didn't like the atmosphere. Susan was very irritated that the trainer didn't seem to get the message that she wanted to see what the club had to offer. Atmosphere was number one on her list, and he seemed to think that price was the first thing to address.

All too often we enter into an exchange with our own goals so much in front of our face that we are unable to see past them to the other person. Momentarily setting aside your own goals will help you clear the way for better communication.

#3: Learn from the past but avoid over generalizing

If someone has always run late in the past and your professionalism or reputation has suffered because you were depending on them, you can learn to have back up contingencies. However just because someone is unprofessional in some areas does not mean they are in *all* areas. If a co-worker is constantly late, to describe

116

him or her as "unprofessional" in general would be inaccurate. Although being late is definitely unprofessional, it would be more accurate to say, "It has been a pattern for him (or her) to be late in the past."

People make this mistake in color watching sometimes too. Just because someone is predominantly Gold does not mean that they never lie or are never late. Because someone is Green and you have never seen them interact with others at work does not mean they avoid social contact everywhere. They may have a fully active social life outside of work.

There is also a difference between occasional occurrences and patterns. If a co-worker got emotional once or twice when you pointed out a mistake, it doesn't necessarily mean they can't handle criticism. It could have been that they did not get a good night's sleep the night before. This time may or may not be just like the last time. We can learn a lesson from this. It is very important that you meet people where they are.

Remember, we are all multifaceted and do not always operate from our dominant color. So pay attention to the current situation. Look at, listen to, and experience the other person before proceeding.

#4: Look for the positive intention behind the behavior

Although you may not understand some people's behavior because it is not the way you would act in the same circumstance, know that the individual has a "good" reason for acting that way. For example, if someone is acting stubborn, selfish, or even hurtful (by anyone's standards) we could look behind the behavior and discover that they have a positive intent or aim, perhaps to stand behind what they think is right or to gain respect. Standing firm for what is right or gaining respect are positive aspirations.

It is interesting to note that people may even admit trying to inflict misery, and perhaps if you asked the person why they were doing it they may not realize what is underneath their actions right away. But if you kept asking, "...and what would that do for you?" you would discover the underlying reason would boil down to a positive one (perhaps only beneficial or positive from their perspective or to them, but positive nonetheless).

Try this and see: when you dig deep enough you'll find the positive intent. Looking for the positive intent of others will reduce negative judgments and allow you to open your mind to dealing with the situation at hand instead of focusing on whether the behavior is appropriate or not.

117

#5: Give others the benefit of the doubt

How do you communicate when you are stressed? Is it any different than when you aren't? Just because someone happens to be yelling at the moment doesn't mean they don't have the capacity to speak calmly. Just because you can't think of your best friend's name right at the time you are trying to introduce them, it doesn't mean you don't know it, does it?

We all get into "stupid states." Give the benefit of the doubt that the other person has the capacity to communicate and get along. If your past experience with that person has always proven otherwise, check to see what *you* might be contributing to the situation. For instance, do you have a tendency to interrupt them by walking up very briskly when they are in mid-conversation? Sometimes a different approach is all it takes to get communication going right.

#6: Keep experimenting— There is no such thing as failure, only results

Every situation is useful. Even if you dislike the results, the knowledge you gain from them is priceless in making better decisions and choices in the future. This book is about getting to know others so that you can understand them at a whole new level. If you try something and it does

not work out the way you intended, try something else. Notice what works and what doesn't. Keep experimenting until you find a way—and you will!

#7: Be prepared to adapt

Have you ever gotten frustrated with others who have a different communication style than yours? Did you ever wish they would make life a little easier and just adapt to your style? For example, some people wish they could just "tell it like it is" without people getting their feelings hurt. In contrast, others might wish that people would "slow down, show some consideration, and take the time to listen." Both parties wish the other would accept their way as the right way.

For example, think about those individuals in America that speak only Spanish. Of course, they wish that others spoke their language fluently. This would help ease their struggle with English. If you had a co-worker who spoke only Spanish, wouldn't you think it was nice if they learned English to be able to communicate with you? On the other hand, they would probably appreciate any attempts you made to learn Spanish to help communicate with them while they tried to learn English.

As in any successful relationship, there is always give and take. The important thing is how flexible you can be to get the result you are after. If you take the stand of "it's up to them to learn my language," be ready for some challenging times. In addition, as you can guess, the *way* you say things in any language can make all the difference in the world in meaning.

Learning new ways to communicate can be like learning a new language. It takes some getting used to it before you feel really comfortable and natural.

#8: Decide what is important to you

Are you willing to learn the language of Green, Gold, Orange, and Blue so that you can be a better communicator? As you know, the more you practice a language the more nat-ural it becomes, and the more fluent you become. Knowing ways to open lines of communication for each color style gives you access to one more tool. You can choose to pick up the tool and use it or not. At least this way you have a choice.

The next chapter provides ways for enhancing communication with the different color styles. Discern how the information applies to the particular people in your life. Some suggestions will be more relevant than others, and some may need to be modified or combined to accommodate the differences in second color combinations.

Chapter 10
UNDERSTANDING BLUE COMMUNICATION

Martin came bounding in the door, an ear-to-ear smile on his face and a twinkle in his eye.

"So how was your vacation?" he bubbled, as he reached out to give his co-worker, DeAnn, a big hug. "We missed you around here."

Gladly returning his friendly, welcoming embrace, DeAnn said, "I'm surprised you even noticed I was gone. It was only three days."

"Are you kidding?" said Martin, beaming with warmhearted cheerfulness. "The place just isn't the same

120

without you. So, tell me, what did you do with your time off?"

"Actually," DeAnn answered, "I just relaxed around the house and caught up on a few things."

"How wonderful. Isn't it great to be able to do that? It always helps me get more centered."

"How was your weekend?" inquired DeAnn.

"Oh it was great! Besides soccer practice, a T-ball game, and gymnastics lessons, we took our little guys to the zoo. They have a new monkey exhibit. We had a whole group of little ones with us, most of the children on our block. It is so fun to watch the kids giggle and see the looks of fascination and wonder they get.

"Mayra and I are 'Zoo Parents,'" Martin continued. "We have a lifetime membership to the zoo. We thought we would give the other parents in the neighborhood a break for the day and take the kids on a safari adventure. Before we left we all made animal headdresses from scraps of fur, cardboard, and paint. You should have seen them. Little Oscar made up a 'zee-la-ger.' It's a combination of a zebra, elephant, and tiger! The children were so proud of their artwork. When we paraded them in the front gates of the zoo there were plenty of smiles and comments from admirers."

"Wow, sounds like you had an action-packed weekend," DeAnn said.

"Well, I think it is so important for children to be able to be creative and self-expressive. It was a remarkable experience," beamed Martin. "Tonight I was hoping to check out a class on dream interpretation and journal writing, but it's our turn to cook so I may not be able to make it."

"Your turn to cook?" DeAnn asked.

"Yeah. There are four other couples on our block that Mayra and I swap-cook with. Each couple takes a turn cooking one night a week. We just make more of what we're cooking, divide it up, and place the meal on each other's porches. It's wonderful to come home and find a surprise waiting on the porch!"

"What a system you have worked out," said DeAnn. "It sounds wonderful."

"Relationships are so important," explained Martin. "That's what life is all about. What's on your agenda for today? Anything I can help you with?"

How Blues Communicate

A Blue's world revolves around people, relationships, and fostering growth in themselves and others. When speaking, they focus their attention first on establishing or re-establishing the relationship. The information they wish to convey is woven into this relationship-building endeavor.

A few words that describe their communication style are the following:

Friendly—Generally very approachable and neighborly, Blues make it a point to acknowledge others. They also enjoy being acknowledged and will attempt to seek a connection with a handshake, smile, hug, comment, compliment, question, or conversation. Their tone of voice may vary from mellow, soothing, and polite to animated, enthusiastic, and excited.

Helpful—Will offer their assistance and may readily volunteer for committees and events they think are worthwhile. Sometimes they can get so caught up in a cause, or feel so compelled to pitch in, that they may offer their help before realizing just how much they already have on their plate. Then they may experience stress trying to follow through on their commitments.

Expresses emotions—Speak with feeling in voice. From tears to laughter, Blues feel and display the dramas of life. Their expressions and body language will usually reveal their moods, and their language may include expressive words and adjectives.

Optimistic—Have so much faith in peoples' good nature that they continue to give situations and individuals the benefit of the doubt or another chance, even when others around them have given up hope. Frequently have a kind word to say and can usually find specific examples of positive qualities in others. When an individual is complaining about another, Blues commonly find something "good" to say about the target of the complaint. May sometimes be so enthusiastic that others misinterpret their eagerness, generosity, or gratefulness as insincerity.

Fosters harmony—Want people to get along and be happy. Often capitulate their own needs for the happiness of others. Will go to great lengths to circumvent conflict. Avoid or minimize conversations that feel too negative or critical, especially if the topic seems harsh toward others.

Empathetic—Able to enter another's world and experience it from that person's point of view. Avoid imposing their own beliefs and have a tendency to change mind or make decisions based on others' opinions or desires.

Takes time to relate—Will usually try to stop what they are doing to connect with others. Attempts to establish good eye contact and give attention. Capable of talking and listening endlessly.

Creative—Imaginative. Embellish points and make use of many-sided examples. Discuss ideas, insights, and concepts as they pertain to people, the human condition, and the future. Style is usually rich and interesting yet can get a bit lengthy. Enjoy it when others are novel, unusual, or challenging. Have varied interests and generally welcome conversation with most anyone.

Indirect—May interpret bluntness, quickness, or loudness as rude. Therefore, may lead up to the point, tell stories, or create a metaphor to enhance understanding. Their conversation may sometimes seem wandering and difficult to follow, even disorganized and disconnected. May avoid the truth if they think it will hurt the other person's feelings. Will use qualifiers and other softeners, such as "I don't want to be any trouble" or "would it be okay if..."

Reads between the lines—May not take things at face value. Instead, try to look behind actions and words for intention and deeper meaning. Pay attention and give credence to hunches, speculation, and intuition.

Personal—Often enjoy sharing stories about many aspects of their life and thus can be fairly easy to get to know. Frequently use "I" statements; what they talk about may also be very intimate. To ensure the other person feels validated or included, they try to elaborate or comment on what others say.

I'm SORRY, I'm ON MY PERIOD AND I'm HAVING VERY BAD CRAMPS TODAY...

Polite and compassionate unless personal values are violated—Blues check before interrupting. Do not use threatening language unless they feel extremely betrayed or endangered. Focus is on relationships, harmony, and comfort. May apologize if they notice the other person is feeling uncomfortable or disregarded. However, when their personal values have been infringed upon they can dig in their feet, put up walls, and become extremely stubborn.

Blue's Listening Style:

During conversation, a Blue is focusing on more than just the words. They are attending to the meaning behind the message. They evaluate what they see, hear, and feel is being communicated, first about the speaker, then the message. They listen for the suggested values and assess whether theirs are in alignment or not. If they are not, then Blues consider whether the values should be accepted or rejected. This is one way of determining how they feel about the speaker. They get a sense of the extenuating circumstances around the speaker and will give the benefit of the doubt if they feel the person is sincere and cares about others.

Once they have determined that it is okay to relate to the speaker, then they discern how they feel about the message. The message will not get through fully if the relationship is not first established.

Tips for Communicating with Blues

Acknowledge Them—First and foremost acknowledge the Blue as a person before diving into your agenda. Find out what is going on in their world. Ask how they are doing and be prepared to hear more than just "fine." They like to let you know how they are doing, not just at work but personally as well. They can get frustrated if they are asked how they are doing merely as part of a ritual, when the person asking is not really interested and does not pause long enough to hear the answer. Some Blues, if asked a question without being acknowledged first, will stop their questioner and say, "Good morning!" to remind them to pause and recognize them as a human being.

However, for them it is better to be acknowledged as part of a ritual than not at all. If you say "hi" to everyone else in the department and they are in the corner cubicle where you might not see them, they will take it personally if you do not make the effort to say "hi" to them also.

Let Them Know You Care—Show them you care about them as a person, that they are unique, and that you care how they feel.

124

Mandy was in charge of a meeting and had ordered sandwiches from a new establishment. She asked one of the women on the committee, Elizabeth (an Orange), how she liked the sandwich from the new place. Innocently enough, Elizabeth thought Mandy really wanted to know how she liked the sandwich so a decision could be made as to whether or not to order from the place again. So Elizabeth responded with, "Actually, it was kind of yucky; the bread was doughy and soggy. I really prefer the other place."

It was obvious to those observing that Mandy was offended by the comment. Noticing Mandy's facial expression and body language, Elizabeth tried backpedaling by saying, "Oh Mandy, thank you for ordering them and trying out a new place. We really appreciate all your effort."

Plainly still flustered, Mandy forced a smile and left the room. Later that afternoon, Elizabeth ran into Mandy. Elizabeth inquired, "Was I a little too blunt at lunch when you asked me about the sandwiches?"

Mandy paused and held her body in a stiff, defensive posture. Her face flushed as she quipped, "Actually, when you said that you didn't like them, I thought to myself, 'Well then, you can get them for yourself next time!'"

Although your top priority and concern may be the project at hand or getting your information conveyed, remember that a Blue's first concern is the relationship. Acknowledge them as a person, confirm the relationship, and recognize their efforts *first* when communicating. If you aren't already a natural at this, the following can help:

Recognize Their Contributions—Use words that express appreciation and care to Blues, such as:

"I appreciate how you help out your co-workers/friends/family."

"I value your uniqueness."

"You are important to me as a person."

"I care about how you feel."

"I really enjoyed your creative approach."

"I'm impressed with your imagination."

"You are valuable to the success of our organization by being so warm, friendly, and caring."

"I enjoy how you see the potential in everyone."

"I value your honesty and sincerity."

"Your participation in the group made it more successful."

Pay Attention to Congruency—Blues are good at noticing the body language of others and are likely to assume that everyone else has the same ability. They can tell if someone is overwhelmed or upset and will try to wait until the "right" moment to approach them, if at all. Often, if Blues are "able" to take on a responsibility, they feel "obligated" to come through for others.

Notice when a Blue is really trying to say "no," and let them know that they will not be jeopardizing the relationship if they do. Their attempt to say "no" may not be very obvious to some. For instance, you might ask if they have time to finish a project, and they may say, "I'm really swamped, but if you are desperate I'll do it." Now, to some individuals that may sound like "Yes, I'll do it!" But check again if you suspect they are just saying "yes" to keep you happy or not let you down. You may end up getting disappointed when they are unable to finish the project because of overload and overcommitment. Their intentions are terrific, yet they can underestimate the amount of time and energy it will take to complete something and then get backed into a corner of not wanting to let anyone down. Although some people do not appreciate this double checking, many Blues actually welcome it.

Blues have every intention of finishing what they promise. However, sometimes their ability to see the details and estimate the time involved can get blurred by their aim to assist and please.

Include Them—Blues can feel hurt when left out or singled out. Encourage them to be involved. Ask for their opinion and consider it in your decision making. Blues thrive on making a contribution and can wither if they feel they or their opinion are unimportant. They want to know how alternatives will affect the people involved.

Have Patience—Blues have a tendency to read between the lines of communication. For some, this is a welcome empathy. For those who have not gained the confidence of a Blue yet, it can be frustrating. However, once you have established enough rapport, Blues often shift suspicion to perception and can tell what you genuinely want to communicate without you having to say it. Continue to foster the relationship, and they will increasingly accept your messages at face value.

Listen for Feelings—When you try to communicate with a Blue, listen to the feelings behind their words. If they are upset, it is better to talk with them privately and allow them to vent emotionally before you try to have an objective conversation with them. Practice patience when helping or counseling a Blue to overcome certain feelings, stress, or behaviors. Don't be condescending. It helps to share a similar experience.

Let Them Share What They Know—Allow Blues to express their feelings and emotions. Listen to their concerns. They enjoy talking about opinions, ideas, and dreams. Blues will often bring up a subject just because they want to talk things through. For best results, don't hurry the discussion. Unless they specifically ask for advice, don't try to solve their

problems. Be patient about their need to process.

Hear Them Out—Blues can feel anything from crushed to furious because someone did not at least listen to what they had to say. If you don't listen, they feel that you don't care. Even if you have already made up your mind, if you just let Blues finish their sentence or story, they will feel more validated. It also helps for the listener to share with the Blue their understanding of what was said. Focus on what you agree upon. For example:

"I understand that you feel silly handing out pencils at a health fair because you think it is a waste of your skills. I get a sense that you think I don't value your skills. Actually it is because I do value your skills with people and your knowledge of the department that I think you are the best person for the job."

I used to get frustrated with my mother because I felt she took too long on the telephone telling me stories instead of getting to the point and getting off the phone. Sometimes when I would call I would give her a time limit. She finally told me that if I did not have at least half an hour to talk then I shouldn't call at all because having any less time made her feel rushed and cut off. She, in turn, allows my Orange needs to be

127

met. She doesn't mind if I multitask while on the phone. I wear my headphones around so I can fold laundry, clean the house, or work on other projects while we talk. She gets her half-hour and I get to move!

Show Appreciation—
Acknowledge their ability to put others at ease.

- Let them know their impact, that they make a difference.

- Allow them to grow and explore. They enjoy learning about themselves and others.

- When motivating them, point out how something is an opportunity to grow, and how it is helpful to and will bring out the best in others.

- Allow them to please you.

Use Gestures of Friendship—
Blues are usually comfortable with a handshake, hug, or sometimes a hand on the shoulder. They love a smile, cards, gifts, and compliments.

Say hello when you see them. Call them by name. Notice when they have been gone for awhile and acknowledge their return. You may even want to ask them about

their trip if their vacation was for pleasure. Give condolences if appropriate. Remember their birthday and other things on the personal side. For example, if you know they own a dog named "Frankie" that they love dearly, or that they write music, inquiries about Frankie or their music would be appropriate.

Although Blues are usually quite comfortable with affection, do not assume it is okay to invade their personal space if they or their body language tells you otherwise. Don't make the mistake of interpreting Blue's friendliness as sexual attraction.

Be Tactful When Offering Feedback—Pay attention to the amount of "constructive" criticism you offer to Blues. You may think you're helping, or being accurate, but Blues may perceive that they are being constantly corrected. If you need to discuss a behavior or misunderstanding, don't shame or embarrass them in front of others. Speak in a soft, modulated manner. Indicate you are meeting with them because you care. List the things they did well first and validate them for their contributions before sharing the challenges you are having. Ask them for their feelings about the situation and what they believe can be done about it.

Blues are sensitive to teasing and sarcasm, so do not poke fun at the unique way they do something or about their generosity. Although Greens may not mind and actually enjoy this kind of ribbing from their peers, most Blues find it uncomfortable and even mean-spirited.

Finish any discussion of problems by focusing once again on their strengths and positive contributions.

If You Are Blue

Because it is quite natural for you as a Blue to have the ability to adapt to the styles of others, you will enjoy reading through the following suggestions. You most likely are already aware of your own communication habits and the effect they have on others. Your willingness to be flexible and learn new skills will come in handy when practicing these suggestions. The benefit is the enhancement of your interactions with others.

Practice Objectivity—Recognize when you are reading too much in between the lines of communication. In the example with the sandwiches, Elizabeth was just commenting truthfully as to whether she liked the sandwiches or not. She was not trying to hurt Mandy, nor was she being unappreciative of her efforts.

If you notice yourself starting to take a comment personally, pause. Note your immediate reaction and ask yourself, "What meaning have I linked to this and why?" You may need to clarify that what you heard is really what they said or meant to convey. Make sure that your definitions match. Notice if there was something in the delivery of the message that

I WONDER WHAT HE MEANT BY 'HELLO'.

could have caused you to second-guess the words. Let go of any pre-conceived notions, grudges, or overly suspicious thinking. And give the benefit of the doubt. (Really pay attention to discern the difference between intuition and old, habitual thinking patterns.)

Next, ask yourself "How can I use this at face value?" And finally, even if it isn't packaged the way you'd like to hear it, be open to the gift of feedback. Be resourceful with what you learn.

Add "No" to Your Vocabulary—It's okay to disagree or say "no" to a request you don't have the time, energy, or desire to do. Be more realistic about time and how much you can accomplish. It's one thing to be optimistic; it's another to be overwhelmed. People can do things for themselves or find someone else to help them. And some things don't have to be done at all.

It's also okay to hear "no." Don't take offense when others make their preferences and boundaries known. It doesn't mean you were wrong for asking.

To reduce feelings of rejection and judgment, practice asking questions for which you expect to receive a "no" answer.

For instance, the next time you visit a restaurant ask your server if you can have a free salad bar with your meal. Ask in the most polite, sincere way so they take you seriously. Think of some creative questions to ask people. Get outrageous. The more you hear "no," the easier it is to understand that it is not a judgment or rejection of you personally. It is just a response.

Speak Up—Say something before you are pushed to your limits. It's okay to be more direct. Most people value feedback they can clearly understand.

Gloria was making omelets for herself and her boyfriend, Adam. She had just finished cracking her last egg and turned to the counter where she noticed a small carton of egg substitutes.

"Where did this come from?" she asked Adam curiously.

130

"I put them there," he said.

"Did you want me to use them?" Gloria asked.

"I was hoping you would—I like them better than regular eggs," he responded.

"Then why didn't you just say so?" she asked. "Why did you just put them on the counter?"

"I didn't want to tell you how to cook. This way, if you noticed them and chose to use them then great, if not, then that would be okay too," he said.

"What about your needs?" Gloria questioned. "If you like them better, I would have liked to have known."

"This is exactly what I wanted to avoid," responded Adam, "an argument over eggs!"

We all have needs. Make yours known. Don't make people guess at them. People will appreciate your frankness more than if you hide your feelings so you won't hurt theirs.

Recognize the Difference Between Politeness and Interest

Notice if others are actually interested in your story or are only listening to be polite. You've probably been in a similar situation yourself when you've stuck around to listen to someone just to be courteous. Since Blues can get so enthusias-

tic about their subject, they sometimes assume others share the same fascination. Discern when to conclude your anecdote, explanation, or comments by watching for cues of body language or listening for exit remarks such as, "Okay then, I've got to go." Ask yourself, "Am I rambling?" Know when to get to the point or get off the subject.

THEN WE SAW THE CUTEST LITTLE ...

Seek Other Avenues

If you find that your need to express yourself is going unmet by significant others or certain co-workers, don't make them feel that they are wrong. Don't try to get them to change or "punish" them for it either. Instead seek out others that enjoy sharing like you do. Find friends to share with. Enroll in workshops or classes in subjects that interest you. Avoid participating in things that you really don't enjoy just to hang out with others.

Chapter 11
UNDERSTANDING
GOLD
COMMUNICATION

Two insurance agents were sitting at a table, eating lunch together. Mike complained that a client had the nerve to turn in a claim for thirty-seven dollars, a year and a half later. Susan asked from across the table, "What is the policy on that?"

Mike said, "I checked into it, and there isn't one that applies."

"Well, if there's not a rule that says *not* to pay it unless it is turned in by a specific time, and it is a legitimate claim, then we should pay it," said Susan.

"But we shouldn't have to pay it. People should submit things in a timely manner. They shouldn't wait a year and a half to turn in a claim and expect us to pay it—it's just not right," Mike insisted.

"I agree that people should be responsible enough to turn things in on time," said Susan. "We should have a policy, something in writing so they know what is expected of them."

Mike replied, "I think so, too. We are having an executive meeting next week, and I made sure that the issue got on the agenda so a policy can be made and guidelines set for its enforcement."

"Terrific, that's the responsible thing to do," agreed Susan. "Way to stay on top of things. I will support you 100%."

How Golds Communicate

In general, Golds have a tendency to come across in a businesslike manner. They speak of structure, responsibility, and the "shoulds" and "should nots" of life. Of course, depending on the situation and what their second color is, they can appear friendly and approachable, yet still cautious. They are usually conservative and firm-minded in their views. Following are traits common to those people with a high amount of Gold.

In Writing—Golds like to be accurate and responsible. Recording information enables them to have all the details for future reference. This way

they don't have to rely on their memory. Instead, they have a sort of physical check list they can look back on to make sure they fulfilled their obligations in the manner they promised. They also have precise documentation in case there is a question about the conversation, timelines or responsibilities.

Purposeful—Unless the situation is a special one, or they are on a break from their regular schedule, Golds will usually state the reason for their conversation up front or early on in their communication. They experience an urgency to stay on their timelines, especially at work, and get frustrated if they feel they are wasting time chatting instead of doing.

Appropriate—Golds try to use proper language, avoiding slang or politically incorrect wording. They also pay careful attention to their timing to make sure it is the right instance to communicate as well as the correct mode. They will pause to find out whether they should be talking to the individual directly, or going through a chain of command. They will also determine whether they should communicate in writing or fill out a form verses making a phone call or communicating in person.

Very respectful, they would not tell a joke that could be taken wrong or fool around in a serious situation. They may share an off-color joke, but it would most likely be amongst friends or in a social situation where that kind of thing is accepted. They will frown upon others that use inappropriate language and even try to guide or correct those that are not following the proper chain of command or norms.

Task Focused—Once the purpose of the conversation has been established, Golds like to stay on topic. It is very frustrating, and often interpreted as rude by Golds when others disrupt the conversation by interjecting comments or changing subjects. Golds may center their conversations around accomplishing the goal at hand. And if the goal at hand is to have a conversation, they like to give their undivided attention to the interaction, making good eye contact and avoiding multitasking as much as possible.

When extenuating circumstances, people issues, or interruptions in arise, they may refuse to spend much time talking about them or figuring out alternative solutions, instead they may try to redirect the dialogue back to the original goal or plan.

Loyal—During conversation, you will notice that Golds speak in ways that support the organizations they work or volunteer for, their spouse and families, their communities and their country if they happen to be a proud citizen. They may mention policies, rules and customs and how they uphold them as well as share how may years they have been working for a company, been married, a member, or what positions they have held or projects they have worked on. They usually feel it would be inappropriate to publicly criticize but may do so if someone has been disloyal or broken too many rules.

134

Predictable—Comfortable with consistency, Golds like to speak and respond in anticipated manners, such as those mentioned throughout this chapter. Rarely will they pull a fast one and spill a surprise request on their listener. Unless they are under a tremendous amount of stress, you can count on them to be consistently reliable in their communication.

Chronological—One communication method that keeps Golds on track and helps them remember details is to speak of events in order, from the past to the most recent. Asked to explain one aspect of a problem, they will begin at the beginning and explain the entire linear process. During conversation, if a step is missing or a Gold gets interrupted before completing the sequence, they may begin their communication over again from the beginning to make sure everything has been included.

When a conversation is first started, Golds may ask for the history or background so they may get their bearings on a situation or project. It helps them to listen. They may like to establish a purpose for the conversation up front, but they don't like to start conversations "in the middle".

Detail Oriented—Rarely do Golds like to talk in generalities or interpretations. They like more concrete details and logistics. For instance, if you are traveling, and ask for directions from a Gold, instead of simply saying, "Take Highway 5 north, exit Watt Avenue south, turn left on Keifer," they will give more details. Their directions will be more like: "Take Highway 5 north about 10 miles, when you see the exits for Howe Avenue and Florin Road, you will know your exit is coming up. Take the Watt Avenue Exit south, when you get to the top of the ramp turn right. Five lights down make a left on Keifer. Go about 3 miles down, you'll go through about 3 stop signs. As soon as you pass the Albertson's Shopping Center on your right, start looking for the post office. The driveway comes up quick.

Status Quo—Because consistency is such a high ranking value for Golds, they often speak of "The way we have always done it." They like to look at the past for reference of how things should be done now. When others suggest a different approach, Golds first response is usually to defend the current approach. They like to get used to things and are not likely to jump into something without it having a proven track record. When someone starts talking about a "new way," Golds just may change the discussion to, the "old way."

Judgments—Before responding to another individual, Golds will first judge whether what the person is saying or doing is right or wrong. Once they have decided, Golds will give their views on the matter, often peppering their conversations with words like, "should" and "should not." They may come across very authoritarian, "That is wrong, what should be done is..." They may also speak in comparatives, "What will the neighbors think? What would George Washington do in this circumstance?"

It is usually very clear to a Gold what the correct action is in a situation. If it is unclear, they like to make it clear by establishing a rule or finding facts to back up their thinking. Once they institute a standard, locate confirming information, or decide upon a certain value, their communication leaves no room for interpretation. They make sure the listener knows exactly what they are talking about and what action is expected as a result of the communication.

Closure—Golds desire completion. They like to be able to finish their sentence or thought. If you are on a phone conversation with a Gold, and you hang up the phone before they are absolutely complete with the interaction, say to take another call or because of a time constraint, they may phone you back to "bring closure" or "close up" the conversation. They do not like to be left guessing about what is expected or where to go from here.

MR. JOHNSON? DID WE HAVE ANYTHING ELSE TO GO OVER AFTER YOU TOLD ME I WAS FIRED?

Golds can get quite uncomfortable with too many options left open and may insist that a choice be made. Their discussions from that point on, center around fulfilling the requirements to satisfy the choice that has been made, accepting no excuses for quitting early.

Accountable—Concerned with law, equal justice, and general standards of order, Golds help us realize that our actions are an integral part of a system and can effect it positively or negatively. They will caution us if we are straying from the principals and use them for their own guidance as well in their decision-making. These general standards of order create a common ground for everyone in the system, be it an organization, family, or community, and establish certain rights and expectations. Golds will inform others of these rights and expectations, not to support their own personal opinions, but rather to help others know what to expect from one another, especially when nothing else seems certain.

Golds may put aside their own immediate interests for the sake of their principles and can lose sight of their own personal needs and priorities. Committed to a specific code of conduct, they do not trust exceptions to the general rule and will communicate this in their interactions.

Golds Listening Style:

Golds listen for details, in order. They can lose their train of thought if the conversation is interrupted or a person speaks off target. They do not want to fill in the blanks. Golds listen for responsibility. They listen for the purpose of gathering information so they know what their part is. They pay attention and ask themselves, "What is my duty? What should I do with the information?"

Golds are concerned with whether something is right or wrong. They are listening to decide the correctness of the speakers intentions as well as their status within the given context. The more they are able to determine the appropriateness of an interaction or response, the more comfortable they are in conversing.

Tips for Communicating with Golds

Be Specific—Fill them in on the details they need to know. Don't overwhelm a Gold with too many abstract ideas or generalizations. When making a request, let them know what specifically needs to be accomplished, by when, and they will get it completed.

Outline Priorities—Be very clear about expectations and order of importance. Golds are most comfortable knowing they are on track and meeting the requirements. Golds generally enjoy working together with others to successfully complete tasks, projects and events. Ask for their suggestions on how to prioritize and plan. Make sure to mention how your plan upholds the organization, family, or community.

Plan Ahead—Knowing what you are going to say before you say it is helpful when conversing with Golds. They like it when you are prepared. If you intend to brainstorm with them, let them know that is what you want ahead of time.

Stay on Target—They can get irritated if you don't complete one con-

137

cept before skipping to another. It helps maintain their attention when you present concepts in chronological order and in a step-by-step manner.

Save Surprises and Novelty—
Golds thrive on predictability, regularity, and efficient use of time and resources. When outlining a plan, mention what has worked in the past. Be practical and financially sound in your appeals. The words "new" and "improved" are less interesting to Golds than "established" or "quality you can count on." Don't switch methods or plans on them without warning or a good, solid reason.

OH BY THE WAY... WE ARE HAVING TEN GUESTS OVER FOR DINNER TOMORROW NIGHT DEAR

A Gold man had been married just a few weeks when he invited his parents over for a holiday dinner. His wife was preparing a festive dinner of ham with all the trimmings. She had just started to put the ham into a baking pan when her husband stopped her.

"Wait," he counseled, "you must first cut the ends off the ham before putting it in the pan!"

Puzzled at the urgency of his request, his wife questioned, "Why do the ends need to be cut off the ham?"

"My mother always cut the ends off the ham. It turns out delicious that way," he informed her.

"But it seems as though that would be wasteful," she declared. "It is perfectly good ham."

"That's the way we've always had our ham," he insisted. "Just try it, you'll see."

Wanting to please him and her new in-laws, the woman cut the ends off the ham before baking it.

When dinner was ready and she began to serve the ham, she turned to her mother-in-law with burning curiosity.

"Why is it," she asked, "that you cut the ends off your ham before baking it?"

Her mother-in-law replied matter-of-factly, "So it would fit in the pan!"

Because tradition is something Golds value highly, they will proudly follow customs that have been passed on to them through generations. In their speech patterns you will notice references to the way things have been done in the past and a tendency to want to stick with what they know and can rely on.

138

Don't interrupt!—When beginning a conversation with Golds, wait until they have finished what they are doing and acknowledge you. Golds find interruptions rude as well as irritating. They like to complete their sentences, thoughts, and tasks, at hand before turning their attention elsewhere. Be polite and greet them before diving into your agenda. Don't bombard them by having two or more people speaking at once. They prefer to listen to one person at a time. Trying to listen to several people talking at once from different directions can cause them stress.

Apologize When Appropriate— Golds are pleased and validated when you take responsibility for your actions. Own up to it when you "blow it" and let them know you are sorry. Trying to cover up your mistakes can make matters worse.

Appeal to Their Strong Sense of Right and Wrong—Make sure your idea or plan supports the appropriate rules or practices. Let them know that you were conscientious in following procedures. Keep in mind they are usually honest, trustworthy and concerned.

Acknowledge their Hard Work— Remember to notice and comment on the effort Golds put forth in various areas. Comment on their work, family, church or community involvement.

Maintain Composure—Golds appreciate it when you are poised. Loudness as well as exaggerated gestures can be interpreted as boisterous or rude.

Be Consistent—Treat everyone fairly. Don't give "special" treatment to some and not others. Don't arbitrarily make exceptions to rules. If a rule is constantly being bent or broken, make one that is enforceable.

Recognize Their Contributions—Let Golds know you appreciate them by using some of the following phrases:

"I appreciate how much you contribute to this (family, organization, committee, community)."

"The valuable time you spend here is highly regarded."

"You are very important to others in this (family, organization...)"

"I appreciate your level of fairness."

"I recognize your honesty and sincerity."

"The time you spend on _____ activities is very admirable."

"Your sense of duty and responsibility is terrific!"

"I appreciate being able to rely on you."

If You Are Gold

Golds are generally respectful and responsible in most areas of their lives. This is also frequently true when it comes to communication. If Gold is your dominant color, you'll most likely size up a situation for what would be most appropriate before responding. However, as you are well aware, not everyone shares your same ideals for what is appropriate. Therefore, conflicts can arise. One of the best ways to show consideration for yourself and others is to appreciate each individual's unique style. Instead of trying to convince others that your way is the right way, use the following suggestions to enhance communication and promote alliances.

Have Patience—When people talk in different directions, do ten things at once, and don't stick to the agenda, be open minded about their communication styles, especially if you are a listener or the one that has approached them for something you need.

Praveen approached Liz and Carrie for some information he needed to complete a project. He first addressed Carrie with his question. Carrie was only three words into her response when Liz excitedly piped in with an idea. Irritated at the inter-ruption, Praveen asked Liz to hold her thoughts so Carrie could finish her sentence. Carrie, waved her hand back and forth quickly in the air as if to erase his request, saying, "That's okay, let's hear what she has to say." Reluctantly, Praveen listened to Liz's idea. Just as he started becoming intrigued with her suggestions, Carrie added in a few more ideas to elabo-rate on Liz's. Praveen glared at Carrie trying to send her the signal that interrupting Liz was inappropriate, but neither Liz nor Carrie seemed to notice as they continued their brain-storming. No sooner would Carrie start a sentence when Liz would inter-rupt it or finish it for her and visa versa. In frustration, Praveen tried harder to regulate who was speaking by requesting that only one person

HERE'S HOW I SEE IT... HEY! HOW ABOUT... AND THEN WE COULD... OH! AND WHAT IF WE... YEAH! AND THEN THERE'S...

speak at a time. Carrie and Liz seemed to completely ignore his requests as the energy of their discussion escalated.

In exasperation, as well as self preservation, Praveen finally said, "Why don't you two just discuss this, jot down your ideas and get back to me."

Carrie and Liz looked at him momentarily puzzled. Shrugging their shoulders they said, "Okay," then eagerly returned to their conversation.

Praveen's frustration actually lead to a great idea. If it is too uncomfortable for you to adapt to a communication style that is extremely tangential, you may want to make your request for information, then ask that they respond to you when they have gathered their thoughts. Of course if you are the "boss" you have the right to expect that others adapt to your style of communication. You could provide an outline of the format in which you would like the information submitted to you. However in either case you risk stifling their creativity.

Consider Other Options—Golds have a tendency to judge very quickly whether a person's actions are "right" or "wrong" on the onset of a conversation. Pay attention to whether or not you are missing the whole point of the discussion because you got stuck on something that you decided was "wrong" in the beginning of the interaction.

Practice Peripheral Listening—Instead of zoning right in on the details, practice discerning the concept or big picture.

Accept Others—Unless you are in a position to supervise others and it is your job to correct their actions, when their values are not in line with yours, it can be fruitless and irritating to try to change them. Know that others have different skills and values than you, and *different* does not mean *wrong.*

Give It a Break—Remember... you are not the general manager of the universe. Be aware of how hard you are driving yourself and others. Take the weight of the world off your shoulders. Relax a little and realize there are just some things that don't have to be perfect.

Chapter 12
UNDERSTANDING
ORANGE
COMMUNICATION

Michelle was meeting Karen's fiancée for the first time that morning. Michelle had hitchhiked across three states to see her sister. She had her morning cup of coffee and was sharing her adventures of the trip there when Karen reminded her that Glen would be waiting promptly at 10:00

142

a.m. to meet them for their planned morning hike.

"Oh, he can just take a chill pill—we're getting there!" Michelle joked, giving no indication that she was willing to move any faster. It had been a long trip and she wanted to relax a little. Karen finished packing a picnic lunch for the day and informed Michelle that it was fast approaching 10:00. She once again encouraged Michelle to hurry along and told her that Glen would not understand their tardiness.

By the time they arrived at the meeting point, Glen was fuming. "You're ten minutes late! Where's your integrity? You made a commitment to be here. I was here on time and you kept me waiting!"

Without hesitation, Michelle looked Glen straight in the eye and said, "You're a jerk! I'd rather hike without you." With that, she turned and tromped up the trail, leaving Glen dumfounded where he stood.

How Oranges Communicate

Of course, as with any temperament, there are varying ranges of the ways Oranges communicate. When Oranges are extroverted, they will demonstrate much of the communication patterns described in the following list. Introverted Oranges have many of the same casual tendencies but usually display less intensity and volume in their manner of speech.

Confident—Whether they know what they are talking about or not, they will come across as if they do. Speak with certainty, sureness, decisiveness. Like to take control of the situation and be in the spotlight.

Loud—Because they don't mind the attention, they may turn up the volume to be heard. Some people find this abrasive, but other Oranges find it refreshing! Can be boisterous and intense. Enthusiastically expressive, they are prone to exaggerate.

Casual—Friendly, playful, inviting. May use slang, "street talk," or even profanity. May use first names of prominent individuals.

Desire to speak in the moment—Generally, Oranges will want to share their opinion the minute it hits their mind. May make comments or promises so quickly that they don't remember they did so, or aren't prepared to back them up.

"Now" oriented—Because Oranges like to live for the moment, they may interrupt others. They like to act now, and "now" doesn't include waiting until you finish your sentence!

Quick—May switch subjects before the listener is ready. Also, hate to wait

143

for an answer. Want to know immediately so they can act "now." May even assume a "yes" response if the person seems indecisive. Appreciate immediate feedback and will swiftly give it.

Brief—Don't usually lead up to the point or spend time with "How are you?" or other greetings. Direct. Get to the point quickly. May not even finish their sentences. Oranges make sure each moment counts. They don't want to waste their time or breath.

Straightforward—Give it pure and simple without trying to soften delivery. Can be very explicit. May even point while speaking. In their world, they would rather not fog frankness with tact.

In Motion—Craves mobility. Possibly will fidget or work on some thing else while you are talking to them. May want you to walk with them as you speak or even conduct business while exercising or recreating. Most Oranges want to be "productive" during a conversation.

Flexible—Although they are usually quick in making a decision initially, they reserve the right to change their mind midstream, and often do.

Varied—Their attention span for things in which they are not directly involved can be minimal. Seek opportunities, options, choices. Switch gears frequently. Most decisions are not final—many times they just want to

get the show on the road so they choose whatever option seems the best at the moment.

Involved—Oranges generally like to laugh, are playful, and will joke around. They delight in spontaneity and action, and may argue just for fun. Extroverted Oranges especially will use large gestures and body movements, visible facial expressions, and an animated voice.

Oranges Listening Style:

Oranges listen for entertainment, impact, relevance and usefulness. Unless you are incredibly engaging or reveal immediately how the information you are conveying is useful to an Orange, they may lose interest, especially if your communication is lengthy. If you fail to stimulate or keep their interest, they will do it themselves, making connections to what you are saying so they can in turn tell you a colorful story of something that happened to them. Their minds can whirl a mile a minute as they playfully hop from subject to subject.

They also try to figure out the motive of the person speaking, what do they want, need or expect from me? They do this almost simultaneously as they look for opportunities for themselves. They want to be able to take action with what is said, be it to share a quick joke, seize a chal-lenge, or perform some feat. They listen in the present and process contextually, usually not linking so much to the past or distant future, but instead figuring out what they can do with the information in the moment.

Tips for Communicating with Oranges

When Oranges are interested in being expedient and clear with their communication they can be very straightforward. Some people may perceive this as brash, inconsiderate, or even aggressive. Golds may interpret Oranges' communication style as rude, Blues may feel it is mean or pushy, and Greens may find it too dramatic or flamboyant. Oranges who have a high amount of Blue as their second color are often perplexed by people's reaction to or perception of them.

For example, many Oranges report that oftentimes servers in restaurants are caught off guard by their directness. An Orange ordering lunch may sound something like this: The server asks, "May I take your order?"

"Yes, this grilled chicken sand-wich...is the bread grilled or the chicken grilled or both? Because if the bread is grilled, I don't want it; it's too greasy. I'll be sick half the day."

145

"The bread is not grilled, only the chicken."

"Good. I'll have that then, and can you leave off the mayonnaise? I'll just have mustard on it, and toast the bread. I'd like to substitute the green salad for the potato salad, unless of course it's gloppy. Is it real gloppy?"

"I'm not sure what you mean by 'gloppy.'"

"Well, never mind then, I'll just take the green salad, but put the dressing on the side. And can I have a side order of mashed potatoes and gravy?"

"I'm sorry, we only serve mashed potatoes and gravy for dinner. We do have French fries."

"French fries are too greasy. See if you can ask the cook about the mashed potatoes and gravy. And, I'll take an ice water . . . thank you."

The server acts offended, and the Orange is perplexed as to why. In the Orange's mind he or she has only asked for something specific and tried to make it clear so that the server would not get the order wrong and have to go through the trouble of taking the food back and starting over again. Of course, some Oranges that read this might say to themselves, "Hey, I'm not that picky. I'll eat anything that's put in front of me." But the ones that like their food in a particular way can relate.

The following general guidelines are meant to assist you in communicating to win the motivation and cooperation of an Orange. Note the particular behavior of the Oranges in your life. You will then be able to know which methods to use with which person for the most success.

Be Prepared to Listen for Straight Content—Keep in mind Oranges are not trying to be rude when they do not slow down to greet you before expressing their needs. They are trying to accomplish a goal. Think of what you are trying to accomplish before attempting to slow them down by forcing them to stop to acknowledge or greet you. It might not be worth it. Let them do their thing and be on their way.

Lighten Up—See how much you can enjoy their playful behavior. Keep in mind that even though their approach may be lighthearted, they are serious about accomplishing their goals. "Casual" does not equal "disrespectful" or "unprofessional."

Use Sound Bites—Oranges get distracted and bored easily, so be direct and to the point. Remember they are multitaskers and thus like to work on several things at a time. This includes having a discussion. If you want to meet them in their world, instead of trying to get them to set everything down or stop their activity for a long discussion, encapsulate your information into small, concise bites, like commercials. Use thirty-second elevator speeches. If you had to tell them something and had only an elevator ride to do it in, what would you say?

Match Their Speed—If you speak too slowly, they will have a tendency to fill in your words for you or move on to another subject.

Move with Them—You will accomplish a lot by having a conversation with them while they walk or do some other physical activity. If they are already on the phone, they usually do not mind being interrupted for a quick question. Check to be sure. Go with the flow.

Appreciate Their Flair—Oranges speak with confidence and flamboyance that can be misconstrued as overbearance. In communicating with Oranges that you know exaggerate, take their overstatements with a grain of salt. Their intentions are usually to entertain or increase the intensity, not to straight-out lie. Is it important to clarify whether they were on hold for ten minutes verses three? If so, ask in a curious or playful tone. Otherwise, why bother? Be amused.

Give Them an Audience—Oranges have a need to share their excitement. Allow them to tell you an adventure or blow off some steam without trying to give them advice or to channel their energy into problem solving just yet. Oftentimes, they just need to get things off their chest. If they are particularly extroverted, they probably won't even want a comment

147

of any kind. They'll supply the entire conversation. Otherwise, to avoid irritating or insulting them, make sure they really want help before offering any.

Offer Options—Give them choices. Oranges need the freedom to choose or they will feel too limited. Ask for their suggestions.

Make It a Challenge—"I'll bet you can't guess what I need you to bring with you!" Invent a game.

Recognize Their Contributions—

Encourage and reward Oranges by saying some of the following:
"What you did just now was great!"
"I particularly value your enthusiasm."
"You are a great leader."
"I know others look to you as a leader."
"Now, let's put your ideas into action."
"I appreciate your ability to influence people."
"I am recommending you for (specific) recognition."
"Remember how you did it this time, so you can do it again."
"Channel these talents of yours so they can provide the greatest benefit for all."

If You Are Orange

We all want validation for our own unique style of doing things. Use the following suggestions to help open lines of communication with those that seem to be stopped by your fashion. When those around you become more aware of your mode of operation and intentions, they will give you more room to be yourself. In many cases, however, people won't have had the True Colors training and may misunderstand your methods. If it is important for you to get along with them at an even higher level, then use the following tips for modifying your own behaviors to build bridges for communication. Once the bridges are established, you will have more freedom to express yourself in your preferred style.

Be Aware of How You Are Coming Across—You may want to "tell it like it is," but some people need to have it wrapped in a nice package. While you might not care about certain things, others do. If it is important to you to be heard, modify your speech to fit the patterns used by your listener.

Wait for a Response before Proceeding—A pause does not equal a "yes." Give people time to think. Your mind may run a mile a minute, but others may prefer to plan before taking action.

Identify Others' Requirements—Some people sim-
ply cannot listen until you acknowl-edge them. Notice if that's the case. Pay attention to whether the listener wants more information or not. Be prepared to take an extra minute. A minute spent now can save you sev-eral later.

Notice When You Are Exaggerating—If you embellish too much, too often, people will not believe you anymore and try to sec-ond-guess you. It can be fun to add some color to your conversations but be aware of the response of others. You might want to save your best sto-ries for those that you know will appreciate them.

When Listening to Others, Keep Your Mind Focused—
Remember, not everyone can switch gears as quickly as you can, or even wants to. Curb the impulse to inter-rupt those you know find it distracting.

Pause before Making a Commitment—Think past the moment to check and see if you can really follow through. Set up ways to remember the promises you made yesterday.

Recognize Others—Others need praise as much as you do. Find out how they like to receive it and give it to them their way.

Use Softeners When Making Requests or Giving Direction—
Using "please" and "thank you" goes a long way with the population. Think of how the other person might like to hear something phrased.

Make a Decision and Stick to It—Leaving your options open may be freeing for you, but it can make others nervous.

Find Other Oranges—Some of the other color styles may take offense to the "straight up" way you communi-cate and interpret a "harmless," play-ful comment as being "mean," "harsh," or "judgmental." Find other Oranges so you can "let it all hang out." This will give you a channel for your energy and help prevent the wrong kinds of communication at inappropriate times.

149

Chapter 13
UNDERSTANDING
GREEN
COMMUNICATION

FLIGHT 223

CAN YOU VERIFY THIS LAST SAFETY CHECK?

Randall, a custodian for several office complexes, came over to his friend Carson's house to borrow a special tool he needed for a project.

While Carson ran upstairs to see if he could find the tool, his wife Shala offered Randall a cup of coffee. They sat at the kitchen table, and Shala

150

shared with Randall that she was thinking about getting laser surgery on her eyes, but her regular eye doctor thought that her pupils might be too big. "He says that the laser can only cut so wide on my eyes," she explained. "At night the lights would catch on the edge of the surgery when my pupils dilate. I don't quite understand why they just can't make the laser a little wider so my pupils won't hit the edges."

"Well, actually," Randall clarified, "the cornea only extends barely to the perimeter of the iris before it amalgamates with the sclera. Expanding the circumference of the laser beam could compromise the integrity of the eye."

Noticing the blank look on Shala's face, Randall lifted his hands, making a fist with one and covering it with the other. "Say my fist is the eye and this hand is the cornea," he began. "No wait," he said. "May I?" He gestured toward a couple of plastic eggs that had strayed from the kids' Easter baskets and happened to be in a bowl in the middle of the table.

Shala nodded her head and said, "Yes, please do."

He lifted the eggs and split them apart. Stacking the sides on top of each other creating several layers, he began to explain. "Laser in Situ Keratomileusis, or LASIK, corrects vision by reshaping the corneal tissue beneath the surface of the eye. An instrument called a microkeratome makes a protective flap from the epithelium that covers the cornea."

He continued his explanation until he got confirmation from Shala that she understood the procedure, as well as the anatomy of the eye. By now, Carson had appeared in the room, triumphant in finding the tool he was looking for. "Speaking of lasers," he said, "did you hear that they recently disproved Einstein's theory about the speed of light?"

Randall perked up in his chair. "I heard that!" he said excitedly. "That corroborates my own personal theory that the speed of light represents the ability to get information in our lives. The limit of the speed of light as being the fastest anything can travel simply denotes our ability to measure movement. We assumed it was the limit of which things could move— movement itself."

"Yes!" Carson said. "It makes me think about instantaneous information transfer. Take what we experience as gravity. I believe that we are going to discover that gravity is an instantaneous effect produced by the proximity of matter or energy. Once we learn to reproduce gravity waves and transform them, we'll be able to send and receive information instantaneously, regardless of the distance."

"I'll bet we discover that our subconscious mind already does this," said Randall, starting down yet another avenue.

Shala wanted so much to participate in the conversation but she could find nothing to contribute. She sat there looking back and forth at the two speakers as if watching a tennis match. After several minutes she got up from the table and drifted out of the room.

"Furthermore, we will have to rewrite our current public paradigm," she heard her husband say.

How Greens Communicate

Greens, for the most part, communicate for the purpose of gaining or sharing information. They automatically have rapport with those who understand their communication style and are excited to share ideas and concepts. They usually have a wide variety of interests and may know quite a bit of information about many things. During a conversation, their attention is usually focused on the subject or matter at hand. It is not generally aimed at establishing any kind of relationship with the person they are communicating with. Yet, as you no doubt have noticed by now, some people like to chat a bit first before actually getting to the topic. When two people have different agendas for a conversation (as in the following story) the message can get lost.

Char had been working on a project for the past week. This morning she had been at it for almost two hours already. The statistics and figures were coming together nicely. She had worked at it much like a puzzle, strategizing where to fit what piece and figuring out what was the best method to present the information in a logical, precise way. All she needed to complete the project were the statistics from her co-worker, Kelly.

Char checked her e-mail. She had sent a message to Kelly two days ago, and again this morning, but hadn't received a response yet. Char tried reaching Kelly on the phone but the line was busy. She really needed that last bit of information so she walked over to Kelly's cubicle. Kelly was just hanging up the phone.

"Kelly," began Char, "do you have those figures for the K-7 project?"

"Good morning, Char," Kelly said.

"Good morning," Char responded. "Do you have the statistics for the K-7 project? I need them to finish up."

"How are you this morning?" inquired Kelly, not responding to Char's question.

"Fine," Char replied.

"Did you get your haircut?" asked Kelly. "It looks great."

"As a matter of fact, I got them all cut," answered Char. "About those K-7 statistics, are they ready?"

"You know, my son missed the bus this morning and my computer crashed twice already. What a morning!" sighed Kelly.

"So is that a 'no'?" asked Char.

"I'm sorry," said Kelly, seeming to just now join Char. "What is it that you need?"

"The K-7 statistics," Char repeated.

"Oh," said Kelly with a bewildered smile. "Why didn't you say so?"

The following will help you gain further insights into the values, motivations, and intentions behind the communication style of Greens. See if you don't notice some of the attributes below in your next interaction with a Green.

Purposeful—Avoid "small talk"—feel it is a waste of time. Like to get to the pertinent information quickly. Have a knack for cutting to the chase or plowing through the "fluff" to get to the point. A classic line of many Greens is "And your point?"

Private—Usually talk more about ideas, information and strategies than relationships or personal matters, especially with co-workers.

Logical—Objective, use analysis to reach conclusions. May seem cold to those who don't understand the Green modus operandi. Although they have plenty of feelings that run deep, they don't usually like to display them freely. Voice and demeanor are frequently modulated.

Think before they speak—Sometimes do not feel the need to speak. When asked a question, unless they are extremely extroverted, like to take some time to ponder before answering.

Irritated at "stupid questions"—Can be bothered when people don't stop to think, look, or try to figure something out before asking a question.

Abhor redundancy—If a person overexplains something, particularly if Greens know more about the subject than the person doing the explaining, they may get irritated or mentally leave the conversation.

Theoretical—Hypothetical, abstract. Speak of new ideas and future plans. Hand movements or models are used to explain concepts. Avoid "tried and true" methods. Seek instead novelty and improvement.

Like the big picture—Greens go for the main idea or concept before honing in on the details and like others to do so as well.

Love to share ideas—Enjoy exchanging thoughts and having discussions with people that understand what they are talking about. Want to establish credibility of speaker before investing time. Like to embellish or upgrade concepts.

Ask a lot of questions—Seek information and facts. May debate. Want pros and cons. Respond negatively to inaccurate information or incompetence. Love to play "devil's advocate." Point out mistakes or exceptions and may argue with what is being said.

Use big words—Are precise and well articulated. May have quite an extensive vocabulary.

Communicate with conviction—Persuasive and convincing, use strong statements. Look for compliance, belief, or agreement in listener.

Wry sense of humor— Can see the humor in situations. Are creative with word puns and vocabulary. Can be especially witty, observant, or sarcastic.

Zena took her daughter to a well-known, reputable medical center. Her daughter needed a physical exam so she could go to daycare. Zena was given a form that instructed, "If your child has a temperature do not send them to daycare."
Zena chuckled to herself and said wryly, "If my daughter did not have a temperature, then she would be dead! Of course I would not send her to daycare."

The medical assistant, not catching Zena's sense of humor, explained, "Oh, we mean 'fever' when we say 'temperature.'"
"Why not just say 'fever' then?" Zena questioned.
The assistant quipped, "Any intelligent person would know we mean 'fever' when we say 'temperature!'"
"Actually," responded Zena, "any intelligent person would be irritated that you say 'temperature' when you mean 'fever!'"

154

Green's Listening Style:

Greens listen for information and want to know the purpose for the communication. Often, they assume the communicator has approached them to solve a problem or to exchange necessary or intriguing material. They tune out with redundancy, extreme emotion, and subjects that are of little interest to them. They seem to automatically click into data gathering and concept or strategy formation. They focus so intensely on thinking about and processing (then reprocessing from several different approaches) the "data" presented that they regularly miss out on the additional messages supplied by non-verbal communication such as tonality, body language and facial expressions. You may be sharing to gain empathy and instead they are concentrating on solving your challenge, offering little or no outward signs of compassion, while all the while in their minds they are demonstrating the ultimate compassion by taking the time to solve your problem.

Tips for Communicating with Greens

When Linda first met Gary she was often perplexed at the long pauses she would get after asking a question. Being an extrovert, she would blurt out thoughts as they hit her. She enjoyed fast-paced conversations. When she would ask Gary a question about how he felt about a subject, the silence that ensued made her uncomfortable. Feeling perhaps he hadn't heard or understood the question, she would often repeat or rephrase it. Gary would assure her that he understood and was just thinking about how to answer her. Linda would insist, "Just tell me the answer. Why do you have to think about it? Whatever is, is. What is there to think about?"

Gary would respond, "I don't want to say something incorrect."

Confused even further, Linda would say, "What do you mean? Just say your answer! What are you doing, making something up?" Linda had an uneasy feeling that Gary was trying to hide something because he was careful to monitor every word that came out of his mouth.

After attending a True Colors presentation, Linda learned that Gary is an introverted Green. She now understands that what might seem like a playful conversation starter to her is interpreted by him as a serious request for information. And, because Greens pride themselves on being accurate, he takes his time to ponder the question at hand before answering. Gary, on the other hand, is now able to detect when Linda is flippantly talking off the top of her head, just making conversation, or is really asking a serious question.

Following are some ways you can help open lines of communication with Greens.

Give them time to think—Greens like to ponder the subject at hand. They like to weigh many possible options before responding. They are not only thinking of the content of their message, but also what would be the most accurate method of conveying it. Sometimes the most succinct response for them is complete silence.

Don't misinterpret their need for information as anything else—Realize they have a need to question and explore. If they ask "why" or "what do you mean" realize that they are seeking more specific information, not trying to read between the lines or interrogate. Be logical and factual.

Give the big picture—Provide an overall context, outcome, or purpose for the discussion. Do you need a problem solved? Are you just sharing information? Give the big picture or end results first, then fill in the details. Remember, don't insult their intelli-

gence by stating or restating the obvious, especially if they know more about the topic than you do.

Stick to logic—Unless Blue is a very strong second color for them, Greens are not usually influenced by emotional appeals. Although they feel their emotions deeply, they usually do not show it and are not swayed when you do. Greens appreciate accuracy. You are better off using logic and facts. Emphasize an opportunity to learn and gain wisdom.

Watch your vocabulary—If you use large words, make sure you know what they mean and how to pronounce them properly or Greens may get annoyed and stop listening.

Notice their humor—Many Greens have a wry sense of humor that can sometimes be misunderstood. Give the benefit of the doubt. You don't have to laugh at their jest, but at least recognize it as humor instead of mistaking it for cruelty.

Debate with them for fun—If you have been deemed a worthy opponent by a Green, take the opportunity to dive into a healthy verbal exchange of ideas. Although they like to be straight to the point and appreciate it when you are too, they also enjoy arguing both sides of an issue. Be prepared to defend your position.

156

Share with them the big picture and your global views.

Speak for a purpose—Greens usually do not like small talk and are the least likely of the color styles to be up on the office gossip. However, once you have gained their trust and confidence, they can open up.

Understand and heed—Their interests may vary greatly from yours so don't be insulted if they don't seem fascinated in what you have to share. They usually won't give things a high priority unless they see the value, logic, or intrigue. Don't continue insisting they listen to matters that only you find satisfying.

Recognize Their Contributions—Let Greens know you appreciate them by using some of the following phrases:

"Your work on this project is valuable."

"You have keen analytical abilities."

"I hope you would like to present your findings to the company."

"I am impressed with your inquisitive mind."

"I am interested in your ideas on this subject."

"That is a fascinating observation; I want to hear more."

"I look forward to seeing your thoughts in action."

"I want you to share some of your ideas with others."

If You Are Green

If you are interested in facilitating smoother communication with others that do not embrace a similar style as yours, the following are techniques for further understanding their language and style.

Add some detail, or not—When asked to describe an experience, be aware of what the other person is requesting. Do they want just the big picture or some details? Some Greens have a tendency to give only the big picture, while others may go into an in-depth explanation. Determine the appropriate strategy for relaying information according to the person you are communicating with.

Ease up—Notice whether your "why" questions are being misperceived as interrogation or as doubt of another person's intentions. If this is the case, use softeners to gain your answers, such as, "Please say more about _____."

Allow emotions—Just because others want to show their emotions does not mean that you are obligated to act or help them in any way. Let others express their feelings. Understand that's how some people process.

Pay attention to other people's needs—Before charging ahead with your own agenda, take some time to gain rapport. A few minutes at the start of a conversation can save much time and frustration later for both of you. Notice the effect your behavior has on others. Is your body language sending signals that you don't want to be approached?

Learn to listen without fixing—Many times people just want to be understood and heard—not every "problem" needs to be "fixed." Before the communication gets too far, politely ask them if they are seeking solutions or just a listening ear. This way you will know whether to listen for details or merely feelings. Simply listening and empathizing is a worthwhile activity in itself.

Acknowledge others' intent—Before offering correction, announce your understanding of the positive purpose behind others' behavior. Skip the scathing sarcasm or condescending tone; instead, validate them with your feedback.

Save the debate—Although you may derive entertainment from playing "mental chess" with others, not everyone appreciates an intense discussion. Achieving a goal while alienating others can burn some bridges you may want to cross later.

Make time for your relationships—Notice what the people in your significant relationships need and appreciate. When feasible to do so, figure out what you can do to accommodate them—even if does not seem practical or logical.

158

Inform others—When you need to process, instead of just fading into your head to figure things out, let others know this is what you are doing. Notify them that you are not tuning them out, you simply would like some time to think. If you really want a challenge, allow others in on your processing. If your nature is to be introverted, experience what it is like to examine externally by speaking your thoughts out loud, as they occur. Let others in on your analysis of the data.

EXCELLENT POINT DEAR. I'M GOING TO GO THINK ABOUT THIS NOW.

Chapter 14
COMMUNICATING
IN COLOR

Fortunately, learning to communicate "in color" is remarkably easy. And it not only improves your interactions, it changes your effectiveness in virtually *everything* you do. It is surprising how many people experience better results in communicating after just a few adjustments to their approach.

The following story depicts all four color styles interacting together. Let's find out how much you have learned. See how well you can determine the colors of the characters in this story:

The Meeting

Simon had arrived early and already been waiting about fifteen minutes for the rest of the committee to arrive. He was sitting at the conference table with his papers neatly in a stack, looking at his watch, when Roland walked into the room.

"Good morning!" Roland said, smiling. "How are you today?"

"Fine, thank you," replied Simon. "And you?"

"Fantastic!" Roland said excitedly. "My fiancée Angela and I went to the park for a picnic this weekend. It was *so* romantic. We ate sandwiches under a big shade tree. We laughed and shared stories. It was such a bonding experience." Roland's eyes glazed over as he sighed, "She is the love of my life." After a pause he seemed to snap back to the room. "How was your weekend, Simon?"

"Well, my in-laws visited on Sunday, so I spent all of Saturday cleaning and reorganizing the house," answered Simon. "I like it 'just so.'"

At 9:00, a woman, Page, entered the room, her face buried in a report as she walked. She took a seat without ever looking up from her reading.

"Good morning! How are you today?" inquired Roland.

After a moment's hesitation, Page looked up and said, "Huh?"

"How was your weekend?" Roland asked.

"Oh," she finally responded, "great."

"Well, what did you do?" Roland inquired.

"I read a fascinating book on the functions of neurons in the brain. The chemical structure and potential energy of the neurotransmitters are mind-blowing."

"Hmmm . . . I see. Sounds interesting," said Roland, trying to sound excited.

"Well, we need to start this meeting," piped in Simon. "We're all here but Laquisha. It is already past 9:00; we have waited long enough. I believe starting meetings on time is important. We'll just have to start without her."

"I'm sure she is on her way. Traffic was really backed up this morning," said Roland, defending his absent co-worker.

"We have an agenda that indicates the meeting starts at 9:00 a.m. She needs to be responsible enough to get here on time. We have too many important decisions to make," said Simon firmly.

"Important decisions?" quipped Page. "We're not building a space shuttle here—we are planning an employee recognition ceremony."

Just then Laquisha came hurrying in the room, talking on her cell phone. "Okay. You bet! Gotta go!" Ending the call, she looked at the committee members for the first time. "So what's up? How far did we get?"

"We?" both Simon and Page chimed at the same time.

"Something came across my desk that needed immediate attention," stated Laquisha. "I took care of it on my way here. The miracle of cell phones! Problem solved in five minutes flat. Now that's what I call action!" she boasted, snapping her fingers back and forth in the air.

"No problem," Roland told her. "We waited for you. You are just on time."

"The employee recognition sub-committee meeting of the ABC organization is now called to order at 9:07 a.m.," declared Simon, glaring at Laquisha. "The first item on the agenda is, of course, to look at what we have done in past years. The date we hold the event is always August 8th, the day this company was officially established. This is our 25th anniversary, and I am proud to say I have been a part of this organization for eighteen of those twenty-five years. It has been a tradition to have the ceremony at the town hall."

"Town Hall is so boring!" blurted out Laquisha. "I swear, it's so old it even smells musty. Let's have a picnic this year!"

"Have some respect for your town hall," frowned Simon. "As I was saying . . ."

"That way we could have some fireworks!" Laquisha continued. "Now, that would be fun!"

"I like that idea!" said Roland. "We could have some fun activities for the employees to get to know each other better."

"It would not be feasible to have fireworks in August," counseled Page. "The combustibility of the grasses in this area is five times the amount that it is in July when fireworks are lawfully allowed outdoors."

"Oh no," Roland worried. "We wouldn't want anyone to get hurt by causing a fire."

"Actually, if we had it at the Sports Arena, fireworks would be possible," Page said, rethinking her last remark. "I was watching a special on the Discovery Channel the other night about the engineering and construction of the Arena. The logistics involved are fascinating. As long as the trajectory of the fireworks at time of ignition is . . ."

"Please!" pleaded Simon. "Let's get some order to this meeting. The event has always been at the town hall. We need to decide on the presentation schedule and the menu."

"But we haven't settled the question of the fireworks yet," insisted Laquisha.

"Fireworks are not in the budget." stated Simon. "There! It's settled!"

"Let's step back a minute and look at the bigger picture," requested Roland. "This is a shared experience.

It's not just a date, a location, and a menu. Think of it as a family reunion. We have our great-grandparents—the founders of our organization; our grandparents—the managers; our mothers and fathers—the supervisors; and other various members of the family, including aunts, uncles, cousins, even the children—all with different needs, insights, and experiences."

"Can you get to the point?" said Page, growing impatient.

"How do we make this a welcoming and memorable occasion for each and every one of them, as individuals as well as a group?" asked Roland.

"Well, it's got to be fun!" said Laquisha. "If the president of the company does that boring speech one more time, I think I'll vomit!"

"The president *must* give a speech," said Simon. The event must have tradition."

"Is there a way we could do both?" asked Roland.

"Why don't we just mail out certificates?" interrupted Page. "It would save us a lot of time and money, and we could all get back to work."

Simon, Roland, and Laquisha all looked at Page, trying to figure out whether she was joking or not.

"I've been thinking," continued Page, now that she had their attention. "If we used a little technology by adding a sound system and some laser lights we could bring this event

up to date yet still keep the traditional speech."

"Tell us more!" the others encouraged.

"I can hook up my stereo to the new computer system. It has a program that can download music and digitally synthesize it to synchronize the beats to laser lights projected on a screen behind the podium. I could run some speaker wire to various speakers strategically placed for a surround-sound effect."

Laquisha perked up. "Yeah! I like it! That sounds like fun!"

"It does spice things up a bit," Simon admitted.

"Now we're talking!" Roland said enthusiastically. "We could have a theme! Maybe '70s since that's when we were founded. We could all dress in '70s garb! Think of the decorating possibilities!"

"Yeah! And we could have karaoke for entertainment," added Laquisha. "There are some great '70s songs. 'Stayin' alive, stayin' alive, ooo . . . ooo . . . ooo . . . ooo, stayin' alive!" She sang. "I'll M.C. the event."

"I can make invitations so people know what to expect," volunteered Simon.

"I'll recruit people for a greeting team to make everyone feel welcome," said Roland.

"I'll make a list of what needs to go in the programs for you to pass out so people know the schedule of events," added Simon. "Now, let me record each person's assignments so we know who is responsible for what," he said, jotting down notes in his daily planner. "This is moving along nicely."

"I'll bring the karaoke machine and some music," volunteered Laquisha. "I'll also M.C.—I've got some great jokes I can tell. Did you hear the one about the . . ."

"Put me down for decorations and a team to greet people as they arrive," said Roland.

"I'm not going!" said Page with an ever-so-subtle grin.

Catching onto her humor, Simon said, "I'll put you down for laser lights and the sound system, and I will be responsible for the invitations and programs . . . We'll need a map with good directions . . ."

Suddenly a woman came into the room, handed Simon a note, muttered that she was very sorry, and quietly left.

"Oh, no!" wailed Simon. "How could this happen? I booked the town hall a year in advance and the secretary to the mayor just informed us that they need the hall on that date! What are we going to do for a location?"

"What do you mean, what are *we* going to do?" questioned Laquisha. "That's their problem. We've got it booked."

"We are talking about the mayor!" said Simon.

"Who cares? We had it first," insisted Laquisha. "Who says we can't have Town Hall if we want it?"

"Well, the mayor, Charles Goodman," Simon pouted. "That's who."

"Charlie?" said Laquisha. "You really want the town hall? I can get it for you!" Without waiting for a response, she took out her cell phone and dialed. "Hey girlfriend," she said casually. "What's this about Charlie using the town hall on August 8th? Is this set in stone?" Laquisha paused while listening for her answer. "How about you using it the week before instead?" she suggested. "Think about it, Aug 1st, beginning of the month, people just got paid, all in good moods, what more could you ask for?" A smile burst across her face. "Great! Then it's all set! Thanks. Say 'hi' to Charlie for me!" Laquisha ended her call, stood up, and looked at the committee. "All right then, that's that!" she said brushing her hands past each other as she walked towards the door. "Let's get the show on the road. Gotta run—I've got some music to find! See ya!" she exclaimed, making her exit.

"Well, how about that!" said Roland. "That was nice of her to make that call and it was really nice of the mayor to change days. What a nice man. I better get moving on those decorations. I can get Paul, Debra, and Teresa—I'm sure they'd love to help."

"I'd better get started on that research," Page said, as she visibly retreated into her thoughts. "I'm going to check all my favorite websites to see what kind of information they have on lasers so I know precisely..." she mumbled, jotting down ideas on a pad of paper as she left the room.

"Well! Look what can be accomplished when we all work together," said Roland, turning to Simon. "Now that was a meeting!"

Simon agreed. "Meeting adjourned," he said.

Simon Says . . .

So, how easy was it for you to determine the dominant color style of each person at the meeting? Write your answers below:

Simon_____

Roland_____

Page_____

Laquisha_____

What color communication style was Simon? If you said "Gold" then you are right. What was it about the way he communicated that helped you determine this? What were some of his actions, words, and intentions? Think for a moment. Pretty obvious, wasn't it? (Early for the meeting, keeper of the agenda, looking to the

past for reference to guide actions in the present, wanting to keep traditional speech, keeping list of responsibilities, booking the town hall a year in advance, respect for authority—heeding the note from the mayor's office, and so on.)

How about Roland? Yes! Blue. How did you know? (Acknowledged each person as they came into the room, expressed interest in them as a person—reestablishing the relationship, asked about their weekend, had kind words to say in Laquisha's defense, spoke in metaphor comparing the event to a family reunion, tried to mediate a compromise between Simon and Laquisha, and so on.)

Page? Laquisha? Yes! Green and Orange, respectively. Again, how did you know? (Page's sense of humor, knowing the logistics of fireworks, wanting to update event with technology. Laquisha's multitasking by taking care of business on the phone on the way to the meeting, straightforward comments about the president's speech, casualness with the mayor's secretary.) Although this was purposely a very blatant example of the four color styles interacting, you may have also detected some subtleties. The more familiar you are with the True Colors concepts, the easier it is to recognize the motivations *behind* the behaviors or words. When you are in conversations with others, notice how easy it is to determine which color style they are operating in (remember everything you've learned so far).

If you are serious about bringing your communication skills to the next level, the following steps will offer you further direction.

Step #1

The first step is to understand the different styles and needs of each color in general. Study the chapters describing the various communication styles so you are familiar with them. Because we all have differing amounts of all four colors in our spectrum, pay attention to broad themes. For example, everyone can be caring, kind, and considerate—not just Blues and Golds. Be careful not to start seeing things as only black and white. If you watch for the overall tone, you'll notice one emerging.

Step #2

The second step is to practice over and over until you no longer have to consciously think about or plan your communication. It just happens automatically. It's like driving a car. When we first learned to drive we had to consciously remember to look, steer, work the pedals, and probably even shift too. We may have overcompensated and driven rather unsteadily. We may have had to remind ourselves to check the

rearview mirror or to remember to use our blinkers. But now driving is so automatic to most of us that it seems the car practically drives itself. It is this way with communicating. When you use the communication techniques in this book, you will start to experience results. It may be more transformational than you realize, and you may or may not already be aware of how quickly this transformation has taken place. You probably have already noticed that as you read, your mind began to use the information to apply it to the circumstances and people in your life.

You may feel more comfortable with some of the methods at first than you do with others. Go ahead and experiment; have fun! You could drive along in life in first gear and get where you want to go. However, when you learn to smoothly shift into other gears you will get there more effectively with less stress.

Step #3—Just for fun!

Find someone with the opposite color style that you can communicate with to bounce your ideas off of. When practicing different ways of communicating, make sure you are clear about the purpose of a conversation. Are you looking to share data and ideas, solve a problem, make a decision, or perhaps just share an interesting story? What about the other person? If you are busy trying to

reestablish a relationship with someone and his or her main goal is to get
information, chances are you will be
more effective if you switch gears into
information mode.

Remember that every time
you try something that does
not happen to work as
favorably as you had
hoped, you are just that
much closer to finding a way
that will! Try something else until you
find what you are comfortable with.
As with driving, the more you practice, the more natural it becomes.

Part IV

WHEN
COLORS
FADE

Self Esteem and
S - t - r - e - s - s

When a person is "shining brightly," they are using their skills, talents, and natural preferences in positive, resourceful ways. They have a sense of worth and self-respect or what we often refer to as positive self-esteem.

Positive self-esteem is important because when people experience it they feel and look good, are effective and productive, and respond to others and themselves in healthy, positive, nurturing ways. People "in esteem" are able to enter into stressful environments without having to tear other people down or patronize them in order to make themselves feel good. On the other hand, many people may experience periods of low self-esteem. For some, this has been a life-long pattern. When a person experiences major or long-term stress, feels they have no control over their circumstances, or perceives they are being threatened or victimized, their self-esteem can start heading downhill, and they can begin to "fade."

In these circumstances, normal behaviors can shift to defense mechanisms carried with us from the past. Skilled, capable people who are successful in many areas of their life may begin to crumble or "fade" under the pressures in other areas.

A lot of things can happen to people, but it is their own interpretation of the event that has the most effect on how they feel about themselves. Obviously, the things we say and do have somewhat of an influence on the way others feel and react to our behaviors, but self-esteem is essentially an "inside job." The foundation of people's level of confidence and self-worth is based on their own beliefs about themselves.

Being able to recognize when we, or someone we know, is "fading" can be the first step in being able to turn it around. Most of us have (or know someone who has) experienced a time in our life when we've felt overwhelmed. It could have been from a traumatic emotional event, unmet expectations, changes in circumstances, or even a deluge of too many responsibilities. When this happens, we will go to great lengths to preserve our identities and get our needs met. We all have different things we value, and when the people in our lives are not operating in the same mode as we are, or circumstances are not cooperating with our plans, there can be a mismatch of priorities or a groping for control.

What Is Happening?

When individuals begin to fade, they will resort to meeting their needs any way they can. Most individuals are not consciously aware of their

169

own coping behaviors. They instinctively turn to actions that meet their immediate need for relief, not realizing the long-term effects those actions can have. For example, with illness some people shut down or seem to act the opposite of their true nature. Other individuals turn to amplifying their natural tendencies. Much like the habit many people have when speaking to a person from a foreign country, if at first that person doesn't understand what we are saying, we say it *louder!* The person still can't understand what we are saying. Now, they just get to misunderstand louder words.

Of course by now you have noticed that what is stressful to one person or color style may be exciting or motivating to another. Although there are variations in the ways people respond to circumstances, there are some general themes among the different color styles. The following chapters describe some typical behaviors one might see when the various colors fade. Any one of the colors could possibly demonstrate any of these behaviors. They are not restricted to the color style for which they are written; they are just the most common for this style. Many of the suggestions for preventing fading, as well as the suggestions for brightening, can be applied across the color spectrum.

It is important to realize our own role in affecting the self-esteem of others. It is tempting to want a magic formula to use to change others' behaviors. The main reason for providing this information is not to provide you with a strategy for *changing* others but to help you understand more fully what is going on behind their behaviors. With this understanding will come compassion and a willingness to do your part to help encourage, bolster, or preserve positive self-esteem in those around you. Remember to pay close attention to what you can do for yourself. Even with all the outside influences, when it comes to self-esteem, it's what you do on the inside that counts.

Chapter 15
WHEN
BLUES
FADE

When Blues shine they appreciate everything and everyone. They behave with honesty and integrity.

They like teamwork and cooperation. Blues usually are contagiously enthusiastic and express their feelings readily. They can be very encouraging. They strive for peace and harmony and enjoy creating things to make life better.

However, when Blues are not getting their needs met, they can begin to fade. It is essential for them to be able to express their authentic self and feel they are making a contribution. Because Blues find great pleasure in contributing to others, they can become overextended. Everyone has their limits to how much stress they can take before becoming immobilized. If they spend too much time on other people's problems, too much energy doing for others, and constantly put their own needs last they can get overwhelmed. If they spend too much time in a relationship or environment where there is constant conflict, rejection, or negativity, Blues may "act out" to try and reestablish harmony in the situation and their own equilibrium.

A Faded Blue

Tammy is a single mother with two teenage sons. Her father's illness was getting increasingly worse, and she had just moved to a "fixer-upper" home. At work, there was a bit of restructuring happening. Her direct supervisor, Vanessa, accepted a position in another department. Tammy had really enjoyed working for Vanessa. She felt that the two of them had a friendship as well as a good

working relationship. "Who knows who will be replacing Vanessa?" Tammy thought apprehensively.

Tammy tried not to be upset with Vanessa for leaving, but somehow she felt abandoned and unappreciated. When Vanessa would try to talk to Tammy about her new position, Tammy found it hard to listen. She would plaster on a smile and nod her head, acting like she was interested, while on the inside, she did not want to hear about it. Tammy found herself avoiding Vanessa as much as possible. Yet when confronted, she gave no verbal clues about her real feelings.

Instead, Tammy felt the need to vent about other issues to her co-workers. She would lament that "no one" noticed the hard work and extra effort she was putting forth at home or work. Her workload was overwhelming, she was not getting enough sleep at night, and to top it off—she was gaining weight. Her co-workers eventually grew weary of listening and started avoiding her.

Tammy's venting soon turned into emotional tantrums—drawer slamming, crying, and even yelling. The slightest conflict would bring her to tears. Her outbursts would catch everyone off guard. Practically the entire staff would tiptoe around her, trying not to set her off. Tammy soon began questioning her co-workers' actions. She started getting mad at them, too—accusing them of sabotaging her or gossiping behind her back.

She would take general comments overheard out of context and act as though they were aimed specifically at her.

When Vanessa's birthday arrived, Tammy refused to help decorate Vanessa's new office or pitch in to buy a card. In the past, Tammy would have been the organizer of such activities, so when Vanessa discovered her office decorated and read the thoughtful card, she assumed that Tammy had arranged it all. Vanessa waited until she could have a moment alone with Tammy. She thanked Tammy profusely and told her how much it meant to her to have her office decorated and to receive such a nice, thoughtful card.

Not wanting to admit that she had done nothing to help, Tammy simply said, "You're welcome. It was nothing."

From Shining to Fading

In attempts to maintain harmony and protect their true feelings, Blues may portray the opposite of what they are feeling. They may not want to let on that they feel hurt, inconvenienced, or unappreciated. They can withdraw their love, concern, or listening ear on the inside, yet still appear like everything is fine on the outside. Some Blues will cry, scream, or lash out in an attempt to divert their own attention, as well as the attention of others, to a different

problem altogether. Keep in mind that this is not something they do on a conscious level, but rather unconsciously. They may even fantasize about running away or having someone or something rescue them from their circumstances.

Following are some of the behaviors you might see when Blues are stressed, experiencing low self-esteem, or not getting their needs met for an extended period:

Characteristics of a Faded Blue

- Misbehaves to get attention

- Lies to save face, inconsistent, pretense

- Withdraws, loses track of personal priorities

- Fantasizes, daydreams excessively

- Cries often and appears depressed

- Behaves in passive-resistant ways

- Expresses emotions by yelling and screaming

Common Blue Stressors

- Conflict

- Overloaded, overwhelmed

- Isolation or being left out

- Rejection

174

• Lack of trust, being "back-stabbed"

• Lack of acknowledgment

• Lack of tolerance

• Aggressiveness directed towards them or others close to them

• Negativity

• Not able to express genuine self

• Not able to share

• Not being appreciated

• Lack of caring

• Insincerity

• Lack of romance or touch

• Lack of cooperation

• Unsure or unsafe environment (i.e., can't ask questions without being put down)

• Rigidity

• Saying "No"

Some of the obvious reasons Tammy was stressed had to do with her overwhelming responsibilities at home. Compounding her challenges in her personal life were the changes at work. She felt rejected by her supervisor, Vanessa; left out when her co-workers tiptoed around her; and isolated by not being able to vent and share. There were a few actions others could possibly have taken, such as Vanessa including her a bit sooner in some of her decision making or her co-workers giving her an empathetic audience in private. However, many times there is little others can do but have some understanding and try not to make things worse. Remember, self-esteem, although influenced from the outside, comes from the inside. When individuals have stable self-esteem they are more able to ask for what they need. So, what can you do to help boost your self-esteem, lower your stress levels, and get your Blue needs met? Read over the following suggestions and decide which ones would be the most helpful to you.

If You Are Blue

Have you ever noticed that sometimes it is easier to spot the behaviors of others than to notice the same behavior in yourself? If you have a high amount of Blue characteristics in your color spectrum, the preceding list will most likely depict some of the most common stressors for you. Check the list of "Characteristics of a Faded Blue" and take an honest inventory. Do you recognize yourself resorting to these behaviors to try and get your needs met? Because we are all unique individuals with different experiences and situations, we will, of course, have variations in the ways we react to stress. In general, though, many of the reactions that Blues have will be manifested in these kinds of behaviors with their other color styles blended in.

Since the world of a Blue revolves around relationships, it is easy to think that if others would just change the way they behave, it would lessen our stress levels. Although this may be true in some respects, you are the one that has the greatest effect on your own attitude, self-esteem, and stress level. By adopting the following behaviors you can gain a new perspective and brighten up.

Learn to Accept "Negative" Emotions—Some people express themselves in assertive ways that can seem rude or mean. Others need space to be sad, grumpy, or alone. Although you may not enjoy feeling "down" and feel it is your job to cheer everyone else up, some people need a period to be alone and process. It's okay to try and redirect the focus of others, but pay attention to whether you are being effective or not. Also, some people enjoy a little conflict or argument. When you try to create harmony out of a situation when others are actually trying to stir things up a bit, it can cause frustration for everyone. Notice when it would be appropriate to allow others the freedom to debate, even if they are loud and boisterous. Sometimes the best action to take is to remove yourself from the situation.

Take a Stand—Notice if you perceive that a conflict exists when it really does not. Many times you have control over a situation and don't even realize it. Stop and notice! It really is okay to take charge. Examine your own needs. Pay attention to what you really want instead of repeatedly basing it on what others want or need. If you spend so much time doing for others, you risk losing track of what would best serve you, as well as them.

Note: Expressing your needs and asking for what you desire does not equate with yelling, screaming, or being "mean."

Many times Blues wait until they are at the point of being steaming mad before they will stick up for themselves. Then when they finally express themselves it comes spewing out with aggressive, defiant indignation.

Instead of getting mad, get assertive. Assertiveness is clear, direct expression of feelings. This expression of feelings does not include stomping on the other person in the process. Feelings can be expressed firmly and honestly with respect for the feelings, opinions, and rights of others. Know the difference between your true feelings and the feelings you put on because they seem more appropriate. It is much better to let people know what you want than to expect them to guess.

Foster Growth in Others by Doing Less—Because of your tremendous drive to contribute, the lines of knowing just how much and how long you should continue to give and do for others may begin to get fuzzy. It's admirable to contribute, but not to your demise. Notice when others can do for themselves and when some things just do not need to be done at all. Be careful not to promote others' dependence on you. Sometimes we dig ourselves in so deeply doing for others that we don't leave them any other option but to depend on us. Do them and yourself a favor and let them grow and

achieve on their own. The following story is often passed around at self-help groups to help participants recognize that sometimes it is the struggle that allows us to grow.

Recognizing the Importance of Life's Struggles

A young student found a cocoon one day and brought it to his homeroom, which was in the biology lab. The teacher put it into an unused aquarium with a lamp to keep the cocoon warm. About a week went by when a small opening began to appear on the underside of the cocoon. The students watched as it began to shake. Suddenly, tiny antennae emerged, followed by the head and tiny front feet. The students watched this unfold, and would run back to the lab in between classes to check on the progress of the cocoon. By lunchtime the creature had struggled to free its listless wings; the colors revealed that it was a monarch butterfly. It wiggled, shook, and struggled, but now it seemed to be stuck. Try as it might, the butterfly couldn't seem to force its body through the small opening in the cocoon.

Finally, one student decided to help the butterfly out of its difficulty. He took scissors from the table and snipped off the cocoon's restrictive covering. Out plopped the insect-like thing. The top half looked like a butterfly with droopy wings; the bottom half, which was just out of the

177

cocoon, was large and swollen. The butter-pillar or cater-fly never flew with its stunted wings. It just crawled around the bottom of the aquarium dragging its wings and swollen body. Within a short time it died.

The next day the biology teacher explained that the butterfly's struggle to get through the tiny opening was necessary in order to force the fluids from the swollen body into the wings so they would be strong enough to fly. Without the struggle, the wings never developed and the butterfly could not fly.

As it is for the butterfly, so too it is for us—we cannot violate the laws of creation. Without struggles a lot of things in life never develop.

Let It Go—Most people already like you. It is a given. You are a wonderful person with terrific talents. You may have evidence to the contrary but why collect that stuff? Instead, if someone does not pay attention to an idea you contributed, or fails to respond when you say "hello," or multitasks in your presence without making eye contact, accept that they are doing the best they can at the moment, given the circumstances. You may perceive their actions as rude, when in reality they are just different. It doesn't mean that you should fail to acknowledge others or purposely ignore them to "give them a taste of their own medicine." Relinquish grudges. Be yourself and don't hold it against them for doing things their way. Don't punish others for not being Blue.

Validate Yourself—Have you ever experienced a time when you felt that you did a hundred things right, yet the one mistake you made is what others noticed? Keeping in mind that feedback is good and useful, take into account the comment about the "mistake." Set aside your judgments about the person, the way the feedback was delivered, and the "meanings" you attached to it. Notice what is useful about the feedback. Focus on how you can incorporate and use it for improvement in the future.

Pay attention to whether you have developed the habit of putting yourself down or focusing on your own shortcomings. You can learn from what did not turn out the way you wanted by taking mental notes about what needs to be done differently in the future. Then, purposefully shift your focus to everything you did "right" instead. Focus on what you want to happen instead of what you do not want.

You naturally desire to experience and express your feelings. Validate yourself for your helping, caring, and contributing. You are blessed with the gift of loving and caring about others. Acknowledge your friendships, your sacrifices, your successes. Let your inner light glow. Be yourself.

Use Your Talents—I was talking to a very stressed Blue the other day in a computer class I was attending. She had taken a different position at her job because she needed the five percent increase in salary that came with it. Before, she had been working with victims of violent crimes and their families. She facilitated groups, answered a hotline, and organized events. She really enjoyed working with people and seeing the progress they made in the programs. Currently she was working with computers, entering data. She had recently been given an assignment to design a new database for her organization, something she had no background or experience in. She really was in over

her head but did not want to give up. Thus, the computer class. She expressed how miserable she was in her new job but she needed the extra money to take care of her family.

If you find yourself in a situation where you are dissatisfied with your job, it usually comes down to two choices: (1) change your mind about your job, or (2) change something about your job. A great book to help you discover the type of work that uses the natural preferences for your color style is *Follow Your True Colors to the Work You Love* by Carolyn Kalil.

Set Boundaries—"Give 'em an inch and they'll take a mile" was probably first muttered by a Blue. Blues pride themselves on being empathetic and not taking advantage of others. They are skilled at noticing when others are overwhelmed. They are careful not to overstep the boundaries of others. However, others are not always as perceptive in these areas. Therefore, it is up to you to set boundaries for yourself and take total responsibility to see that they are honored. If you continue trying to be everything to everyone, chances are, someone is going to get let down, and often that someone is *you*. If it has become a chore and is causing you stress to try and keep up with things that seem to go unappreciated or are taken for granted—drop it! Keep the things in your life that give you the most satisfaction. Remember, it is not "mean" or "harsh" to set and maintain a boundary. It is actually courteous, informative, and beneficial. Contrary to what you might expect, people will respect you for it if you do so with caring firmness.

To find out more about how to set and announce your own boundaries, survey people you respect and find out how they set and announce theirs. Use several techniques until you find one that suits you. Who knows? It may be the first one you use!

Look before Leaping—Being a "possibility person," you may have a tendency to project idealistic qualities on others or have high expectations for outcomes. When circumstances don't meet your expectations, use your innate ability to pick out the positive intent behind someone's behavior or see other opportunities in the situation. As much as you might wish that people would reciprocate the love, friendship, or contributions you provide them, it is not always going to show up in the form you would desire.

I remember a cartoon I saw in a calendar published by the Hope Heart Institute (Seattle, Washington). It was of a little bunny that was staring at a small door that had a sign on the doorknob that read, "Closed." The bunny had a sad look on its face. What the bunny was not noticing was a big door right next to the other one.

This door had a huge "Welcome" mat in front of it. The door was wide open and you could see a gigantic carrot garden inside. There were signs posted amongst the carrots, "Jumbo Carrots—Free!" The bunny was too busy focusing on the closed door to see the wide open one. What are you focusing on that is preventing you from seeing other possibilities?

Take Care of Yourself—Again, remember to pay attention to your own needs. Many times we are so busy doing for others that we let our own health and well-being suffer. Are you getting enough exercise, sleep, and nutritious foods? What do you do for stress relief? When was the last occasion you had a massage or took time for yourself? When taking a plane ride, the flight attendant explains that in an emergency, the oxygen masks will fall from an overhead compartment. If you were with a small child, who would you put the oxygen mask on first—yourself or the child? Although as a parent your instinct might be to "save" your child first, then yourself, the flight attendant always instructs the adult passengers to put their own masks on first. This is because if anything were to happen to the adults, the child would have little chance of surviving without them. If you don't take care of yourself, how will you ever be able to authentically express yourself or fully contribute to others?

Express Your Unique Self—Find ways to express yourself. Do you need to dance, draw, or sing? What is it you have been putting off? When Blues are not expressing their true selves they can get confused, depressed, and frustrated. It is so emancipating to be able to release the pent-up desires at last. Although many times Blues will gauge what they do upon the approval they get from others, ultimately they are much happier when they end up following their bliss instead of their blisters. One way to do this is to seek out other Blues. If you find yourself surrounded by color combinations that don't appreciate or bring out the best in you, you still have choices. One would be to have them read this or other books on True Colors. This will help them gain an appreciation for your gifts. Another choice is to join clubs or attend classes where other Blues are likely to be. Try yoga, meditation, a dance class, or whatever else you are interested in.

How to Help Brighten a Blue

If you happen to have Blues in your life that you think may be fading, there are some things you can do to support them in their brightening process. These suggestions work best when Blue individuals are actively putting in the effort to address their own needs. However, these tips are still very effective in helping you help prevent a Blue from fading.

Some of the following suggestions may be out of your comfort level just now. But if you have a genuine desire to learn and grow, they will quickly become a natural part of your behavior. To help brighten Blues, offer them:

Validation—Blues like feeling that people care about them. It makes them feel good about themselves and their relationships with others. People who display any form of acknowledgment that says, "I value you; you are unique; you are important to me as a person; I care how you feel," create a sense of self-esteem, self-respect, and worthiness in Blues.

Notice them; pay attention. Give praise as well as personal and social recognition. Thank them for their contributions. Compliments paid to Blues about their natural compassion, their creative approaches to human understanding, their ability to work with others, and their sensitivity to the feelings of others makes them glow with pride. Notice when they have gone the "extra mile" or done something very creative or unique. They enjoy gifts of a personal nature: a note, a card, something handmade. Say hello and remember their name. They desire acknowledgment that they exist and are human.

Acceptance—Practice tolerance, patience, appreciation, and reassurance. Offer opportunities to "fess up"

without being rejected. Include them. Involve them in teams, relationships, and friendships. Provide ways for them to obtain support systems and social contacts.

Harmony—Blues have an innate urge to make everyone around them happy. They feel it is their duty. If someone is sad, it is up to them to cheer them up. If two people are arguing, the Blue will find the positive points of each. Blues really can put themselves into the shoes of others and empathize. Therefore, if you know Blues that are fading, keep arguments with others out of their vicinity. Even if it has nothing to do with them, they will still feel obligated to try and make it better.

Kindness—Be positive. When fading, Blues can be especially affected by criticism. Discern what they are going through or experiencing. Show sensitivity; give personal support and empathy. Save negative comments or stories for others who appreciate them. Blues are most comfortable in environments that are warm and friendly, and allow for personal interaction, individual creativity, and expression. Allow them to express their feelings.

A Listening Ear—Blues get frustrated if they are not given opportunities to share. They want to be able to share their day and dramas. Give them opportunities to verbalize. Don't wait until they are screaming their needs. Approach them before they get to the boil-over point.

Warmth and Human Contact— Gestures of friendship such as a light touch, a pat on the back or shoulder, a handshake, a hug, or a gentle smile are very heartwarming. Oftentimes a hug can soothe a fading Blue. Smiles are a welcome sign of acceptance. Be accessible. Blues want and need warm and genuine human contact. When they go too long without it they can feel left out, unappreciated, and invisible. They try to consider the feelings, needs, and desires of others and wish it was reciprocal.

Avenues for Growth and Expressing Creativity—Blues fade when they have to endure routine too long. They require mental stimulation, inspiration, and challenge of their potential. Whether it's drawing, painting, acting, singing, dancing, talking, they way they dress, the flair of their performance, or communicating—going too long without an outlet may make them burst! Let them release their creativity, uniqueness, and individuality.

Limited Requests—Blues are prone to overcommit themselves and may fade when they become overwhelmed or exhausted. Limit the number of requests you make of

them. Pay attention to their needs and priorities. Offer your help.

Love and Romance—Blues welcome compliments and intrigue. Instead of seeing them as a mushy romantic or fantasizer, appreciate their love of the dramas and nuances of life. If you are in an intimate relationship with a Blue, think of something they would personally enjoy. For example, tuck a "love" note somewhere for them to find unexpectedly.

Trust—Keep confidences. They need a confidante, friend, or someone they can tell their deepest secrets to without worrying they will tell someone else or judge them for their actions. One way to earn their trust is to share something personal about yourself.

Chapter 16
WHEN GOLDS FADE

When Golds shine they like to do things to help. They are task and structure focused as well as serious and hardworking. They like to plan ahead and keep things organized. They care for their health and are dependable, reliable, and conscientious. Golds—above all—are respectful, responsible, and cooperative. Ordinarily, they place traditions and family time high on their priority lists.

However, when Golds are fatigued, stressed, or otherwise pushed to their limits they can dig in their heels and become overly rigid, self-righteous, and possessive. Their normally positive, helpful attitude can turn pessimistic, negative, and highly opinionated. They may worry about things they have no control over and get compulsive about the things they can control. They may get physically sick and are prone to complain about their symptoms in explicit details to others.

A Faded Gold

One semester, when I was teaching health classes at California State University, Stanislaus, we had just returned from a short Thanksgiving break. We were addressing the topic of stress management. I had asked my class what kinds of things cause them stress, and had already written several responses on the board, when one woman, Betty, called out, "My husband!" The class laughed as I added it to the list of other stressors. After a few other students contributed their responses, Betty yelled out again, "My husband!"

We all laughed even louder this time as I acknowledged her humor and underlined "My Husband!" on the chalkboard. Wanting to finish getting

all of the class's thoughts on the board before getting any details or explanations about them, I encouraged the class to continue sharing the rest of their stressors. For a third time, Betty yelled out, "My husband!"

We all laughed again. This time there was no moving on. Burning with curiosity and still smiling with the rest of the class, I approached Betty. "Please share with us, what is it about your husband that stresses you out?"

Betty braced herself on her desk as she struggled to stand. The smiles of amusement shifted to concern as she turned around to address the class. "I have fibromyalgia," she explained. My body aches constantly and I can't sleep well."

Everyone gave their full attention to Betty as she continued. "For Thanksgiving, I made it quite clear to my husband that all I wanted to do this year was rest. It is a tradition in our family to make a huge turkey dinner with all the trimmings but I was just too darn tired. I have a hard time getting out of bed and moving around the house, let alone cooking a feast, so I told him, 'I am not doing Thanksgiving this year!' But do you think he understood? Do you think he had any sympathy for me? Oh no! He whined, 'But we always have Thanksgiving dinner; it just won't be Thanksgiving without it!'

"I'm telling you, the man stresses me out! What did he expect from me?

185

I try to keep the house clean, take care of the kids, hold down a part-time job, and go to school. I can barely get to my doctor appointments I'm so busy and in so much pain. So I told him, 'If you want Thanksgiving dinner you'll just have to cook it yourself. I need some rest!' With that, I turned and went upstairs to rest.

Do you think he was quiet so I could sleep? Oh no! I should be so lucky. I couldn't believe the noise the man was making! I could hear pots and pans clanging, cupboard doors banging, and him rustling around downstairs. Why me, I thought? Why can't he just be quiet so I can sleep? I pulled the pillow over my ears to try and drown out the noise. I tossed and turned, growing more irritated with every sound. Finally, I had just drifted off to sleep and guess what happens? Yep! My husband! He comes knocking on the door.

'Honey, wake up. Dinner is ready.'

Did the man not understand me? Did I not tell him all I wanted to do was rest? The man stresses me out. So still sleepy and aggravated more than ever, I got up to see what he was fussing about. I dragged myself downstairs and into the dining room.

Much to my surprise—he had dinner all spread out on the table. There was turkey and potatoes and even candles lit. I was impressed. I started to feel a bit guilty about all my complaining, that is, until I went to sit down and saw my kitchen!

I could not believe it! What a mess! What was he thinking? Do you think I can eat when my kitchen is dirty? No way! How could he do this to me? How dare he make more work for me! All I wanted to do was rest. And now I've got hours more work to do. So he offers to help. And you know what he does next? (We were hanging on the edge of our seats in anticipation.) He takes the rag and gets it wet in the sink and he sloshes the water all over the counter. Then he takes the rag and sloshes it all over the stove . . . (At this point Betty noticed the blank stares on our faces.)

"Don't you get it?" she said making hand motions in the air in demonstration. "You're supposed to take the wet rag and wring it out. You wash one little section. Then you wet it and wring it out again and wash the next section. You don't slosh water everywhere! You complete one section before moving on to the next! The man drives me crazy! I told him to get out of my kitchen. I spent three hours cleaning up the mess. Dinner was cold, and I never got my nap! I'm telling you . . . The Man Stresses Me Out!"

From Shining to Fading

Normally Golds thrive on responsibility. Usually, it is a source of strength for their self-esteem.

However, this internal drive to be dependable and do the right thing, along with their desire to belong, can at times result in them taking on an overwhelming amount of duties. The feeling that they are the only ones that can carry out the duties can be so overwhelming that their body shuts down from the overload and they can become physically sick. In essence, if they will not take a break, their body does it for them. During times of stress and tremendous challenge, Golds' already existing need for consistency can intensify to an inordinate demand for control and excessive resistance to change. When the environment around them lacks rules, organization, and clear expectations they can become narrowly focused and overly system bound. They may complain that others are not doing their part or are doing things "wrong." In their own way, they are trying to relieve their stress while at the same time bring order to chaos; remain loyal to their families, organizations, and communities; and above all, be responsible.

Characteristics of a Faded Gold

- Complains and behaves with self-pity

- Exhibits anxiety and worry

- Reacts physically to stress

- Judges self and others harshly

- Exhibits "blind herd" mentality

- Becomes controlling, rigid, and close-minded

- Displays negative attitude

Common Gold Stressors

- Lack of follow through—when others don't do as they promised

- Taking on too many responsibilities

- Irresponsibility in others, untrustworthiness

- When things are not put back where they belong

- Not adhering to schedule or plans

- Lack of closure—having to switch what they are doing without completing it first

- Many things going on at the same time

- Indecision, leaving options up in the air for too long

- Change—especially frequent, unplanned, or unanticipated

- Unclear expectations; lack of rules, instructions, or guidelines

- Not knowing where they fit in, lack of membership or belonging

187

- Lack of consistency, leadership, or master plan

- Lack of cooperation—when others don't carry their own load or do their part

- Not being appreciated

- Neglect of family time or traditions

- Waste

- Incompetence—when someone who lacks the necessary skill is left responsible

- Missing deadlines, not enough time to complete tasks

- Rule breakers; rules or policies not being enforced

- Disorganization

- Tardiness—either being late themselves or others being late

- Interruptions

Not surprisingly, Golds seek to maintain a certain equilibrium of responsibility. Too much or too little can cause them stress. Their self-esteem can plummet when they are unsure of their roles or do not feel they are useful. Sometimes lack of closure on projects or even issues from the past can cause them to worry or disturb them in the present. They can become frazzled by situations where they feel they have lost control.

The following suggestions are ways for Golds to reinforce their self-esteem and lower their stress levels. If you are Gold, determine the underlying cause of your stress. Is it lack of closure on a past issue? Not feeling needed? Too many responsibilities? Keep looking beneath the surface to figure it out. Once you realize the cause of your stress, it will help you choose which areas you will want to concentrate on. Try the following suggestions that apply to your circumstances to discover which ones work best for you.

If You Are Gold

Validate Yourself—Acknowledge all the things you accomplish and all your contributions. You are respectful, responsible, and loyal. You try very hard to do a good job. Know that your efforts are appreciated even if it isn't always expressed in a way that you recognize.

Get Involved—Find a place to belong. Volunteer for a hospital, retirement community, or school. Join a service organization, support group, church, etc. Take a class on something that you enjoy and contribute to the success of the class.

Be Responsible...For Yourself—Take the time to take care of yourself.

188

You have an obligation to spend time nourishing your health and well-being. How can you possibly perform your duties if you yourself are in no condition to do so? It is of utmost importance that you explore and find avenues for self-preservation. Set aside time for yourself and place as much value and priority on it as you do on your other responsibilities. Spend this time doing things you enjoy.

Enough Is Enough—Set realistic limits. Go home when your shift ends, leave your work at work, call in sick when you are not feeling well. The house doesn't have to be "clean-clean" all of the time. Realize that you will never be absolutely 100% caught up to your own high standards. It's okay. Sometimes the best use of your time at the moment is to rest and recuperate.

Focus on What You Can Control—When things around you seem to be unraveling, notice the areas that you do have control over. One of them is your perception of the event. Pay attention to the words you are using to describe a situation. Do you label it as a disaster or an opportunity to learn something?

Start New Traditions—Are some of your traditions adding more stress than pleasure? Maybe it is time to enlist some help or modernize a tradition. Just because it's always been done a certain way does not mean it is still the best way. Embrace change and explore new ideas.

Give Yourself a Break, Delegate—Be aware of trying to drive others as hard as you drive yourself. Learn when things are good enough. If you are able to let go of having things accomplished in a certain manner, you open up all kinds of possibilities for delegation of responsibilities. This will leave you more freedom to focus on other matters. Realize that sometimes others are eager to pitch in and help.

DISHES CAN WAIT.

Bring Closure to Past Issues—
Because Golds honor tradition and ceremony, sometimes that is just what it takes to bring a past issue to completion. Eve Delunas, Ph.D. describes in her book, *Survival Games Personality Play*, some creative ways to perform a ceremony. "These ceremonies can be formal or informal; they can take place in or out of the therapist's office. They may involve writing, speaking, announcing, presenting, eating, drinking, building, creating, burning, burying, planting, cleaning, gifting, or journeying—and even flushing a toilet."

Leave Leeway—All of your time does not need to be scheduled with productive activities. When scheduling, leave some wiggle-room for unexpected events. Reframe your ideas of what is responsible to include relaxation.

Lighten Up—Enjoy the process, not just the success of completing a goal. Inform others of your needs without nagging. Although it is always a good idea to let others know what your expectations are, let go of what they "should" or "must" do.

How to Help Brighten a Gold

Some of the very same suggestions for relating to Golds from the earlier chapter are excellent ways to help them keep stress levels to a minimum. Following these tips will help ensure that you are not adding to their pressures.

Acknowledge Them for Their Contributions—Golds work hard to be responsible—above and beyond the call of duty. When they are taken for granted it can be disheartening for them. Let them know how much you

appreciate their contributions. Comment on their planning, organizing, thoroughness, efficiency, and assistance to the organization or family as a whole. Hold a recognition ceremony to acknowledge their accomplishments. Give them gifts, cards, plaques, or other awards. Although they may not admit it or request it, they enjoy tangible recognition.

Be Responsible—If you said you would do something, honor your commitment. Do what it takes to follow through in a timely manner. Be thorough and accurate. Golds are dependable, and they expect that others will be too. If you have an appointment with a Gold, be on time or even early. They interpret it as a sign of respect and responsibility when you are on time and, of course, disrespect and irresponsibility when you are late.

Be Consistent—It is very stressful to almost anyone and especially Golds when they are treated inconsistently, for example, if they are respected one day and treated negatively the next. Knowing what is supposed to happen or what is expected is a very secure feeling for them. Once a rule, norm, or procedure is established they want to be able to count on it. If a rule is not enforceable, then change it so it can be. Making exceptions all the time can

undermine the efforts of Golds who are trying to abide by the rules and do their best to see to it that others abide, too. Also, stick to the schedule. As mentioned, Golds flourish with predictability. They appreciate it when things start on time and end on time. Keep with your agenda if at all possible. Golds usually have their own time planned in a fairly tight schedule. If you don't stick to yours, it can throw theirs off tremendously.

Show Respect—Demonstrate respect for them, for authority, and for the organization by not gossiping or complaining unless you have suggestions for improvement. Clean up after yourself and put things back where they belong. When you leave messes it can be very irritating and frustrating to Golds, who just cannot leave it that way. If something is out of order, they feel compelled to make it right. If you know Golds that are fading, remember to at least not create more work and frustration for them.

Provide Clear Expectations—Golds appreciate knowing where they stand and what is expected of them. To leave them guessing is one of the most stressful things you can do to a Gold. If they do not know the rules or procedures, they will take the initiative to try and establish some for themselves. And, if they have guessed wrong and violated some unspoken

191

rule, they can be crushed. After all, they were doing the best they could under the circumstances, and now their attempt to be responsible has been stained by the feeling that they have done something "wrong." They try at all costs to be "right" and appropriate.

Conserve, Don't Waste—Golds find it very irresponsible to throw away things that feasibly can still be used, to order things in greater quantity than needed, and to consume precious time in inefficient ways. If too much time is spent doing things that could be done more efficiently if others were more conscientious, responsible, or organized, it can be draining to a Gold. Notice how things can be reasonably done differently to save time, energy, and resources.

Plan Ahead—Be especially careful not to wait until the last minute to make requests or changes with Golds who are already under a great amount of stress. This may cause them to become overbearing and rigid, even snappy or bossy. It's always a good idea to give Golds the time they require to be thorough in completing a project. This becomes even more important if they are already pushed beyond their limits.

Give Them Responsibility—Golds can feel worthless and bored without some kind of responsibility where their efforts contribute to the family, organization, or community. Many times people make the mistake

of not wanting to impose on others by asking for their assistance. They may avoid delegating tasks, especially around holidays. But responsibility can be just what a fading Gold is seeking. Golds enjoy doing their part to pitch in. With this in mind, pay attention to whether the Gold you are dealing with is faded from boredom and lack of duty or because they are overwhelmed. If it's lack of participation that is causing them to fade, invite them to participate. If they are overwhelmed, by all means give them some room to relax a little.

Honor Their Traditions—What is important to you? Golds place a high priority and value on their traditions. This can sometimes get in the way of other people's enjoyment who may want to do things differently for a change. Keep in mind that Golds find rituals and ceremonies comforting, a sort of solid foundation to stand on. Traditions help keep the past alive and are important for making transitions to the next year, season, relationship, job, or even task. If your intention is to help brighten up fading Golds, embracing their traditions or supporting them by helping to create new ones are great ways to do it.

Encourage Them—Let them know you think it is equally important to their other responsibilities for them to schedule time to take care of themselves. Find out their interests and encourage them to pursue ways to get involved.

Chapter 17
WHEN ORANGES FADE

When Oranges shine they are versatile, spontaneous, self-confident, resourceful, and decisive. Their playful manner can brighten up a mundane chore and add fun to a workday.

However, Oranges can be very intimidating when they are stressed or low on esteem. They can become exceedingly pushy, overly aggressive, and confrontational—even physically violent. Placed in an overly restrictive environment, they will go to great extremes to gain their freedom or control.

A Faded Orange

Roy is a talented carpenter. Using tools and figuring out how to build things just comes naturally for him. He could practically build a house all by himself if he wanted to. His skills range from pouring the concrete for the foundation to tiling the roof. Knowing he was talented contributed to Roy's natural cockiness. He enjoyed being the center of attention in most circumstances, and he loved to take charge.

As a subcontractor, Roy had accepted a job putting up a new housing division. He enjoyed showing off his skills to his co-workers who were not as experienced. The crew virtually adored Roy and would, almost without question, follow his lead. He was assertive and confident. He seemed to always know the quickest, most cost-effective way to get a job done. He would find ways to finish projects, even if he had to do it himself. He enjoyed the challenge. In fact, just to spice things up, Roy would cajole the men into making

bets with him about who could do something faster or better. If they were reluctant, he would harass them until they did. Of course, when he bet, he never lost, even if he had to cheat just a bit to win.

Roy also had a habit of stretching his lunch hours, horsing around, and generally not following his foreman's directions. Leo, the foreman, was tired of Roy running the show. Roy would overrule Leo's decisions and practically take over projects, telling the rest of the crew what to do.

It wasn't long before Leo started taking verbal digs at Roy, downplaying his skills and denigrating his techniques as useless or idiotic. When Roy would recommend a better way of approaching a task, Leo would overrule it and insist the crew follow his instructions. If Roy made a clever joke or funny comment, Leo would immediately scold him and remark that he would never amount to anything if he didn't get serious about his work.

One day Leo reprimanded Roy in front of the whole crew, so the next morning Roy decided to be later than "usual." Instead of taking his coffee and donuts to the work site, Roy sat in the coffee shop and enjoyed a leisurely breakfast. "Leo isn't going to tell me what to do," he thought to himself. "After all, I always complete my jobs on schedule, if not ahead of time. Who cares if I'm a little late showing up?"

By the time Roy finally showed up at the construction site, Leo was fuming . . . and Roy was pleased. He walked right past Leo with a smirk on his face and began his work.

"Good morning," Leo said. "Nice of you to finally show up."

"I thought you'd appreciate it," retorted Roy.

"This isn't funny, Roy," said Leo. "Where is your sense of responsibility?"

"My responsibility is to show up and get the job done!" taunted Roy. By now the rest of the men on the crew had paused and started to gather around in anticipation of a showdown.

"Your responsibility includes showing up on time!" Leo shouted, losing his composure.

"On time is when I @!%# get here!" retorted Roy.

"You had better start showing up on time or you're fired!" threatened Leo.

"@!%# you, old man! You can't fire me 'cause I @!%# quit!" blasted Roy. "Who cares about this @!%# job anyway! I can find a job anywhere! I don't need this @!%#!"

Roy seized a large wrench that was lying nearby and hurled it at a huge bay window, shattering it on impact. He grabbed his tools and huffed off the site and into his pickup truck. He put a tape in his tape player and turned it up full blast. "Take this job and shove it!" the lyrics blared. When the song came to an end, Roy spun his truck in several circles in the dirt, blowing up quite a cloud of dust. "@!%# you!" He yelled as he pulled away from the audience at the construction site. Of course, he made sure to wave his arm out of the window—complete with a one-finger salute.

From Shining to Fading

I'M REALLY GOING TO REGRET THIS IN ABOUT 5 MINUTES.

It's the times when Oranges act before pausing to determine the consequences that cause the most trouble for themselves and others.

For instance, they may not want to wait for the "go ahead" from a spouse or boss and may make snap decisions they later regret. Add the criticism of others on top of this ill thought-out decision, and you are sitting on a powder keg.

Oranges are made to be on the go. If they are required to remain stagnant for long periods, they can get very restless. Their urge for immediate gratification and action can get them into trouble if they are not careful. To try and circumvent the drain that boredom, lack of money, time constraints, or other restrictions can cause, some Oranges may turn to stimulants such as caffeine, nicotine, or other drugs to help them regain their energy or spark. They may defiantly break rules, challenge others, and even stir up trouble just for entertainment.

Characteristics of a Faded Orange

- Acts rude and with defiance

- Breaks rules on purpose

- Fails to complete things, runs away, quits job

- May joke or tease inappropriately

- Overly competitive, manipulative

- Lying and cheating behavior

- Violent behavior

Common Orange Stressors

- Lack of freedom or choices, feeling trapped

- Being forced to do something another person's way

- Not being able to use their skills

- Rigidness

- Strict guidelines or rules

- Forced to keep quiet or not participate

- Insufficient attention

- No sense of humor

- Waiting, slow actions

- Indecisiveness

- Traffic or car problems

- Routine

- Lack of sex

- Details, paperwork

- Inactivity, restriction of physical movement

- Lack of money

In the previous story, Roy was provoked quite a bit by his foreman, Leo. He denied Roy his own style and stifled him when he tried to use his skills. He belittled him for being playful and minimized his talents as inadequate. This would probably be a tough situation for anyone to handle. However, the way in which Roy reacted was not very resourceful—coming to work late on purpose, swearing at his foreman, and throwing things. There are better ways to channel your energy.

When their self-esteem is low, Oranges will use their powerfulness to instill fear in others. It may be a fear that Oranges will lose their temper, neglect their responsibilities, otherwise embarrass, or even leave the person, job, or situation. If you are Orange, use these tips to help you get along with others and keep your Orangeness an asset, not a liability. Stop and think about the information before making a judgment about whether it will work for you or not. Just because you might not notice the effect of your behavior on others or may label your actions differently, doesn't mean they don't exist.

If You Are Orange

Your quick thinking and demand for action can get you ahead of yourself. Since you usually enjoy operating in a rush of adrenaline, you might have a tendency to arrange your life so you are constantly on the edge and perhaps putting others on edge as well. What you may find fun and exhilarating, others may perceive as stressful. In fact, the people in your life that are depending on you may not find your behavior very fun at all. So how do you get your own needs for freedom, spontaneity, and attention met without trampling others in the process? The following are some suggestions:

Go Have Some Fun!—Instead of trying to get a majority of your needs for fun and games met at work, where it could be detrimental to your employment status or even the health and safety of yourself and others, find other avenues. What do you like to do for fun? Get out. Go motorcycle riding, to amusement parks, concerts, or camping. Joke around, sing, play in the rain, splash in the mud. It is important to your overall well-being to include play in your life. Do it safely and legitimately.

Get Hands-On—Use your love of tools to create. Build something—if not a house then a sand castle. If you want to develop your skills, take a class on auto repair, sculpting, landscaping, glass blowing . . .what are you interested in? Choose something and go for it!

Move That Body!—Get some physical activity. Exercise: pump iron, jump rope, climb trees. When stressed, go for a walk, jog, or run to cool off—but do come back when your thinking clears. Get out and dance, roller skate, bike ride, something that will get you in action—now!

Find Other Oranges—It can be very stressful to have to guard every word and action in order not to upset those around you. Having other Oranges who will not take your complaining as insults and can hear your words through your colorful language is like being able to breathe fresh air.

Focus—Concentrate on one thing and complete it before starting something else. Reduce distractions by turning off your phone or putting away projects that are not a priority at the moment.

Prioritize—Decide what is most important and what has to be addressed. Complete the most important project before moving on to the next one.

Make an Impression—You can be in the spotlight in a variety of ways. Choose inspiring, motivating ways. At work, be the best you can be. Let your actions speak for themselves. It is much more impressive than getting attention for breaking the rules. Capture the interest of others by sharing your triumphs at appropriate times. Display your trophies and be proud of your accomplishments. At play, practice your skills, pour yourself into your endeavors.

Reward Yourself—Be aware of any tendency to set high goals in the moment, then get overwhelmed and disappointed in the next. Remember

to notice the things that you do accomplish. Pay attention to achievements along the way to the big one. Set up a system of immediate reward. For instance, if you are trying to quit smoking, instead of feeling like a failure for slipping and smoking one cigarette, reward yourself for all the ones you did not smoke.

Compete—Get involved in competitions and games. Take charge of arranging events if that's what it takes. Join a sports team, create a contest at work, challenge your neighbors to a cook-off. Find ways to compete that won't jeopardize your job, health, or budget.

WELL? WHATAYA THINK?

Start Your Own Business—If you are tired of conforming to the rules and procedures of others, why not be your own boss? It is important to either find ways to love what you are doing or do something else. If you are wise enough to research your options and plan ahead in your investments of time, money, and resources, owning your own business can meet several of your needs all at once.

Keep Healthy Habits—Notice when you may be slipping into unhealthy, compulsive behaviors:

- Lacking sleep because of too much partying or "extracurricular" activities

- Using drugs

- Drinking too much

- Smoking

- Gambling or taking financial risks

- Overeating

- Taking physical risks (i.e., driving over the speed limit)

- Overindulging in sex

Take inventory, then take action! Figure out what is most important to you and what is or isn't working in your life. Join a group or elicit the help of others for suggestions as to how they may have overcome unhealthy habits. Grab hold of your life with the same enthusiasm that you grab hold of the moment.

How to Help Brighten an Orange

Oranges are generally optimistic and enthusiastic. If you are flexible and want to encourage them, little effort will be required to enhance their self-esteem. You can add a bit of excitement to your life by allowing an Orange to entertain or provide ways to create a contest or game. They love to perform and volunteer readily for leadership roles that involve taking risks. When you understand their temperament, core needs, and values, you can provide them with an environment that allows and encourages them to express themselves. Not only will you engender their respect and appreciation, you will ensure their future cooperation and support. They will comply with home and work rules when you allow them "time-outs" or private counseling instead of a public showdown.

The following are suggestions for preventing Oranges from fading or burning out. These suggestions can also help Oranges that have faded to brighten up. Some of them may fit with your values and rules of operation; others may not. The fact is, they do work. Only you can decide if they are right for you and the various relationships in your life. There is a big difference between encouraging Oranges to shine versus allowing them to bulldoze over your needs. It may take a bit of fine-tuning to incorporate these changes into your relationships.

Understand Their Need to Multitask—Understand their need for variety and for accomplishing more than one thing at a time. One of the biggest complaints about Oranges' behavior is that they do not pay attention or make good eye contact. Quit expecting them to. They really are able to work on other things while talking to you. Waiting to get their full attention seldom does much good. They may indulge you by looking at you but their mind will be elsewhere.

Allow Them Freedom and Choices—Oranges want options, including doing nothing if they choose. Just knowing they can opt out of a situation or have other choices can give them a sense of comfort and lower stress levels. Do not impose unnecessary duties, schedules, or rules just for your sense of control or comfort. They will inevitably find ways to get around

them anyway. Give them opportunities to offer solutions based on their experiences. Respect their relaxed ways. Leave room for spontaneity. Share your sense of humor.

Grant Them Attention—Let them show off their skills. Recognize the impact of their presence. Validate their talents. You can stimulate Oranges to greater achievement by providing tangible incentives for jobs well done; rewarding their cleverness, creativity, and ingenuity; and praising their ability to accomplish things.

Be Consistent, Not a Bully—Oranges often rebel against discipline and will resist an order if given too rigidly, without any leeway for creativity or flair. It threatens their self-esteem and puts them down. Be firm and direct with them, but not challenging or threatening. Formulate ground rules for behavior with their input "up front." Enforce the rules consistently. Discuss options. That way, before they take any liberties, you give them permission to do what they love doing.

Make It a Game—Appeal to their sense of adventure by making a bet, dare, or contest. If it feels like a "have-to" it is not fun. Do the unexpected. Tell them they can't do something. For example, "I'll bet there's no way you can have this done by

Monday—only an expert could do that. It's just too much." Chances are they'll prove you wrong. Create a competition and make the payoff—if they lose—go to the one they have been trying to manipulate.

Supply Immediate Feedback—
Give them recognition and straightforward critiques. Let them know immediately when they violate a rule. If you let it slide, most likely it will happen repeatedly. Equally, give them instant acknowledgment for a job well done. Note their quickness of action, their flair and skillfulness.

Get Out of Their Way—Oranges are concrete problem solvers who need hands-on activities. The thought of sitting for hours doing one thing seems like a slow death-sentence to them. Give them the freedom to demonstrate their ideas verbally and physically. So many people unknowingly stifle the flair and productivity of Oranges by bogging them down with rituals, routines, and personal rules. Although this is not the way to inspire them, Oranges do like to be efficient. You may be surprised at the proficiency they can achieve. If they are given the freedom to develop their talents, they may feel more compelled to pay attention to the ground rules.

This is because they can focus their attention of doing a good job rather than the perceived restrictions placed on them.

Appreciate Their Directness—
Allow them to be open and expressive. Of course, this does not mean that it is okay for them to swear at a board meeting or do similarly inappropriate things. What it does mean is to give the benefit of the doubt. Remember that most Oranges have an agenda and are looking for the shortest route to reach their goals. They may not take the time to say "good morning," "please," and "thank you" —they will sometimes leave these words and rapport-building rituals out of their vocabulary because they are looking straight at their target and aiming to get there quickly.

Some people may think they are doing Oranges a favor by trying to "train" them to pause and say "hello" before allowing them to continue with their agenda. Although this may work when trying to train children, if you have not had much success or are aggravating the situation, skip it. Oranges find it condescending and controlling. Respect is relative anyway. Watch two Oranges interact. Notice if either one is insulted by the other's bluntness. Usually, it is a relief to them to be able to cut to the chase.

Be Confident—Speak and move with confidence. If you are too wishy-washy, some Oranges get an irresistible urge to walk all over you. However, be careful to recognize the difference between assertiveness and aggressiveness. The latter can trigger a fight with an out-of-esteem Orange. Be direct and clear on what you expect.

Move with Them—Oranges find predictable routine tedious and boring. Frequent change of pace and variety will help eliminate much of their stress. Don't make them sit still while they talk with you. Be willing to walk from room to room or conduct business while playing a sport.

Chapter 18
WHEN
GREENS
FADE

IM SURROUNDED BY MORONS.

When Greens are in esteem, they are some of the most exciting people to be around. Their passion for improvement and visionary ideas can be awe-inspiring!

Their tenacity for creating solutions and their expansive knowledge base are a magical combination for seeing concepts brought to fruition and introduced to the world. They

204

have natural abilities for decision-making, being objective, and weighing the data to be considered. They are envied by those that wish they were able to stand their ground and express their point of view with conviction and confidence. Greens' love of their work and high expectations are admired by those stuck in jobs they hate. Although they may not be very involved socially in the mainstream, they are pleasant to be around. If you earn their trust, you can experience their deep, caring feelings and lasting friendship.

However, when Greens are experiencing low self-esteem, their patience is thinner than ever and things that may have only irritated them previously become unbearable. Like Dr. Jekyll and Mr. Hyde, Greens can shift from an otherwise intelligent, rational person to someone who is critical, uncompromising, condescending, and harsh. Their typical wit and amusing sarcasm can become intentionally caustic ridicule. Their composure may switch from their usually objective demeanor to judgmental, demanding, and controlling. Or, they can become withdrawn, ritualistic and detached—not interacting with others, refusing to take part.

A Faded Green

Jack slouched in his chair with his legs extended straight out in front of him. His arms were crossed in front of his chest. Instead of sharing in the smiles and laughter of the other audience members, he sat in obvious defiance with a deadpan look of boredom and irritation on his face.

This was the last workshop of the two-day staff retreat. Not being given any other choice, he had already attended the required workshops on team building, collaborative change, and appreciating diversity. His mind was stagnant and bored. His comments had been met with impatience, and his questions with exasperation. How else was he supposed to keep his mind from going comatose if he couldn't give or get any decent input? He was almost trembling inside at the thought of having to sit through this last workshop.

The facilitator was one of those smiling "rah-rah cheerleader" types. She had started an interactive exercise activity. It was a version of the old "telephone" game. Several people were given a cartoon illustration to view. After looking at the picture, they would tell the person next to them what they saw, that person would tell the next one, and so on down the line until the last person in the row was told the story. When all groups were finished, the last person in each row stood up to tell what their story turned out to be. The participants were bursting with laughter as they listened to story after story.

Rolling his eyes, Jack let out a deliberately loud groan. "What the heck do these people find so amusing?" he thought to himself. "This is such a waste of time and brain cells. This is stupid."

Suddenly Jack stood up and stormed his way to the front of the room, abruptly snatching the microphone from the instructor's hand. "EXCUSE ME, PEOPLE!" he yelled aggressively, scowling first at the instructor, then at the audience. "We all learned this in the second grade," he barked. "I know I did! Can we just get to the point? You guys are all acting like a bunch of idiots! Why do we have to endure these touchy-feely games to make a point? 'A message can get misconstrued if you do not get it straight from the source. Check your facts to make sure they are accurate.' There, that is the point. Now can we get on to some information that we don't already know?"

From Shining to Fading

Not all Greens lash out when their fuse runs short. Some won't speak at all and will withdraw their cooperation, input, support, or even their love. They've been known to cut off a relationship or friendship and not look back. Others refuse to make decisions or may get overly obsessed with unrealistic expectations—pressuring others through intellectual arguments, requiring things be absolutely accurate, correct, and perfect. Or, quite the opposite, some Greens drop their standards, fail to implement ideas, become apathetic, and retreat into their "cave" (as John Gray puts it).

Characteristics of a Faded Green

- Behaves indecisively
- Refuses to comply or cooperate
- Withdrawal, aloofness
- Put-downs and sarcastic remarks
- Refuses to communicate, the silent treatment
- Perfection tied to performance anxiety
- Highly critical towards self and others

Common Green Stressors

- Blocks imposed on their ability to display intelligence
- Overly sensitive people
- No flexibility
- Being limited to standard curriculum
- People who don't try to solve their own problems
- When they don't understand or know something
- Equipment failure

206

- Incompetence
- Not enough time to gather data
- Unfairness
- Boredom
- Lack of independence
- Rules that block progress
- Stupidity
- Redundancy
- Routine
- Nothing new to look forward to
- Emotional outbursts
- Mistakes
- Ignored recommendations
- No system in place or failure of others to use system
- Made to look stupid or incompetent

From the preceding story and list you probably can understand what triggered Jack's response. He had no choice but to sit through workshops that he was not interested in. His questions and comments were met with irritation instead of attention, and he did not enjoy the invasive nature of the "touchy-feely" activities. However, had his self-esteem been strong in the first place he would have figured out a way to be more resourceful. He could have made up

his mind to support those around him in their growth.

If You Are Green

If you are Green and feel yourself fading, it is time to shift your focus outward. You are a big-picture thinker in many areas, so use this ability and apply it to your personal situations. What you focus on is what becomes real for you, so relocate your focus to more empowering thoughts and ideas. What possibilities are you not noticing? Expand your thinking to include empathy for others and their journey in life.

Balance Your Critiques—Refrain from "punishing" or getting irritated at others for not living up to your expectations and high standards. For each drawback or mistake you notice, find a positive point. Pay attention to how much control you really have over a given situation. If you are stuck in a situation where you have to sit through a boring lecture, discover what you can learn or find ways to support others. Take action to change the things that you can and recognize the things that you simply cannot so you can channel your energy into other pursuits that are higher on your priority list.

Honor Your Independence—You are not anti-social, a misfit, or unfriendly just because you prefer

207

independent activities. Don't force yourself to get involved with activities you are not interested in just because of social pressures. If you are involved in activities to stretch your comfort zones and are growing from the experience, that is one thing. But if you find that you are feeling less alive and fulfilled, lacking somehow, because you are not enjoying it, shift your attention to the things you do like. You have the unique ability and nature to be content and enjoy solo activities. Enjoy them!

Validate Your Interests—Visit a library; buy a computer and hook up to the web; visit universities, museums, and research centers; take classes. Feed your hunger for knowledge. Many Greens mention that people have called them "weird" because of the topics of conversations and endeavors they choose to involve themselves in. There are plenty of others with similar interests. It's just a matter of finding them.

Pay Attention to Your Physical Condition—If your health goes down the tubes because you are not taking a break to exercise and eat right, how do you expect to have your full capabilities to work at your potential? Design a strategy for maintaining your health. Investigate programs and create one that fits your particular needs. For fun, chart your progress.

Smile—Interacting with others in a friendly manner can open up worlds. If you are not used to smiling and relating with others on a "personal" level, try an experiment. Make it a point to notice others, not just the people that you know and like. Smile at them as you pass them. (Seriously, a simple smile can change the way that others perceive and relate to you.) Shift your focus outward in the presence of others. Notice the effect that it has.

Prioritize—Learn to discern the difference between things that really do need to be perfect and those that just need to be done. Spend your energies perfecting the important ones. Weigh the investment versus the payoff. Is it more useful to you to have someone behave according to your standards and be unhappy or to have someone be happy at the sacrifice of perfection?

Invite Yourself to Make Mistakes—It is a required criterion for success to be able to adjust and make refinements. Think about what you feel that you cannot do and give yourself permission to try. Allow for results that are less than perfect the first time out. Challenge yourself to see how well you can do an average job on something. If you do an average job, you win! If you end up doing a better than average job, you still win.

Recognize You Can Only Change Yourself—You can definitely have an influence on others. Though you may be able to help them change, they must be the ones to make the change. Realize that people are responsible for their own behaviors and attitudes.

Reach Out to Others—It may be a habit of yours to try to solve your problems all by yourself. Although this is resourceful in many situations, there are times when it is beneficial to seek answers with the help of others. Who can you confide in or turn to for personal, not just work-related, assistance?

help.

Read—Pick up a copy of *A Guide for Rational Living* (1997), by psychotherapists Albert Ellis, Ph.D. and Robert A. Harper, Ph.D. It offers a revolutionary approach that "can teach any intelligent person how to stop feeling miserable about practically anything." This book contains no-nonsense methods, backed by hundreds of research studies, for changing self-defeating behaviors. It set new standards in the field of psychology, providing answers to help people deal with their lives more effectively.

How to Help Brighten a Green

Most Greens want understanding and their own space, not a whole lot of emotional attention and doting. Usually most Greens will not confide in anyone when they are having difficulties. If they do, it would be only a choice individual or two. If Greens confide in you, they are usually to the point of seeking solutions or suggestions, otherwise they would not bother to mention their problems at all. To cope with challenges Greens have a tendency to isolate themselves or bury themselves in their work. They may even turn to mind-altering alternatives, such as drugs or hypnosis; fringe organizations; or the metaphysical realm, to find solutions to whatever it is that is bothering them. But if you pay attention, you can tell when they are fading. Sometimes there is little you can do besides understand and not take things personally.

The following are ways that you can support Greens in their brightening process. If you follow these suggestions on a regular basis in relating to the Greens in your life, it can help prevent them from fading.

Provide information when they request it instead of getting defensive because they ask—Greens aim to be accurate and competent in their endeavors, so before they decide on a direction for action they like to have all the data. Don't dismiss their questions or scold their requests for proof. Just remember: "inquiring minds want to know."

Recognize the value and usefulness of their work—Accept their futuristic, idealistic nature and quest for perfect performance. Provide opportunities for them to choose tasks that are difficult and challenging. Although Greens like acknowledgment for their ideas, creativity, and competence, they will not seek it out as readily as others. Let them know their contributions are important and their work appreciated. Don't go overboard with the emotional displays and stick to the specifics of why you find their work so valuable.

Understand their emotions are deep—And that's where they like them—kept down deep, not on their sleeve. Quit expecting the Greens in your life to display extremes of emotion. They may not want to say "I love you," or show a lot of affection. For many Greens it is just not in their nature. Greens are a lot like cats. Some cats love to give and receive affection; others will run away if you approach them. Some come to you at their own pace. And, some breeds won't accept or show affection altogether, no matter how hard you try. Greens have their own way of showing ardor. Usually, it does not include public displays like holding hands and kissing in front of an audience. However, there are numerous variations. Some Greens show plenty of affection—when they want to—and they like it when you do, too. The key is knowing the difference between your needs and desires and theirs. If both parties respect the wishes of the other then they can get along without compromising their own needs.

Notice when they are being affectionate or complimentary—Greens can have covert or subtle ways of showing affection or giving a commendation. It may appear in the form of a joke or even a nod of the head accompanied by a smile. Sometimes they are disappointed when people miss their intended recognition, yet they usually will not turn up the volume to make it more obvious. Instead they will just let it drop. Pay attention to their unique style of demonstrating approval or affection. You may be surprised to discover what you've been missing has been there all along. You just didn't recognize it.

Honor their privacy—When they are reluctant to share personal anecdotes, don't pry. They will share when you have earned their trust. If they don't eventually open up, that's okay too. Many times they prefer to talk about ideas and events, rather than relationship or personal issues. It is the same way with pet owners. They have the most fun sharing stories and challenges with others that also own pets. Seldom is someone who does not like or own pets very

interested in the subject. If you enjoy discussing personal issues, find someone else who does too, and give the Green a break.

Allow them independence—Greens have the ability to be content with solo activities. Just because you may need to be surrounded by people does not mean that they do. Don't label them as antisocial or pressure them to get involved in activities that simply are not of interest to them. Yes, it is beneficial to experience a variety of things, but just because you enjoy an activity does not mean they will. Greens like to feel included but not coerced.

Demonstrate logic for rules—Their need to understand the reasoning behind rules and procedures, and their reluctance to obey them blindly, comes from the fact that they are usually thinking of a better way of doing things. Make sure you have a valid explanation of why things need to be done a certain way. Be open to listening to their ideas for improvement. Perhaps it is time for a change in the rules.

Consider their ideas—Sometimes people are so intimidated by Greens' imaginative concepts or style of explanation that they may avoid listening to their ideas. Hear them out. Ask them for data or to research something. Give them a creative project. Open your mind to new options and ways of looking at things. Allow them the freedom to get a little wild with their ideas.

Understand their sense of humor—Greens' minds can detect comedy in most any situation. Their wit seems to be never-ending. If their sarcasm is a bit too much for your taste, simply let them know without placing a lot of judgment and drama around it. If they get a rise from you, they are likely to do it again just to get your goat. Be aware that most Greens are not trying to harm others by their cynicism, they are simply pointing out the incongruity of life—which they find amusing. Don't take their humor personally.

Realize that love of their work does not mean they love you less—Don't try to force them to make you their priority. Learn to live in conjunction with their fervor for their work. Allow them opportunities to increase their knowledge and demonstrate their competence. How many ways can you find to be interested in their work?

Pay attention to what they need and want—Your idea of showing how much you love them might be to give them a hug or cards and candy. They may want you to show your love for them in a different

way. Be open to their needs and desires.

Calling All Colors

You may have noticed that there were several suggestions throughout the chapters that were applicable to all the color styles. When anyone fades, no matter their color spectrum, there are things to pay attention to. Are you getting enough sleep? How is your activity level and the quality of your food intake? The following are general tips for everyone:

Get Quality Sleep—Going to bed at the same time and waking up at the same time on a regular basis helps to prepare the body for sleep. Other preparations include a sleep routine. For instance, if you always take a hot bath, put on a pair of pajamas, then brush your teeth to get ready for bedtime, your body will get the signal that it is time for sleep. Stay away from watching late night programs on TV that will keep your brain awake thinking, concerned, or scared. Pay attention to your caffeine consumption. Drinking coffee or soft drinks into the afternoon can interfere with your sleep at night. So can drinking alcohol. One might think that a nightcap before bed would help with a sound night's sleep. Although you may feel drowsy, the quality of sleep after consuming alcohol is much poorer than if you don't consume it.

Exercise—Physical activity is one proven way to actually clear stress hormones from the body. During times of stress our body depends on a "fight or flight" mechanism, which gears the body up to either fight or run away. Many times, instead of running or fighting off the stress, the best we can do is to honk the horn. It is important to get exercise that moves the larger muscles of the body and gets the heart rate up. It is common for individuals to think that being busy throughout the day is enough. It isn't. Take a walk, swim, bicycle, join a fitness club—find a way to fit regular exercise into your day.

Eat Wisely—Skipping meals can make your blood sugar plummet. Without enough oxygen getting to the brain, how can anyone function at full capacity? Make sure you eat regular meals that are high in nutritional content. On the other hand, overeating can make you feel lousy too. Eat foods that make you feel good long term, not just for the moment. Consuming too much sugar, processed and "junk" foods might perk you up momentarily but can zap your energy in the long run.

Plan Reentries—When you are feeling drained, it can help to take a quick shower or do some grooming like brushing your hair, washing your face, changing your clothes, putting on a big hat, or at least a big smile!

Beyond True Colors

By using the True Colors concepts there is much you can contribute to solving conflicts, opening lines of communication, and understanding the actions of others. However, some things are definitely outside your area of influence. On occasion, you may run across someone with mental illness, on heavy medications, abusing drugs, or who has serious psychological issues. Although following these guidelines is useful, it is not enough to overcome the influences of these circumstances. When a person's emotional well-being or self-esteem is extremely low, they may need to seek professional help. Use your common sense to know the difference between things over which you have some influence and those over which you do not.

Because this book is meant as a guideline, not an in-depth study of the color styles, it is not a substitute for personal counseling. Remember to take advantage of other resources also available to you. If you or the people in your life are under a significant amount of stress or suffering from extremely low self-esteem or depression, check out the variety of books,* tapes, classes, and self-help groups in your community.

*A terrific book I used to help guide me in writing some of the tips for this section is Survival Games Personalities Play by Eve Delunas, Ph.D., Sunink Publications (1992). It is a fascinating book that includes case studies describing the games associated with each of the four personality styles.

213

Chapter 19

BALANCING YOUR COLORS

TURNING UP THE INTENSITY

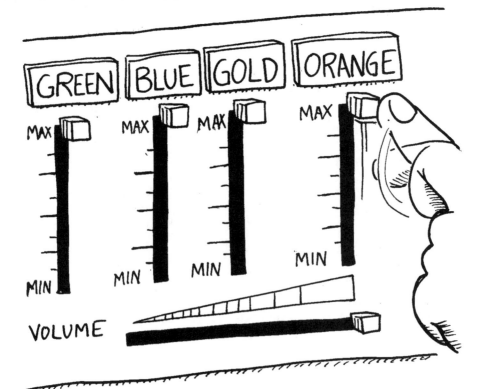

How to Increase Your Least Bright Colors

Reading about the different color styles has given us a deeper understanding of the motivations behind behaviors. And, we know that every color style and combination has something of benefit to offer.

Some individuals recognize the benefits so much that they favor the characteristics of another color style over their own.

Jake, an Orange-Green, shared with me that he wishes the other colors in his spectrum were brighter. "I am constantly stressed, I seem to just always operate that way. I am so driven that I can't *not* be productive. I wish I wasn't bugged by the tiniest imperfection, or feel I have to constantly achieve. My Blue-Gold friends don't seem to have those problems. They seem to have their lives together and are so content. They are satisfied with their secure 9-5 jobs and love raising their families. Sometimes I feel like they can't relate to me and vice versa."

Jake is not alone. There are Blues that wish they could maintain their emotions and composure in more situations; Golds that wish they didn't always feel compelled to complete work before feeling comfortable enough to play; Greens that wish their intentions of making another person feel special wouldn't get sidelined because a fascinating project captured their attention instead; and Oranges who wish they could stay more focused and operate within guidelines, without the irresistible urge to seize the opportunity of the moment, or use a shortcut.

Admiring the traits of others is healthy as long as you aren't feeling that it is wrong or bad to be who you are. As we grow and experience different aspects of life, we are constantly evolving. It is of great benefit to be able to operate in a variety of modes by strengthening or *"brightening up"* our other colors. The great thing is—it isn't necessary to wait for a life experience to push you to your next level of development. You can start practicing now to enhance the characteristics you desire.

For a simplistic example, let's say that Jake is right-handed or right-hand dominant and wants to get better at writing with his left hand (a less dominant trait). He doesn't have to wait until he breaks his right arm and is forced to write with his left to start practicing. If he begins writing with his left hand now, and continues to do so on a regular basis, he can become really good at it.

He will remain right-hand dominant, *but now he'll also be good at writing with his left hand too!*

On the other hand (pun intended), some of us may be so proud of our strengths and gifts that we may not take the time to consider what we are missing out on by not developing the other colors in our spectrum.

Zeke's dominant color style happens to be Orange-Green also. "I love my color style, the other colors suck! I am glad I am not ruled by my emotions or stuck in a rut."

Although it is fun to be validated for being the unique individuals that we are, remember that our strengths magnified can become liabilities. Desiring structure is admirable. Becoming extremely demanding and rigid is not. Flexible is fine, flaky is frustrating.

It is the individual contributions of each different color style that make up the combination needed to get projects finished, keep organizations operating, and societies functioning. Since we are all evolving and our potential is limitless, we are all able to brighten the other colors in our spectrum.

Ideally, this brightening process starts with embracing and appreciating our own primary color style then progresses to brightening our other colors. It is in being able to access an assortment of modes that gives us the greatest flexibility and thus the most personal power in situations. Personal evolution thus becomes a choice within one's control, rather than some random occurrence influenced by the circumstances we find ourselves in.

Take a look at the various suggestions for brightening up the different color traits. Pay particular attention to the ones that are currently the least bright for you. What ways can you brighten each of the colors in your unique spectrum?

Increasing the Blue

If Blue is not one of your most dominant colors, these suggestions might appear a bit strange or uncomfortable to you at first. You don't have to try them all. Choose ones you think will assist you in opening up areas that you feel are not yet developed. This is not to say that we must change. Many of us expand our comfort zones and acquire new skills naturally over time. These tips are offered only to those interested in speeding up the process of intensifying their less bright colors.

Seek Harmony—Be nice. Before speaking, put yourself into the other person's position. Notice how they might feel receiving your message (not how you might feel, but how they might feel). Use softeners when making requests or giving directions. Use words such as "excuse me," "please," and "thank you." While you might not care much about certain rituals, others often do. Think of a very nice person you know, someone that seems to get along with everyone. Ask yourself, "What would they do in this situation?"

Listen—Experience what it feels like to give your undivided attention. Make as much eye contact with others as they are comfortable with. Pay attention to the feelings behind the words. Allow them to finish their sentences without filling in words or thoughts for them. Let go of trying to "fix" the problem, and just listen.

Take Care—Notice the needs of others. What could you do to assist them? It could be as simple as offering to take their coat.

Practice Positivity—Focus on what is good or beneficial about a situation or person. For each negative thought or comment you come up with, counter it with three positive points. For example, if you think someone is a jerk, three positive counter-thoughts could be "How can I help this person? What can I learn from this situation? What is good about this right now?"

Foster Feelings—Cry, laugh out loud, express a range of emotions. Use the following list to "try on" an emotion a day. Distinguish between a whole range of emotions—just to

experience what it feels like. It will also polish up your positivity. Discover how many ways you can express your "emotion of the day." Notice any physical cues in your body that will help you distinguish your feelings. Pay attention to the subtle differences between similar emotions, as well as the drastic differences between the dissimilar ones. See if you can actually get in touch with the emotion, although "fake it till you make it" is fun too.

"Try on" These Emotions and Feelings—

affectionate

amazed

compelled

curious

delighted

elated

enthusiastic

excited

exhilarated

fabulous

glad

gracious

groovy

hilarious

intrigued

invigorated

invincible

joyful

lucky

marvelous

motivated

pleased

refreshed

relaxed

sensational

stunning

thrilled

tickled

vivacious

Of course you can always choose to express a plethora of negative emotions too. However, these usually come quite easily to many of us and therefore it's not typically necessary to practice them. Practicing negative emotions can be uncomfortable or in some circumstances even dangerous, and those who choose to might want to do so in the company of a good friend or under the supervision of a mental health professional.

Rev Up the Romance—Say "I love you" out loud. Write a love note. Buy a gift or do something for someone that isn't necessarily practical, logical, or responsible. Instead, give them something that fits their taste, such as flowers, candy, or even a stuffed toy. Set the atmosphere by playing soft music, lighting candles, and preparing a special meal. Stop and think. What unique gesture would show them that they are special?

Touch—Give or accept a hug. Read the book, *Vitamin T Is for Touch* by Bob Czimbal and Maggie Zadikov (Open Book Publishing, Portland, Oregon). It is a terrific guide to enjoying and increasing the amount of appropriate touch in your life.

Acknowledge—Pay attention to others and cultivate the habit of expressing the positive things you notice or validating people for just being human. Everyone has intrinsic value, whether you can recognize it or not. "Nice job!" "Great haircut!" "Thank you!" are all wonderful ways of expressing acknowledgment. Sometimes we think other people know how much we appreciate them and so we don't verbalize or other-wise demonstrate it. Another way to show appreciation is to write notes or thank you cards, or buy small gifts.

Get Esoteric—Just for fun, get your palm read. Visit an acupuncturist, join a yoga class. Learn how to use cre-ative visualization and enhance your intuition.

Join a Cause—Volunteer to assist a human betterment movement such as passing out gifts to the needy at Christmas, volunteering your time at a local hospital, or visiting a senior liv-ing center.

Seek Self-Expression and Exploration—Write in a journal, sing, dance, write some poetry. Have discussions about the meaning of life. Read self-help books such as Tony Robbins' *Awaken the Giant Within* (Simon & Schuster, New York).

Stir Up the Spirituality —Get out in nature. Learn to meditate. Pray.

Attend a religious service. Visit a retreat center. What will it take to release your spirit and connect with the universe?

Refresh Relationships —Make a phone call, write a letter, get in touch with friends and family. Join a team. Keep in mind that how you work together as a group is as important as what you accomplish.

Increasing the Gold

If Gold characteristics are not very dominant in your temperament, the following are some ideas to brighten up your Gold. Enhancing your Gold can increase your profes-sionalism as well as lower your stress by helping you improve in the areas of time management and organiza-tional skills.

Respect Time Lines—Be on time for meetings and appointments. Plan to be there early to give yourself enough leeway to at least make it on time. If you are not comfortable leav-ing a lot of latitude because you get bored easily with the extra time, bring a book or other project to work on in case you end up waiting. Usually, though, you'll find the extra time is a welcome gift. It helps calm nerves and allows space for extra prepara-tions that you may not have had time to address in the past.

Follow the agenda in meetings as much as possible. Jot down ideas that pop into your head if it is not the proper time to share them at the moment. Usually, ideas presented at the proper time in the agenda are given more precedence than those that are announced out of turn. When people are able to stick to an agenda, usually much more progress is made. Just for fun, practice watching the clock or being timekeeper for a meeting.

Plan Ahead—Think of what you will need to take care of before an event arrives. Don't wait until the last minute. Instead, mentally rehearse what will be occurring and notice what you will need to do to prepare.

For instance, if you are heading on a trip, think of the days you will be gone and what leads up to your departure. Pay attention to the preparations required and make a list. Use the list as a guideline and reminder of what needs to be accomplished. Prioritize your list so the important and time-dependent items get completed first. Add to the list as new ideas come up. Keep track of your list and keep it handy. As you complete each item check it off the list. Create a budget and stick to it. Knowing how much money you have to spend ahead of time reduces the stress of trying to figure it all out later.

Stick to Decisions, Plans, and Commitments—After making an arrangement or choosing an option, stay with it and follow through. Do the research ahead of time so you aren't compelled to change your mind after the data comes in. Go the extra mile to ensure you can stick to your word. Honor the plans of others and experience what it is like to have some structure and predictability. It's fun to be able to count on decisions.

Rediscover Tradition—Investigate your family tree or look into other traditions and customs. Discover the heritage of your organization or community. Read up on a little history. Discover the pleasure of partici-

MAX

Max—
Back in
a week

pating in a traditional meal or custom. Revitalize old traditions or establish some new ones for your family and repeat them year after year. It gives family members something to look forward to.

Multiply Your Manners—Pick up a book on etiquette and read the sections that apply to your life and circumstances. Notice what other highly respected individuals say and how they behave in situations. Interview others to find out if you have any habits that you are not aware of. You may be surprised to find that you have a few slang words in your vocabulary or habits such as nail biting, fidgeting, or playing with your hair that might come across as unprofessional. Perhaps the way that you dress or your grooming could use a

few adjustments. Start by asking family members and close friends, then move on to co-workers. Reassure them that you will benefit from their feedback and won't take comments and suggestions personally. Tell them how much you appreciate their contributions to improving your decorum.

Prioritize Your Time—If your time management skills are not meeting your needs, attend a class on how to use a daily planner system. Just purchasing a planner does little good unless you know how to use it properly and then do so. Planning can cut down on wasted time and open up opportunities for you to accomplish more of what you really want to be doing. Classes on project management are also useful.

Think before You Speak, Act, or Interrupt—Pause before responding and think to yourself momentarily, "Would this be appropriate? Is this politically correct?"

My mother has a saying: "When in doubt, leave it out." She taught me to think of this phrase whenever I wasn't sure if something was proper or not. For instance, if I were contemplating wearing blue jeans to an event and was wondering if it would be too casual and perhaps disrespectful, I would think of this phrase and opt to wear something a bit more dressy. If I were thinking of pointing out the pitfalls of someone's idea that they were

221

very enthusiastic about, I would pause and think "when in doubt, leave it out." I would readjust my thinking and focus on the positive point of the idea first.

If you are contemplating "speaking your piece" and it really will not contribute anything but hurt feelings, anger, or ego, leave it out. If what you have to say will forward the action on a matter, by all means go for it!

Check Procedures—Be aware of any tendencies you may have to take shortcuts—circumventing lines of authority can threaten your credibility as well as your livelihood. It can also end up jeopardizing your safety and the safety of others. Although you may have the agility to get yourself out of a tight spot, others may not. Get informed. Find out what the rules are in the variety of circumstances you find yourself. How many times have you repeatedly driven down the same street and wondered what the speed limit was or some other traffic question? If you are on the other side of the street going the opposite direction and a yellow school bus has its flashing red lights on, are you required to stop? If

you live in California the answer is yes! Pay attention when the laws change; get a booklet from the Department of Motor Vehicles— they're free and could save you lots of time, money, and emotional turmoil.

What are the regulations in your neighborhood? Is it lawful to play your stereo loudly at 7:00 a.m.? How about at work? Do you know where your policies and procedures manual is? Do you know the safety guidelines?

Do you ever read instructions or follow a map? It's amazing how many hours my co-workers and I have spent in the past trying to guess or figure out functions on the computer. We would start by surveying those closest to us for answers, then look for others to ask or fiddle around with several options. My co-worker, Teresa, would pull out an instruction manual and have the answer for us within seconds! Now, I'm proud to say, if it takes us more than a few minutes to figure out a function, we either use the "help" feature or get out the instruction manual and solve the problem in minutes. Teresa is proud of us, too!

Get Organized—One of the best books I have ever read is *Clutters Last Stand* by Don Aslett. It is a guide for de-junking your life. It gives instructions for cleaning out closets and sorting through drawers, boxes, medicine cabinets, garages, etc. It is one of the most emancipating feelings to be rid of the stuff that is constantly getting in the way.

Determine Details—Pay attention to the style and needs of the people you are relating with. If you are used to giving big picture, ambiguous answers to individuals seeking specifics, practice honing in on some details. When giving directions or answering a question, offer some specifics. For instance, one time my friend was pulling into a gas station and asked, "How close am I to the pump?" I answered, "You've got room." A more precise answer would have been "about three feet."

Belong—Join an organization, club, guild, or association and participate fully. Take on the responsibility of facilitating an event or being responsible for some duties.

If you have a tendency to misplace items such as your keys, establish a routine. Have a designated, convenient place to put your keys. Always put them there.

Go shopping for organizers for your closet, office, or cupboards. For fun, color-code files, computer disks, or even the clothes hanging in your closet!

Increasing the Orange

If you are looking for ways to increase your flexibility, spontaneity, and enjoyment of the present moment, the following will help you turn up the intensity on your Orange characteristics. Of course, some of these ideas may seem far-fetched if your Orange is not as bright as your other color characteristics. Usually, it's beneficial to stretch your comfort zones, as long as you are not putting yourself at any physical or psychological risk or compromising your integrity. These suggestions are meant to nudge you in the direction of enjoying the moment and going with the flow—not to encourage you to break rules or make you look silly. Whether you feel silly or not, as you incorporate these methods into your days, you'll get increasingly pleasurable results. What you enjoy may be quite different from what others enjoy, and there is no reason you have to incorporate new behavior into your repertoire. But if you are like many people, all you need is a little jump-start to open up more avenues for intensifying your zest for life! So here are some possibilities.

Do Something for the Fun of It—Dive into an activity with abandon. Forget about schedules and duties for the moment and allow yourself to fully partic-ipate. Instead of questioning whether the activity is pro-ductive, logical or responsi-ble, ask if it would bring you joy. Worry less, live more. The deadlines and responsibilities will still be there when you are finished. Why drag them with you into the moment? Let go, have fun, giggle.

Savor Your Senses—Most of us already enjoy plenty of good food. But do you stop and savor it? Do you pay attention to the way it smells, feels in the mouth, or its texture? Do you make noises when you eat—"yummmm"? When you eat, slow down and appreciate the sensations of the whole experience. Enjoy the experience of a mud bath, or just relax in a bubble bath at home while you listen to soothing music. Get a massage. Savor the smell of fresh cut flowers. We have at least five senses: taste, touch, sight, hearing, smell—what ways can you find to experience them more fully?

Express Yourself Openly—To start, find a safe audience, such as a good friend or co-worker that would be willing to hear you out with no holds barred. Share openly your opinions and comments. Let go of the fear of being judged or of not being politically correct. Vent, share, talk about whatever you'd like to at the moment.

Negotiate—The next time you get a "no" or "can't be done" answer, and you really feel there could be a way—don't give up. Come up with alternatives and back them up with evidence of how they would be viable. Extend your imagination.

Visit a flea market and haggle with the vendors for a better deal than the price that is marked. If you really want to stretch, venture onto a car lot and negotiate for a low price on a car. Just for fun. Leave your pocketbook at home. This way you have nothing to lose. The time you spend

will be like taking a crash course in negotiating skills. Observe the tactics or techniques the sales people use to try to get you to buy.

Lighten Up—See the humor and fun in situations. Share a joke, get playful. Depending on the situation, let yourself get casual and comfortable. Leave a few things undecided. Keep some options open and go with the flow.

Stretch Your Comfort Zones—Follow an impulse. Get some variety. Try new ways. For example, drive a different route to work in the morning, try a new restaurant or something new on the menu. Jump in and troubleshoot in a situation without planning. Take a vacation and leave half a day open with no schedule—just follow a whim, or do whatever activity comes

225

up at the moment. What is it that you have always wanted to do (within reason, of course) but have hesitated to do because of lack of skill or confidence? Just as an experiment to see what it feels like, take on a challenge or charge forth with a desire. Do so without any expectations for the outcome, and you may even double your pleasure.

Take an Acting or Public Speaking Class—This is an excellent way to experience the fun of using big gestures, loud voices, and variations of energy levels, intensity, and enthusiasm. Not only can it increase self-confidence, it can also provide avenues for discovering and experiencing a variety of personality styles.

Play to Win—Have you ever participated in an activity and stopped short of your potential? I once attended a seminar in which we actually played a game of "Simon Says." There were 2,000 people in attendance, and I figured I'd play until I got out—no big deal. It only took about three minutes before I was out of the game. After about fifteen minutes there were only ten participants left standing. The seminar leader asked the audience how many had said something like this to themselves before they started: "I'm going to win this. I'm going to play full out. I'm going to participate with my whole heart and soul. I'm

going to go for it!" Out of the 2,000 people, only 12 raised their hands, and 10 of them were standing on stage!

My friend John often repeats a phrase that his father would tell him as a child: "There are those who make things happen, those who watch things happen, and those who wonder what happened." Which are you?

Share a Story—Think of ways to make your stories interesting and perhaps a bit larger than life. How many adjectives can you use to creatively describe something? Instead of simply saying "there was a spider," you could say "there was this creepy, crawly, hairy, black and brown spider." Rather than saying "the music was loud," think to yourself "how loud was it?" What can you compare it to? Use some enthusiasm and intrigue. One way to practice is to get children's books and read them out loud with full animation and expressiveness. For amusement, pick up a romance novel or horror story and notice how the author can make the words come alive in vibrant, descriptive terms.

Create an Adventure—When you find yourself in a situation that is starting to cause stress, look at it through a child's eyes. For instance, if you are getting tense because it's raining and you are getting muddy, go with it—play in the rain, get muddy!

Or if you are waiting in an airport and have just found out that your plane has been delayed, instead of groaning and waiting in your seat, reading a book or making some phone calls—create an adventure. Go exploring. What would an eight-year-old do? There are usually stores and restaurants to investigate and even airplanes to watch. Take a long time in the bathroom. Eat popcorn by tossing it in the air and catching it in your mouth. If you are traveling with others, it can be even more fun. What games can you play? Try "I Spy." For instance, you look for something red and say, "I spy something red." Everyone looks for and tries to guess the red object you have spied. Whoever guesses gets the next turn. The possibilities are endless.

Activate Your Body—
Exercise, get yourself moving! Turn on some music and sway, swing, or bounce to the rhythm. Sing. You don't have to know the words to a song to belt something out—make something up! Go for a walk, dance, hike, swim, or sail. Roller skate, jump rope, ski, or find an exercise class. However you can find a way to get some movement, do it.

Accept Attention—When you do something funny or awkward, instead of being embarrassed, relish the attention. Laugh with your audience; play with the situation. If you did something wonderful and people have not noticed, call it to their attention. If they did notice, accept their praise. Enjoy it and know that it brings great pleasure to others when you accept the gift of their compliments.

Increasing the Green

How easy would it be for you to find the ultimate lowest price on a car, design an action plan for developing a new product at work, teach a child about the rotation of the planets around the sun, or search the Internet for a little known fact? If your initial reaction is anywhere from "huh?" to overwhelmed, you may benefit from brightening your Green. Being able to say "no" with firm conviction, to stay calm in the face of conflict, or to make more objective decisions are aspects of Green behavior we all admire. Use the following suggestions to turn up the intensity of your Green.

Think Long-Term—Look at the big picture instead of dealing with the most pressing issue at the moment. Slow down enough to prioritize the important versus the urgent. Speculate as to what effects today's actions will have on tomorrow's objectives.

Stop and Contemplate—Instead of making a quick decision or response, pause to think. Gather some data and scrutinize the facts. What are the pros and cons? Actually write out a chart or list and give points to which data weighs the heaviest and is the most important. Before acting or answering, consider several options. Give yourself time to think about different ways to express or do things. Make a decision based on what would be the most logical, instead of on how you feel.

Solve a Problem for Yourself—Before turning to others for assistance, try to figure out a challenge on your own. Read instruction manuals, try various alternatives, get creative.

Ask "Why?"—In college, I was taught analytical reasoning. We were told to look at a research paper and see beneath the obvious—what the author wanted us to think—and find the facts beneath. It helped me to ask more questions in order to delve for hidden facts or even manipulation.

Just as with analyzing research papers, it can be beneficial to explore beneath the surface. When you are presented with something that you are unsure of, instead of just taking the person's word for it—ask. Get your questions answered.

Exercise Objectivity—When someone behaves in a way that is outside of our rules for appropriateness, it can trigger a reaction we may think is as natural as a knee jerk. Actually, it isn't natural. It is learned! Ever notice how some people get upset over the same things you do—and some don't? As a matter of fact, we have all experienced situations when something upset us one time and yet didn't at another. If we're not paying attention, we can get connected to behaviors and react like Pavlov's dogs hearing a bell. But we don't have to be victims of these automatic behaviors. The following are some ways to respond more resourcefully to produce the results you desire instead of letting the situation control you.

Remember you have choices.

It may not seem like it at the moment you get triggered, but you have a choice whether you will waste your energy getting upset or channel it in a more useful way. If someone offered you a million dollars to not be upset, could you find a way? Sometimes it is an issue of motivation, not lack of ability. It's your choice to simply react to the situation or to respond more resourcefully. *"It's a fool who takes offense when none is intended, and a bigger fool who takes offense when one is intended."*
—Brigham Young

Check your facts.

Do you really know what happened or are you upset by something someone told you, what you think you saw, or the meaning you attached to an experience? Are you overreacting because this event has been stacked upon numerous past events? *"People are disturbed not by events, but by their views of those events."*
—Epictetus

It's a great idea to double check information to make sure you and the other person are speaking the same language and have the same understanding. Don't make assumptions about information. Find out for sure. This can save everyone a lot of time and frustration.

Also, make sure you are not overlooking the obvious or not-so-obvious. Are there options you haven't thought of yet? If you can discover new ways to look at a situation or chunk it into smaller parts, it is easier to understand.

Take action!

It is a good idea to pause, breathe, and mentally step out of the situation for a moment to get a more objective view. Decide what would be the most appropriate and mutually beneficial action to take—then do it! Of course for some, that can be easier said than done. So sometimes we do nothing instead. Although this is a natural, occasionally useful method, many people never get to the point of dealing with the conflict. They prefer to bury it where it keeps festering and oftentimes bursts into flame at a later date.

After you have taken time to examine the situation for a while, but not long enough to let it fester, decide on a course of action. Say "no" when you need to, without apologizing. Give a logical explanation and expect a rational response. Keep in mind that "rational" does not include being indignant! Sometimes, in order to muster up enough courage to say "no" or express their point of view, people act self-righteous or angry. Instead, express yourself matter-of-factly.

Debate the Other Side of an Argument Just for Fun—The dual benefit: Since you are not emotionally vested in winning, because you are arguing the opposite of what you really believe, if you concentrate, you can experience what it's like to argue a point without your emotions taking over.

Practice Being Precise with Your Words—Challenge yourself to learn a new word a day to expand your vocabulary. If you encounter a word you don't know, look it up.

Stretch your Sense of Humor—See if you can recognize word puns in people's speech throughout the day. You'll be amazed at how much you hadn't noticed before. If you really want to have some fun with this, comment creatively with your own new words. Start simple. For example, when your husband tells you he is going to "hop in the shower," you might respond, "You're not going to skip or jump, just hop?"

Record Ideas—Document your discoveries and thoughts. Actually take some steps to implement them, even if it is sharing your idea with someone you trust. Create a graph or chart to explain your inventions. Design models and schematics for further clarification.

Explore—Look up something on the Internet. Visit a library or other resource center. Ask yourself, "What else can I find out about this subject?" Then look for it. Read something about math, science, magic, philosophy, or technology. Watch the Learning Channel. Take a journey to a distant place. Visit research centers, planetariums, and libraries.

Balancing Your Colors

Notice that as you brighten up the other colors in your spectrum, you are still able to access your most dominant traits when you want to. As we develop various aspects of ourselves, we gain an appreciation for the ways others operate.

The executive director for an insurance company shared with me that to assist in brightening up the colors of his employees he purchased several brightly colored shirts in each of the four colors. In meetings he asks his staff to choose a color different from their most dominant and "operate" in that color for the meeting.

"It is fun to watch the Oranges wait their turn, Greens practicing compassion, Blues logically explaining a project, and Golds tossing ideas out on the table. We all have a great time expressing ourselves in creative ways."

As we continue our evolution through the stages of our lives, we naturally integrate the different colors in our spectrum. This balancing enables us to operate in a variety of situations with more ease and confidence. Knowing your True Colors and brightening the colors in your spectrum is one way to accelerate your journey and gain the desired flexibility to understand and relate to yourself and others at a whole new level.

Part V

APPLYING
TRUE
COLORS
IN YOUR LIFE

True Colors in Every Aspect of Life

As you stop and think about the insights you have gained so far by reading about your colors and the colors of others, you'll realize how knowing this information can cause shifts in the way you interact with the people in your life. You'll notice that although every person is unique in many ways, the values, preferences, and motives you are able to recognize can give you clues as to what a person may think, say, or do in certain situations. It can also help you understand the intentions behind their actions. Instead of resentment you'll find compassion. Animosity will be replaced with understanding and potential conflicts with cooperation. You'll discover yourself applying the concepts of True Colors in virtually every aspect of your life.

From Animosity to Understanding

Ann was on a committee that was planning a statewide conference. The committee had only met twice and already chaos and animosity were rampant. Several members seemed to consume the meeting time by suggesting ideas, ordering pizza, and joking around. Other members were irritated at the time-wasting and attempted to gain control by confirming tasks to be completed and giving orders. Ann

tried her best to facilitate harmony in the group by taking on tasks and giving her attention to everyone, not just the outspoken. She was extremely uncomfortable with the conflict between members and although she knew she was making positive contributions, thoughts of quitting the committee ran through her mind. It was at this point, thank goodness, they had a guest speaker in their general meeting. The woman conducted a presentation on True Colors! Ann found the information about the different colors fascinating and immediately began thinking about how she could apply the information in her own life.

A week passed and the committee met at a hotel so they could take a look at the facilities. The group was interested in obtaining several small rooms for "break-out" sessions and was told by the hotel to look at the El Dorado Room. As they were walking into the room, they noticed there were about five people already there. Ann, not wanting to be rude or intrude upon the people, said in a loud whisper, "Wait! There are people in the room. Let's come back later."

Jules, one of the most outspoken of the committee, darted to the front of the group, waving them on. "Oh, who cares? Let's go in; we'll only be a minute."

Ann stood dumbfounded as the group filed past her into the room. She felt that her opinion had been negated and overruled. Her mind

233

started heading into a direction of hurt feelings and misunderstood intentions, when suddenly she clicked out of it. "Wait a minute," she thought to herself. "Jules is an Orange. She didn't mean to negate me as a person. She simply was trying to 'just do it.' She just wanted to charge forth with her agenda." Ann was able to immediately let go of the angst she had started to feel and instead appreciate the "charge-ahead character" of Jules. What could have possibly turned into a slow-burning grudge instead had dissipated because of the understanding that True Colors provided.

Much to her surprise, on the way out of the room Jules acknowledged Ann for her politeness and apologized. "Sometimes my Orangeness gets a bit ahead of me. Thank you for being such a team player."

During the conference, because the committee recognized the caring concern for people that Ann consistently showed,

they chose her to monitor each room to make sure the speakers and participants were comfortable. She made more handouts if needed or asked the hotel to adjust the heat when necessary. She did a fantastic job of anticipating people's needs. For instance, if she saw a speaker clearing his throat repeatedly and looking around, she would appear with a freshly poured glass of water.

During lunch, several attendees wandered around looking for places to sit. Wanting to make sure they were comfortable but not interrupt those that were already seated, Ann asked the hotel personnel to bring out more chairs. This way, if she saw people unsuccessfully searching for a seat, she could offer to place chairs at any table they would like. This seemed to be a good system—until the bill came at the end of the conference. The catering captain stood with Ann explaining that he would have to charge her for the twelve extra chairs that were brought out.

"We charge for lunch by the chair," he told her.

Had she known this, she would have never asked for more chairs. She would have gone around to the tables and found the existing chairs. "But we did not have twelve more people for lunch," she told him.

THANK YOU FOR BEING SUCH A TEAM PLAYER !

She tried several ways to communicate to him that they should not have to pay the extra charges because in actuality there were no extra people eating lunch. But he was not budging.

"We charge by the chair," he repeated firmly.

Getting more uncomfortable by the minute, Ann suddenly recalled that Wendy was a Green. Maybe she could explain the situation to the catering captain in a way he would understand. Wendy was quickly brought into the conversation, clipboard in hand.

"Look," Wendy said to the man, showing him the figures she had tracked and calculated on her clipboard. "This is how many people attended the conference; this is how many people paid for lunch. This is how many people actually showed up for lunch. I know. I took their tickets. I counted them as they came in the door. This is the number of people that ate, and this is the amount of money we are paying you."

The man looked at Wendy and said, "Okay."

True Colors is not an excuse for bad behavior

It is important to realize that knowing your True Colors does not give you free reign to behave in unacceptable ways. It is ridiculous to think that it is okay to be late for work and

say to your boss, "Oh I'm just Orange, this is the way I am." It's just as ridiculous as thinking that all Oranges have a tendency to be late. We all have preferred ways of operating. Preferences do not necessarily equate to skills or competencies. Be careful not to stereotype or lock yourself into your color style. Use this knowledge to unlock your self-expression and to validate yourself for your preferences. And remember—you can always brighten the less dominant colors in your spectrum.

Recognize what you can gain by brightening your other colors

I was conducting a True Colors presentation for an elementary school staff that had just finished establishing a policy regarding interdistrict agreements. These agreements govern when a child who lives in one school district can be allowed to go to a school in another district. The policy was needed because in the past decisions were based more on who begged the most to get into their school than on any clearly designated criteria. It had caused a tremendous amount of stress for Wanda, the secretary, who was the one to have to deal with parents seeking an application. It was her job to fill out the paperwork and let the parents know if their child was accepted or not. Wanda was relieved to finally have something in written form that she could rely upon. Included in the policy was a deadline date for applications.

Three weeks after school had been in session for the new year, and two days after the deadline date for interdistrict agreement applications, a mother came into the office and requested an application for her children. Wanda informed her that she had missed the deadline date, but that she could try applying next semester. The woman was furious! She had been in Europe over the summer and had just gotten back. How was she supposed to know there was a deadline date? She had counted on getting her kids into this school. School was already well into session, and they had missed enough already. She accused Wanda of being to blame for her children not being in school yet.

Wanda held her ground. She was glad to have the new policy guidelines to stand behind and gave the woman a copy of the policy. Wanda apologized for any inconvenience and again suggested that the woman could apply for her children to attend next semester. The woman would not have it. She insisted on seeing the principal. Wanda told her that it would not do her any good. It was policy.

Hearing all the commotion, the principal appeared. He ushered the upset woman into his office. After about half an hour, the two emerged from his office. The principal handed a completed application to Wanda

and said, "Please process this for me and see that her children are admitted to the school as soon as possible."

The woman glared smugly at Wanda, as if to say, "Nah-nah-nah-nah-naaah-nah!" Of course, Wanda was embarrassed and humiliated. She was only doing her job, and now she was being made out to be the "bad guy." She was angry with the principal for not supporting her and the new policy.

The principal was Blue-Orange. After training in True Colors, he realized his contribution to the problems created by not sticking to policy and why it was so important to Wanda, who was Gold-Blue, to have his cooperation and support. Her needs for consistency and fairness were being sabotaged by his "quick to accommodate and keep the harmony" attitude. Recognizing his own tendencies was the first step in adding the necessary skills to still honor his Blue-Orange desires while embracing and supporting policy.

Just a little insight can help you understand the actions of others

It is important to make accommodations for others who's style happens to be your least dominant preferences. Put yourself in their shoes.

Ed is a family practice physician. His patient load is overwhelming. He

Part V

sees an average of thirty patients a day. From the moment he arrives at work he is ordering charts, diagnosing conditions, and writing prescriptions, as well as a stacks of other duties. He moves steadily from room to room, dealing with whatever challenge is presented to him. He is constantly concentrating on what he needs to do to serve each patient's needs, so when he walks through the hallway to the next room he does so without stopping to connect with his co-workers. They used to think Ed was antisocial or mad at them.

CONGRATULATIONS ON
YOUR NEW ARRIVAL !

They would say "hi" to him, and he would respond, "hi" and continue straight to his next patient without pause. He rarely, if ever, attended any social events such as Christmas parties or luncheons. In fact, one time his staff invited him to a baby shower and he didn't even know the woman was expecting—and she was eight months pregnant!

His staff explained that before experiencing True Colors, they always mistook his seriousness for being mad, his not paying attention to social events as being antisocial, and his lack of acknowledgment as being pompous. Now they understand more about his natural tendencies. So now if they want him to know something,

they call it to his attention. When he is jolted out of his concentration for the task at hand, he can recognize their needs more readily and does so. His staff has a new understanding and admiration of his skills and vice versa. He actually enjoys the pleased responses he receives when he surprises his staff with gifts during the holidays. He has taken up the habit of using an expressive word for the day. When people greet him with the usual "Hi, how are you today?" he responds with something like "sensational" or "golden."

Sometimes trans-formations are so dramatic it's almost amusing

Many of you probably have already noticed some subtle changes in your relationships and level of acceptance of others as a result of learning the color concepts. You can recognize more easily when you are, or are not, getting through to someone. Now you have some vocabulary and

237

insights at your fingertips. You'll continue day by day to discover ways to use this information in many situations—to reduce antagonism, confusion, and conflict and increase compassion, understanding, and cooperation.

After determining that her ex-husband, Sam, had predominantly Orange characteristics, Cindy decided to try a new motivational strategy with him, one that would appeal to his sense of adventure and challenge. It had been a sticky divorce and many of Cindy's, as well as the children's, items were still at their old house where Sam was living. If Cindy asked Sam to please bring an item with him when he picked up the children for visitation, he would inevitably forget or refuse. Because she was not welcome at his house and she wanted to keep the peace, she had to find another way to motivate him. Being a Green, Cindy was willing to devise a strategy. Instead of asking him to bring the items, she appealed to his Orange personality style by making a game out of it. "I'll bet you can't guess what I need you to bring," she would challenge.

"Your bike!" he would guess.

"No, guess again."

"The tea kettle."

"Wrong room, try again."

"The rocking chair!"

"Yes! You're right. Can you guess what else?" She would continue with the guessing contest until he determined all the items. The amazing thing was that he would remember to bring every single item, without fail. Cindy admitted that sometimes she felt weird or even manipulative playing this game, so she would occasionally just straight out ask him to bring something. Of course when she did this, he would inevitably forget. Anytime she created a contest, game, or challenge he would come through with flying colors!

Respect vs. Manipulation

The interesting thing about communicating with others in their "color language" is that to those who do not understand the benefits, it may seem manipulative at first. It is such a sad disservice when people misinterpret respect for manipulation. When you learn to speak another language to be able to talk to your neighbor, colleague, friend, and loved one are you being manipulative or respectful? Of course it depends on your intent. If your intent is to open up lines of communication, then you are being respectful.

Pay attention to the needs of others, through the eyes of others, not only your own

Another terrific way to show your respect and consideration for others is to notice what they need and value. Sometimes in our aim to please, we don't notice that we are contributing in a way that would make us happy, but not necessarily in a way that would make others happy. Our intentions may be very honorable, yet the results might not be as good as they could be if we had looked at a situation from more than just our own perspective.

Colleen absolutely loved holidays, especially Christmas. She had always derived such pleasure from upholding the traditions of decorating the house, making a home-cooked meal, and opening presents around the tree. When her three children were not yet in school, her husband worked outside of the home and she stayed at home to take care of them. Because she was at home, she took on the sole responsibility for making sure the holiday was a memorable occasion. She would pull out her grandmother's recipes and make homemade apple pie. She helped the children make ornaments, and they decorated the house together.

However, when the children were old enough to go to school, Colleen took on a part-time job. By the time the last child graduated from high school, Colleen was working full-time outside of the home as well as taking on some bookkeeping clients for a home business she had started. As the Christmas season approached Colleen became increasingly stressed. Now her days were spent at work and her nights were spent doing bookkeeping. Her children were married and had children of their own. Instead of cooking and buying presents for her family of four, she now cooked the holiday meal and shopped for fourteen! Since she had always been the one to prepare all the festivities, she tried her hardest to continue the tradition. Although circumstances had changed tremendously, she never asked for any help. Her children tried to volunteer a few times to assist her but she always turned them down. She felt it was her obligation to come through as she had always done in the past. What once had been her favorite time of year had now become the most stressful.

In early December Colleen attended a True Colors workshop at her office. During the session she discovered she had many Gold characteristics. It helped to explain why she felt a driving sense of duty to uphold traditions. She also learned the values of the other color styles. She recognized many Blue as well as Gold traits in her children. Knowing this, she realized that her children were being respectful in allowing their mother the honor of carrying out the traditions, while at the same time probably yearning to contribute. Only a few days after the workshop, Colleen had the opportunity to ask her children to pitch in for the upcoming holiday.

They were delighted! They had not wanted to rock the boat by insisting that she accept their help. They knew how much joy it brought their mother to prepare for the holidays. They did not want to be rude or make it seem as though they did not appreciate her efforts. But they wanted greatly to be part of the preparations and were relieved to have her finally accept their help.

Colleen shared with me that it was one of the happiest holidays she ever had. She had started a new family tradition of everyone pitching in and preparing together!

One of the greatest benefits of knowing True Colors is the validation you get for your own style

You are a unique combination of characteristics. And, although society may try to force its opinion on us about the way we should be, through the media and other pressures, we recognize how unrealistic that really is. Take weight management for instance. It's one thing to want to watch your weight for health reasons; it's another to try to lose weight because of the feeling that you don't measure up to some imaginary "ideal." You are an awesome individual with your own set of values, likes, and dislikes. Deep down we know what is right for us. When we behave with integrity and are able to show our True Colors, it is a freeing experience.

I remember one time recently in a True Colors workshop that I was conducting, a young woman motioned for me to come over to where she was sitting. "I'm Orange!" she beamed.

"Good," I said, "then you are sitting at the right table."

"No," she said, "you don't understand . . . I AM ORANGE! All my life I was trained to be Gold. I did not think there was any other way to be. I thought there was a 'Gold Standard' the way everyone should be. I had no idea that there were other people that felt the way I do or valued the same things. I have gone to counseling over the guilt and inadequacies I have experienced. I have never felt more validated than at this very moment. Thank you!"

She continued, "The greatest thing is that I know I have choices. I still can choose to behave as a Gold, but I know I don't have to. If I feel like letting a little of my Orange show, it is not wrong, bad, or better—it is just different."

240

Chapter 20

IN LIVING COLOR

Seeing in Color

By now, you are better able to recognize what energizes you and how it may differ from what energizes your least dominant color style. Enter interactions with a willingness to learn. Notice that their reality is as valid as yours and keep an open mind so you can gain something by interacting with them. People are constantly sharing with me how after they learned about True Colors they attended a family or community event and watched people's behaviors in a new light. They were tickled to be able to recognize the color characteristics various individuals were displaying.

Speaking in Color

Many people that have been exposed to the True Colors concepts are amazed at how quickly and easily—even spontaneously—the color language is brought into so many of their conversations. They find themselves saying things like, "Oh, it's the Blue in me . . . " or "You are being rather Gold . . . " See if you don't notice this happening as well. The next time you are in a conversation with someone who has enthusiastically chosen a subject you are interested in, or especially ones you are not, become aware of what color is motivating them. You'll be surprised and delighted to discover your world turning colors!

Living in Color

Those who really embrace True Colors will find themselves applying the concepts in virtually every area of their lives. One time a co-worker approached me and said she was going on a blind date and knew that the man was Blue. She wanted to know what I could tell her about Blues! I was surprised that she knew the man was a Blue, and further intrigued as to how she knew he was, if it was a blind date and she had never met him before. She told me that a friend of hers told her he was a Blue. How did the friend know? True Colors is contagious!

It is fun to recognize the color styles and combinations of styles in the people around us. The next time you watch a movie, notice each character's style and see if you can determine their most dominant color. This is fun to do with TV shows and storybook characters as well. Take The Wizard of Oz, for instance. Can you guess the colors of Dorothy, the Tin Man, the Scarecrow, and the Lion? How about the Wizard?

Everyone adds value

There is no "best" type of color style, and everyone is a different combination. Keep in mind that you are more than just your most dominant color. The whole is greater than the sum of its parts. Be proud of your color spectrum and allow others enjoyment of theirs. Think of ways to bring out the best in people by recognizing their needs, values, and talents. See how many ways you can elicit their True Colors while maintaining your own.

Share True Colors with Others

More and more people are experiencing the benefits of True Colors and sharing them with the people in their lives. The more people around you that know the concepts, the easier it is to communicate, understand behaviors, and solve conflicts. Share this book or spread the benefits by contacting True Colors and getting a workshop or presentation at your school, work site, or community event. In the meantime, keep these key points in mind:

"Do unto others as *they* would have you do unto them."

As you know, some people don't want to be treated the way you like to be treated. Take hugging, for instance. I love to hug! When I was younger I used to assume that because I liked receiving hugs as much as giving them that others would also like to be hugged. Wrong! As you may have already discovered, some people do not always appreciate a hearty hug—especially from a stranger. I also like to speak loudly and directly and enjoy it when others do the same. Still, I meet people that prefer softer tones as well as a softer approach. When we treat people only our way, it can increase tension and resistance levels. Our willingness and

244

ability to adapt our behavior to the circumstances as well as to the people we relate to, is essential for our personal effectiveness. Learning the language and customs of others not only lowers tension and resistance levels, but also demonstrates the utmost respect. It helps to build relationships and collaborations.

True Colors is only a model; it takes real life to validate it

Although True Colors can give you tremendous insights into the behaviors of yourself and others, it certainly does not explain or solve everything. Through training and reading this book, you can learn the guidelines. Life is where you learn to apply them. There are variations within all color styles; color watching is only one filter through which to view human behavior. Use this as a powerful tool to combine with other methods that work for you.

Do you have some stories to share?

How has True Colors affected your life? How has it validated your desires or allowed you more self-expression? What have you learned about relating to and connecting with others? Would you like to share your story with others that are interested in enhancing their relationships and increasing their understanding? Would you like to see your story appear in a future book about True Colors? Write to me and let me know your adventures and discoveries! How are you showing your True Colors?

Mary Miscisin
P.O. Box 277453
Sacramento, CA 95827
Mary@PositivelyMary.com
www.PositivelyMary.com

References and Resources

Baron, Renee. *What Type Am I?* Harmondsworth, England: Penguin Books, 1998.

Briggs-Myers, Isabel. *Introduction to Type*. Palo Alto, California: Consulting Psychological Press, Inc., 1990.

Delunas, Eve. *Survival Games Personalities Play*. Carmel, California: Sunlink Publications, 1992.

Kalil, Carolyn. *Follow Your True Colors to the Work You Love*. Wilsonville, Oregon: Book Partners, Inc., 1998.

Keirsey, David, and Marilyn Bates. *Please Understand Me*. Del Mar, California: Prometheus Nemesis Book Company, 1984.

Kroeger, Otto, and Janet Thuesen. *Type Talk, The 16 Personality Types That Determine How We Live, Love and Work*. New York: Dell Publishing, 1988.

Kroeger, Otto. *Type Talk at Work: How the 16 Personality Types Determine Your Success on the Job*. New York: Dell Publishing, 1992.

Robbins, Anthony. *Awaken the Giant Within*. New York: Simon and Schuster, 1992.

Teiger, Paul, and Barbara Barron-Teiger. *Just Your Type: Create the Relationship You've Always Wanted Using the Secrets of Personality Type*. New York: Little, Brown and Company, 2000.

True Colors Inc.
www.true-colors.com

Our vision at True Colors is to foster positive, healthy, productive communities whose successes flow from the natural dedication of each person. Our powerful, customized "edutainment" workshops, books, workbooks, videos, live shows, and events have empowered millions of people during the past twenty years and helped to realize this vision.

The following are some of the True Colors resources people across the country are turning to for improved communication in their personal and professional lives.

Also available from True Colors

Follow Your True Colors to the Work You Love

This innovative course in career planning is a must read for college students. Author Carolyn Kalil, a gifted educator, career counselor, and speaker, introduces students to the True Colors personality system to help them better understand their natural strengths and talents. They become equipped to identify careers in which they will thrive and find true satisfaction—work they will love! A terrific resource for any career counselor.

True Success

Written specifically for today's teens, *True Success* introduces high school students to the True Colors process and guides them toward careers that fit with who they are. Author Carolyn Kalil leads students through a journey of self-discovery to help them gain a better understanding of their natural strengths and identify careers in which they will find true satisfaction.

Reading Colors—The Art of Teaching to Their True Colors

Make reading come alive for young students with the help of True Colors! This fun-filled yet practical book by veteran teacher Jean Marie

Miscisin helps teachers identify the True Colors or "personality" of their students and create lesson plans to get every child excited about reading. Includes a True Colors comparison chart and oodles of creative ideas and activities for maximizing reading performance.

Meaningful Conversations: Connecting the DOT and True Colors

Bursting with an infectious passion for teaching, this brilliant and inspirational book helps educators rediscover the magic of reaching the hearts of students. In her delightful style, educator and author Ann Kashiwa, reveals how to identify the True Colors of students and use that information to connect with the core of each child for maximized success in the classroom. A welcome "shot in the arm" for today's teacher, *Meaningful Conversations* is a must read for educators of all backgrounds and grade levels. And parents, too!

True Parenting

In *True Parenting,* Kathy Hayward, a veteran facilitator of parenting workshops, guides parents through the True Colors process to determine the Color Spectrum of each family member and the family as a whole. This information becomes a springboard for developing improved parenting skills, greater communication in the home, and more meaningful family relationships. Includes fun-filled activities for the entire family!

Dare to Dream

Super Bowl champion Curt Marsh challenges readers to dig deep and pursue their dreams, whatever their circumstances. Curt talks about the physical and emotional pain he endured when a football injury led to the amputation of his right foot above the ankle. He shares many of the life lessons that have inspired him to rise above his challenges and pursue his passions—including the True Colors process. *Dare to Dream* will inspire you to embrace change and diversity, discover true toughness, set goals and develop plans to achieve them, and much more!

Victory Beyond the Scoreboard

At last comes a practical guide with intelligent answers to the social, ethical, and behavioral concerns surrounding youth sports. Full of innovative ideas for making sports more fun and less stressful for children and their families, *Victory Beyond the Scoreboard* clearly outlines how to create a winning partnership among players, parents, and coaches. Authors Cliff Gillies, an award-winning high school principal and coach, and John Devine, a veteran coach of twenty years, have teamed up to offer this "play book" for guiding young athletes. Includes tips for selecting the right sport and program, helping children deal with athletic successes and failures, using sports as a catalyst for family-building, and more!

Sports Management Journal

The *Sports Management Journal* is an easy-to-use workbook written specifically for school coaches and parents of children in sports. In this wonderful companion to *Victory Beyond the Scoreboard*, author Cliff Gillies presents tear-out exercises to copy and use in daily coaching and parenting. You'll also find a proven design for coach-parent teaming, games for teaching respectful communication, charts for athletic achievement and improvement, the True Colors personality assessment system and cards, and much more.

Action & Communication Guide

Our popular *Action & Communication Guide* will help identify the "personality" of your classroom and provide effective ways to help you better relate to each student. Features a durable binder and four "colorized" sections—one for each personality type. Eighty-eight pages full of valuable insight for creating a stimulating classroom environment, for motivating learning and achievement, and for gaining cooperation, plus more.

To order additional copies of *Showing Our True Colors* or any of these True Colors resources, please contact us at:

True Colors, Inc.
3605 West MacArthur Blvd. Suite 702
Santa Ana, California 92704

Telephone: 800–422–4686

E-mail: info@true-colors.com

Web Site: www.true-colors.com

Word Cluster Sort

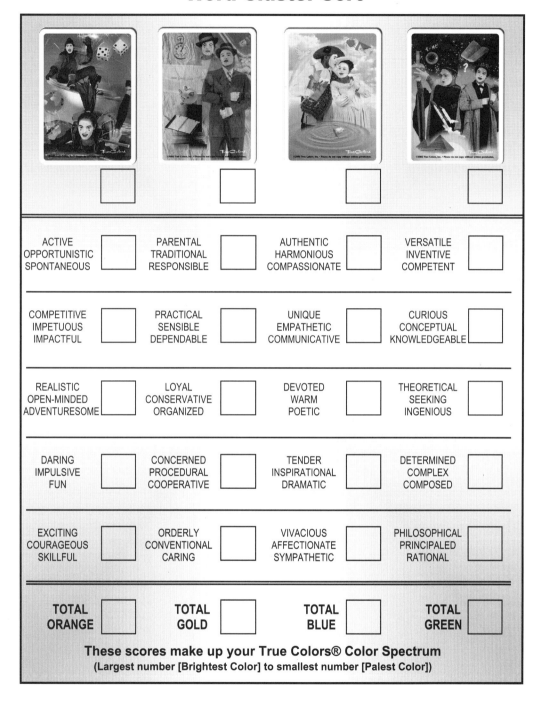

ACTIVE OPPORTUNISTIC SPONTANEOUS		PARENTAL TRADITIONAL RESPONSIBLE		AUTHENTIC HARMONIOUS COMPASSIONATE		VERSATILE INVENTIVE COMPETENT	
COMPETITIVE IMPETUOUS IMPACTFUL		PRACTICAL SENSIBLE DEPENDABLE		UNIQUE EMPATHETIC COMMUNICATIVE		CURIOUS CONCEPTUAL KNOWLEDGEABLE	
REALISTIC OPEN-MINDED ADVENTURESOME		LOYAL CONSERVATIVE ORGANIZED		DEVOTED WARM POETIC		THEORETICAL SEEKING INGENIOUS	
DARING IMPULSIVE FUN		CONCERNED PROCEDURAL COOPERATIVE		TENDER INSPIRATIONAL DRAMATIC		DETERMINED COMPLEX COMPOSED	
EXCITING COURAGEOUS SKILLFUL		ORDERLY CONVENTIONAL CARING		VIVACIOUS AFFECTIONATE SYMPATHETIC		PHILOSOPHICAL PRINCIPALED RATIONAL	
TOTAL ORANGE		TOTAL GOLD		TOTAL BLUE		TOTAL GREEN	

These scores make up your True Colors® Color Spectrum
(Largest number [Brightest Color] to smallest number [Palest Color])